BUILDINGS OF

New Orleans

The Society of Architectural Historians gratefully acknowledges the support of the following, whose generosity helped bring Buildings of New Orleans *to publication:*

Gill Family Foundation

Myra Malkin

 Louisiana Endowment for the Humanities

 National Endowment for the Humanities, an independent federal agency

National Park Service, Heritage Documentation Programs, HABS/HAER/HALS Division

Ellen B. Weiss

Lee Ledbetter

VergesRome Architects

Anonymous

Initial and ongoing support for the Buildings of the United States series has come from:

National Endowment for the Humanities, an independent federal agency

Graham Foundation for Advanced Studies in the Fine Arts

Donald I. Perry Fund

Founders' Fund of the Buildings of the United States

Society of Architectural Historians

Southeast Chapter, Society of Architectural Historians

Historic Hibernia National Bank (6.13).

BUILDINGS OF

New Orleans

KAREN KINGSLEY
LAKE DOUGLAS

UNIVERSITY OF
VIRGINIA PRESS
Charlottesville | London

University of Virginia Press
© 2018 by the Society of Architectural Historians
All rights reserved
Printed in the United States of America on acid-free paper

First published 2018

9 8 7 6 5 4 3 2 1

Library of Congress Cataloging-in-Publication Data
Names: Kingsley, Karen, author. | Douglas, Lake, 1949– author.
Title: Buildings of New Orleans / Karen Kingsley and Lake Douglas.
Description: Charlottesville : University of Virginia Press, 2018. | Series:
    SAH/BUS city guide | Includes bibliographical references and index.
Identifiers: LCCN 2018002829| ISBN 9780813941349 (cloth : alk. paper) |
    ISBN 9780813941356 (pbk. : alk. paper)
Subjects: LCSH: Architecture—Louisiana—New Orleans—Guidebooks. |
    Architecture and society—Louisiana—New Orleans. | New Orleans
    (La.)—Buildings, structures, etc.—Guidebooks. | New Orleans
    (La.)—Tours.
Classification: LCC NA735.N4 K56 2018 | DDC 720.9763/35—dc23
LC record available at https://lccn.loc.gov/2018002829

Contents

How to Use This Book

This book is divided into four main sections—thirteen tours of the City of New Orleans in Orleans Parish, two tours of adjacent parishes (Jefferson and St. Bernard) and their historic suburbs, and three tours along the Mississippi River. The building and landscape entries within each tour are arranged in the order they are encountered as one moves along.

The City of New Orleans tours begin with the Vieux Carré, the oldest section of New Orleans, and then follow with tours that to a large extent reflect the chronological and spatial evolution of the city.

Each entry in the first three sections is identified by a sequential tour number and the name of the property (e.g, 1.1 Jackson Square), with historic or alternate names in parentheses. On the next line appear the primary date(s) of construction and the name of the architect or designer (if known; if the work has undergone a subsequent, substantial addition or alteration by another architect or designer, that date and name appears as well), followed by the address and other location information.

The three day trips from New Orleans (one downriver and two upriver) are each written in narrative form, with key sites (which do not carry entry numbers) set **boldface** for ease of identification.

Given the thousands of historic buildings in the City of New Orleans and thousands more in the surrounding areas, this book is far from comprehensive, offering instead as broad and inclusive a representative sampling of the city's architectural and urban traditions as possible. Only those buildings, structures, and landscapes extant at the time of writing are listed, but a visitor should be prepared to find that a few of the works addressed may no longer exist or may have been substantially modified. We trust that our readers will always respect the property rights and privacy of others as they view the buildings.

Foreword

The primary objective of the Buildings of the United States (BUS) series, and this City Guide, is to identify and celebrate the rich cultural, economic, and geographic diversity of the United States of America as it is reflected in the architecture of each state. The series was founded by the Society of Architectural Historians (SAH), a nonprofit organization dedicated to the study, interpretation, and preservation of the built environment throughout the world.

The BUS series will eventually comprise more than sixty volumes documenting the built environment of every state and many of their cities. The idea for such a series was in the minds of the founders of the SAH in the early 1940s, but it was not brought to fruition until Nikolaus Pevsner—the eminent British architectural historian who had conceived and carried out the Buildings of England series, published from 1951—challenged the SAH in 1976 to do for the United States what he had done for his country.

The authors of each BUS volume and city guide are trained architectural and landscape historians who are thoroughly in-formed in the local aspects of their subjects. Although the great national and international architects of American buildings receive proper attention, outstanding local architects, as well as the buildings of skilled but often anonymous carpenter-builders, are also brought prominently into the picture.

The BUS series and city guides, as well as this specific volume, have received generous and ongoing support from the donors listed on the funders page at the front of this volume, as well as the many individual members of the SAH who have made unrestricted contributions to the series.

We thank the authors, the University of Virginia Press, the SAH Board, and the members of the BUS Editorial Advisory Committee listed at the front of the volume.

The Society of Architectural Historians
Buildings of the United States

Acknowledgments

The authors owe thanks to many individuals who helped in innumerable ways to bring this book to completion. Foremost, our thanks go to Pauline Saliga and the staff at the Society of Architectural Historians and to Mark Mones and the University of Virginia Press. Design and production of the book were guided by Anne Hegeman and Cecilia Sorochin, and Nat Case created the maps; we thank them as well.

We are particularly grateful to John Klingman (Tulane University School of Architecture) and Julie Nicoletta (University of Washington) for their insightful and valuable comments on the manuscript in process. Jennifer V. O. Baughn, Delos Hughes, Joan Kay, and Robert Salzar generously helped provide photographs for the book. Thanks also go to Guy W. Carwile (Louisiana Tech University) for building information and for photographs.

Organizations and people whose resources and assistance were invaluable include Kevin Williams at the Southeastern Architectural Archive, Tulane University Libraries, and staff at The Historic New Orleans Collection, Special Collections at Louisiana State University's Hill Memorial Library, Baton Rouge, and the Louisiana Endowment for the Humanities. Thanks go to various colleagues at Louisiana State University, including Elizabeth Duffy (Office of the Dean, College of Art and Design), Erin Voisin and Dana Tuminello (Office of Sponsored Programs), and Vincent Cellucci (Communications across the Curriculum Program).

And special thanks to Debbie de la Houssaye.

BUILDINGS OF
New Orleans

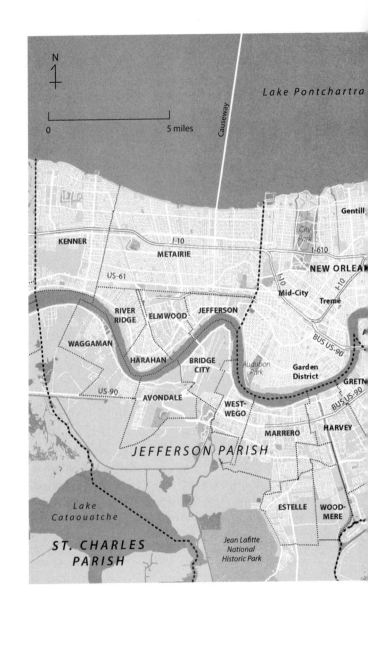

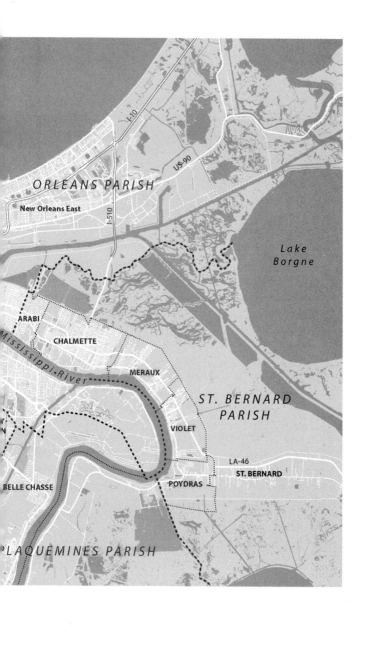

Orleans Parish

NEW ORLEANS

Cradled in a curve of the Mississippi River and contained on the north by Lake Pontchartrain, New Orleans has fluid boundaries; like an island, the city can be approached only over water. Its elevation is ten feet above sea level next to the river and well below sea level in many places. With its saucerlike shape and with an average yearly rainfall in excess of sixty inches, New Orleans must depend for its survival on an extensive and sophisticated system of pumps, floodwalls, and levees. The city's physical growth paralleled the natural levee formed by the Mississippi's deposits, spreading into the swampy center and toward Lake Pontchartrain only when these low-lying areas were drained beginning in the early twentieth century. This growth pattern can be tracked in the types and styles of the city's residential architecture: from neighborhoods of Creole cottages to urban town houses, shotgun houses, bungalows, and the low-ceilinged, ranch-style houses built after air-conditioning became standard. Although New Orleans neighborhoods contain some of the oldest buildings in the nation, much of the city's fabric dates from the twentieth century.

Jean-Baptiste Le Moyne, Sieur de Bienville, selected the site for New Orleans in 1718, naming it for the French regent, Philippe, duc d'Orléans. Bienville learned from the native peoples that this location, which he intended as a trading post for the Company of the West (and had been similarly earmarked for the Company of the Indies), offered a shorter route to the Gulf of Mexico via Bayou St. John and Lake Pontchartrain than that provided by the Mississippi River, and it was this route into the Vieux Carré that much of the new community's commerce flowed.

The core of New Orleans is the Vieux Carré, laid out in 1721 on a grid plan by engineer Louis-Pierre Leblond de La Tour (c. 1670–1723), and his assistant, Adrien de Pauger (d. 1726). This basic plan of New Orleans remained unchanged throughout the eighteenth century, although ownership of the colony (and surrounding territory) changed over time. France ceded the colony to Spain in 1762, then it passed back to France in 1800 and

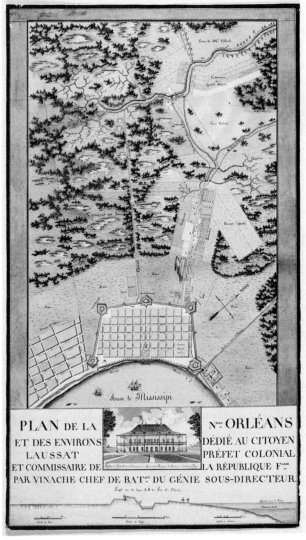

Plan de la Nouvelle Orléans et des Environs Dédié au Citoyen Laussat Préfet Colonial et Commissaire de La République Française *[Plan of New Orleans] by Joseph Antoine Vinache, c. 1803.*

was sold to the United States in 1803 as part of the Louisiana Purchase. The territory became the State of Louisina in 1812.

The surrounding cypress forests provided building materials for the new city, but disastrous fires in 1788 and 1794 led the Spanish governor to issue regulations that buildings of more than one story must be constructed of brick and, if the bricks were set between wood posts in the type of construction known as *briquette-entre-poteaux*, that they be covered with stucco or lime to help fireproof them.

By the end of the eighteenth century, new suburbs were laid out downriver and upriver from the Vieux Carré, and New Orleans grew rapidly in the first half of the nineteenth century, especially after the Louisiana Purchase (1803). This growth accelerated after the first steamboat navigated the Mississippi to New Orleans in 1812, for cargo could then be transported upriver as easily as down. By 1840, only New York had more business than the port of New Orleans, and with a population of approximately 102,000, the city was the nation's third largest, just behind Baltimore and just ahead of Philadelphia.

The city was captured by Union forces early (April 28, 1862) in the Civil War and was occupied for the remainder of the war. Economic recovery began in the 1870s but was relatively slow until the end of the century. Residents weathered devastating outbreaks of cholera (1832 and 1849) and yellow fever (1853 and 1905), as well as the effects of storms from the hurricane of 1915 to Hurricane Betsy in 1965. A construction boom in what is now known as the Central Business District (CBD), lasting from the 1890s to the Great Depression of the 1930s, was accompanied by residential development. Shotgun houses predominated in the newly drained sections and, ornamented with varied and fancy overhangs, brackets, and cornices, they offered individuality within uniformity. In New Orleans today, the less affluent nudge the wealthy in a multiplicity of small and distinct neighborhoods, often separated by no more than a street.

Although the railroads ended New Orleans's monopoly of the Mississippi River valley trade, the port nonetheless remained a significant one, and the city's riverfront was occupied by wharves for maritime use. Completion of the Inner Harbor Navigation Canal (familiarly known as the Industrial Canal; **3.14**) in 1923 linked the river with Lake Pontchartrain and, later, the Gulf via the Intracoastal Waterway. Following World War II, the city benefited from revenue generated by oil and gas industries. Between 1959 and 1970, the built-up area of New Orleans approximately doubled in size; suburban expansion in the 1970s, east across the Industrial Canal and west into neighboring Jefferson Parish, left much of the inner city to decay. The late 1970s began to see a reversal of this trend, but the economic recession of the 1980s proved challenging to neighborhoods and the downtown economy.

Nevertheless, neighborhood groups, nonprofits, and commercial developers have initiated programs and developed projects to renovate and restore historic buildings. By the turn of the twenty-first century New Orleans was blossoming and new buildings, restaurants, and festivals attracted locals and increasing numbers of tourists alike. Then, in 2005, Hurricane Katrina and the subsequent failure of the levee system that resulted in devastating flooding and loss of life brought the city's resurgence to a sudden halt. In the years since, New Orleans has made a remarkable recovery. Although its population is less than before the hurricane (decreasing from approximately 455,000 in 2005 to just under 390,000 in 2015) and some residents were never able to return to their devastated neighborhoods, other areas have experienced a rebirth with new and restored buildings. Tourists flock to the city and numerous former commercial highrise buildings and warehouses have been converted to hotels and apartments.

French, Spanish, Carribean, and African influences characterized New Orleans architecture until 1803, when Anglo-Americans who flocked to the city began to introduce Eastern Seaboard fashions. Architects were attracted by the opportunities this booming city offered. Among those who settled here in the nineteenth century were some of the nation's premier architects: James H. Dakin (1806–1852), James Gallier Sr. (1798–1866), James Gallier Jr. (1827–1868), and Henry Howard (1818–1884), and, from France, Jacques Nicholas Bussière de Pouilly (1804–1875). They crafted a unique architecture from the city's diverse heritage, one that was also sympathetic to the difficult climate and site. In the twentieth century, architects and firms have made major contributions to the city's extraordinary built landscape: Emile Weil (1878–1945); Charles A. Favrot (1866–1939) and Louis A. Livaudais (1871–1932), who formed Favrot and Livaudais in 1895; Moise Goldstein (1882–1972);

Leon C. Weiss (1882–1953) and F. Julius Dreyfous, who established a firm in 1919, expanded as Weiss, Dreyfous and Seiferth when Solis Seiferth (1895–1984) was made partner in 1927; and Nathaniel C. Curtis Jr. (1917–1997) and Arthur Q. Davis (1920–2011), who formed Curtis and Davis. Koch and Wilson, Architects, the partnership of Richard Koch (1889–1971) and Samuel Wilson Jr. (1911–1993), did its most important work in historic preservation in southern Louisiana. Koch, working with Wilson, spearheaded the State's federal Works Progress Administration (WPA) efforts to document Louisiana's historic architecture for the Historic American Buildings Survey (HABS). Today, architects working here and architecture are in the mainstream of American design, with several local firms receiving national recognition, and prominent national firms designing buildings here. Many local architects have had ties to the Tulane University School of Architecure, which has been training professionals and promoting architectural culture in the city since 1894.

New Orleans has an unmatched culture of public display compared to other American cities. In the days before air-conditioning, the heat dictated outdoor living on galleries, porches, or stoops. In modest neighborhoods, this tradition lingers. Streets are also the setting for Mardi Gras and other ritual activities and parades, many generated by religious festivals. The city's high water table has affected death as well as life: the deceased are often placed in elaborate above-ground tombs, giving local cemeteries both the appearance and the appellation of "cities of the dead."

Most of the buildings in New Orleans are constructed of wood, and because of the high annual rainfall, heat, humidity, and termites, they need constant repair. Without human or natural intervention (drought, flood, freeze), vegetation grows out of control. Depending on one's point of view, the city can be characterized as looking either dilapidated or picturesquely decayed and antique. In many older sections, overhead electricity and telephone wires tangle with the branches of oak, magnolia, and crepe myrtle trees to form a sheltering canopy that contributes to New Orleanians' often parochial inclinations.

Since New Orleans lies within a crescent bend of the Mississippi River—thus its nickname, the Crescent City—the street grid merges roughly in the center, which often makes finding one's way a challenge. For New Orleanians, locations and directions are identified not by compass points but rather on the basis of their relationship to the Vieux Carré—that is, upriver or downriver—and to Lake Pontchartrain (lakeside) and the Mississippi River (riverside).

Vieux Carré

The Vieux Carré (old square), also known as the French Quarter or simply the Quarter, was designed in an eleven-by-six-block gridiron plan. A public square, the Place d'Armes (now Jackson Square), faces the river and dates from the colonial period as a military parade ground that evolved, when military uses became obsolete, into an open space in the community's center. The early-nineteenth-century levees along the Mississippi River, while not nearly what they are now in terms of height or location, were spaces for early evening public perambulations, and, according to an 1806 account, the site of "traffic *de coeur*" that resulted in *plaçage* (extralegal) arrangements among local residents of different ethnicities. Here, as elsewhere and later in the nineteenth and early twentieth centuries, open spaces often facilitated public social interactions among all, regardless of race, class, economic status, or the letter of the law; this changed beginning with enforcement of Jim Crow laws in 1896 and held sway through enforced segregation policies until the mid-1960s.

Although fortifications surrounding the settlement were planned, they never amounted to much more than a ditch and palisade. Of the four planned corner forts, it was only in 1792, under Spanish rule, that one, Fort St. Charles (San Carlos), was built (1792), and it was demolished in 1821. The Old U.S. Mint (**4.1**) now stands on that site at the foot of present-day Esplanade Avenue. Eighteenth-century city plans show large freestanding houses set in elaborate geometrically organized gardens (which probably did not exist). By the early nineteenth century, as the population increased, buildings fronted directly on the street and were provided with interior courtyards to shelter their occupants from street noises and odors and to accommodate domestic services. As a consequence of the two major fires (1788, 1794), the earliest extant structure is the Ursuline Convent (**1.29**) of 1749–1752, and approximately seven-eighths of the Vieux Carré's buildings date from the nineteenth century. This unique mix of institutional (i.e., religious, educational, governmental) with commercial and residential structures forms the most complete historic neighborhood in the nation.

In addition to Creole cottages, two- and three-story brick row houses similar to those of eastern cities became popular in the early nineteenth century, as exemplified by the eleven brick houses on the 1100 block of Royal Street. Many structures combined commercial functions at ground level and residential space above, sometimes with an *entresol*, a shallow story between the ground floor and principal floor to provide storage for the shops, although this was sometimes used as living quarters for the store owner. Beginning in the mid-nineteenth century, two-story iron galleries were added to many existing buildings, such as those on the Gardette–Le Prêtre House of 1836 (716 Dauphine Street), which give the Vieux Carré its filigreed character. Greek Revival details also became fashionable, especially for door and window frames.

By the early twentieth century, the Vieux Carré had become shabby, disreputable, and as a cheap place to live, the home to newly arrived immigrants, particularly Italians, including many from Sicily. Among the many artists attracted to the area were Enrique Alferez (1901–1999), Alberta Kinsey (1875–1952), and brothers Ellsworth (1861–1939) and William Woodward (1859–1939), who gathered and exhibited at the Arts and Crafts Club (active from 1922 to 1951). Writers, too, notably William Faulkner, Frances Parkinson Keyes, and Tennessee Williams, have given an aura of Bohemian glamor and a mystique to the Vieux Carré. In the 1930s, this renewed interest in the historic quarter was instrumental in the formation of an early preservation movement, led by local preservation activist Elizabeth Werlein.

From the late 1940s onward, the Vieux Carré faced a major challenge from the proposal, developed by Robert Moses, to construct an elevated expressway along the riverfront that would have severed Jackson Square from the Mississippi River. Citizens' objections were crucial in the long battle to defeat this plan (1969) in the face of unanimous support of business and political leaders. In the 1970s, after maritime industries consolidated or moved elsewhere along the river, riverfront spaces were renovated for public use as initiatives to encourage tourism and reacquaint the city with the river. Among them was the Moonwalk (1.8) on the riverfront and pedestrian streets around Jackson Square and throughout the French Market area aimed at creating tourist amenities. Waterfront attractions continued to be added into the 1990s with the construction of Woldenberg Park (1.8) and the Aquarium of the Americas (5.1), and a recently (2016) initiated planning process aims to refurbish these riverfront pedestrian spaces and unify them into a cohesive pedestrian experience.

Today, the Vieux Carré faces the danger of losing its identity because of too many tourist attractions and overrestoration that could make it a caricature of itself. A recent dramatic decline in owner occupancy and permanent residency (from 10,000 permanent residents in 1980 to fewer than 3,000 in 2010) has become a serious threat to its survival as a viable neighborhood.

Although each of the Vieux Carré's streets has a distinctive character, the area closest to the river and toward Canal Street, including upscale commercial Royal Street and tawdry, raucous Bourbon Street, is largely the business, commercial, and tourist sector; the area downriver from Jackson Square is more residential. The buildings described here are unique or represent particularly fine examples of architectural types belonging to this extraordinarily rich built landscape. To appreciate fully the character and individual buildings of the Vieux Carré, one needs to walk the area street by street.

1.1   Jackson Square

1720s, Pierre La Blond de la Tour, engineer; Adrien de Pauger, assistant; 1800s renovated, Joseph Pilié; 1840s renovated. Bounded by Decatur, St. Peter, St. Ann, and Chartres sts.

Arguably one of the most important urban spaces in America is the ensemble of buildings and adjacent open spaces that comprise what is now known as Jackson Square. Dating from the city's beginnings in the early 1720s, the community's central open space was, as in other French colonial communities, a square laid out by eighteenth-century military engineers amid a local landscape of swamps, bayous, and impenetrable vegetation. Graphically documented as early as 1726, the Place d'Armes, originally a bare open field for military drills, parades, and civic functions (including public executions), was open on

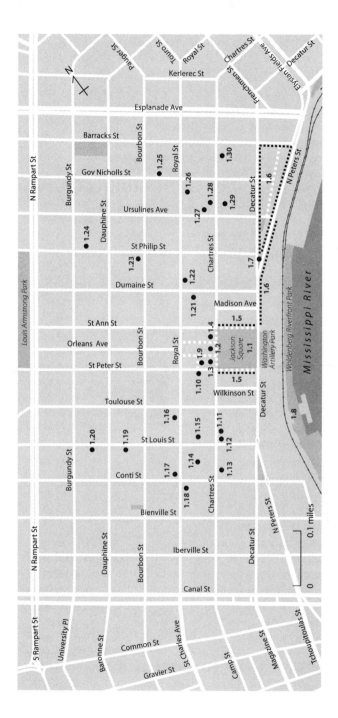

Toulouse St
Pauger St
Royal St
Chartres St
Elysian Fields Ave
Decatur St
Kerlerec St
Frenchmen St
N

Esplanade Ave

Barracks St
Bourbon St
N Rampart St
Burgundy St
Gov Nicholls St
Royal St • 1.25
• 1.30
Decatur St
N Peters St
Dauphine St
Ursulines Ave • 1.26 • 1.28
• 1.27 • 1.29
1.6
St Philip St
• 1.24
Chartres St
Dumaine St • 1.23
• 1.22
1.7
1.6

Louis Armstrong Park

Madison Ave
• 1.21
1.5
St Ann St
Bourbon St
Orleans Ave
Royal St
• 1.4
1.2 Jackson Square
Washington Artillery Park
Woldenberg Riverfront Park
Mississippi River
St Peter St • 1.9 1.1
• 1.10 • 1.3
1.5
Toulouse St
Wilkinson St
Decatur St
1.8
• 1.16
• 1.15 • 1.11
Burgundy St
• 1.20 • 1.19
St Louis St • 1.12
Conti St • 1.17 • 1.14 • 1.13
• 1.18
Chartres St
N Peters St
Bienville St
0.1 miles
N Rampart St
Dauphine St
Bourbon St
Iberville St
Decatur St
0
Canal St

S Rampart St
University Pl
Baronne St
Common St
St Charles Ave
Camp St
Magazine St
Tchoupitoulas St
Gravier St

one side, with municipal structures (the Cabildo and Presbytère; **1.3** and **1.4**) and St. Louis Cathedral (**1.2**) facing the Mississippi River. Residential and commercial structures lined the upriver and downriver sides. Nearby was the French Market (**1.6**), a public marketplace on the banks of the Mississippi River that had evolved over time from a Native American trading site into an active cultural and commercial crossroads. It remains today, although its original function of offering produce, meat, and fish to local residents has now changed into selling non-local trinkets to tourists.

A plan from 1808 shows the square planted with rows of sycamore trees perpendicular to the river, but by the 1840s the space had fallen into disrepair. The wealthy and influential Baroness Micaela Almonester de Pontalba gained control of property facing the square's upriver and downriver sides, and she demolished existing structures and commissioned identical brick buildings to face the square (**1.5**). She is even credited by some for designing (or redesigning) the structures and supervising their construction. Containing commercial uses on the ground floor and residential units above, they are widely acknowledged as being the first apartment buildings in America. She also supported renovation of the square into a more fashionable design reminiscent of a nineteenth-century French urban park. A second casting of Clark Mills's equestrian statue of General Andrew Jackson for the square's center was installed in 1855, and the square was renamed in Jackson's honor as a tribute to his heroic leadership of American troops in the victory over the British forces at the Battle of New Orleans (1815) at nearby Chalmette (**15.2**).

Many accounts of the period, including those of architect Benjamin Henry Latrobe (1819), journalists John Paxton (1822) and Frederick Law Olmsted (early 1850s), and architect Thomas Wharton (1854), document contemporary impressions of Jackson Square and its central role in the city's life. Visual evidence, from the midcentury onward, show a space that is cosmopolitan, urbane, and spacious.

In the late 1870s, city officials leased riverfront access to expanding railroads in exchange for their development of commercial wharves, an accommodation that encouraged economic, urban, and commercial expansion but effectively separated the city and its residents from the Mississippi River. This situation remained until about a century later, when events converged to reestablish a relationship between local residents and the river. As maritime industries left the downtown riverfront, elected officials realized that tourism could become a viable component of the local economy and that tourist-related amenities would make the community a more attractive destination. Architectural preservationists had by the 1970s established a substantial community foothold with vocal and persuasive arguments for the preservation of the city's unique architectural heritage. A notable victory ("The Second Battle of New Orleans") was the cancellation in 1969 of a six-lane elevated riverfront expressway, proposed by Robert Moses, which would have passed along the riverfront in front of Jackson Square. The combination of these elements resulted in projects such as the award-winning refurbishment of Jackson Square into a pedestrian space (mid-1970s, Cashio Cochran Sullivan, landscape architects). The square remains the center of New Orleans, and, much as in the past, this iconic urban landscape and the adjacent riverfront developments are the focus of the community's civic and cultural identity.

1.2   St. Louis Cathedral (Basilica of St. Louis King of France)
1849–1851, J. N. B. de Pouilly. Chartres St. at Jackson Sq.

St. Louis Cathedral, facing Jackson Square and the Mississippi River, stands as perhaps the iconic symbol of New Orleans. From the earliest days when people arrived by steamboat at

the river's bank, it has served as a formal gateway to the city. Completed in 1851, the present cathedral replaced two earlier structures on the site: Adrien de Pauger's church of 1724–1727, which burned in 1788, and that of 1789–1794 by Gilberto Guillemard, the architect for the Cabildo and the Presbytère. In 1793, the church was made the seat of a diocese, giving it the status of a cathedral, and Benjamin Henry Latrobe designed the clock tower in 1819.

After the Cabildo (**1.3**) and the Presbytère (**1.4**), the two buildings that flank the cathedral, were heightened with mansard roofs in 1847, the cathedral was rebuilt, in part to keep it in scale with the new development and emphasize its importance but also because the structure was in need of repair and too small for the congregation. J. N. B. de Pouilly's design was similar to that of Guillemard and also called for brick stuccoed on the exterior, but included a columned three-story rather than a two-story facade. The new design included a longer and wider nave, an openwork central steeple of cypress and iron, and, at each end of the facade, a three-story octagonal tower with a spire. Unfortunately, the central tower collapsed during construction in 1850, bringing down some of the roof and walls. Although it was probably the fault of the contractor, John Patrick Kirwan, who did not allow enough time for the mortar to set, de Pouilly was dismissed and Alexander Sampson hired to supervise construction. The final result was a three-story facade with paired Doric columns flanking central, round-arched openings on the two lower levels and paired pilasters on the third, balanced by horizontal moldings to create a harmonious design. All these elements project only slightly from the wall's surface, resulting in a planar surface that conveys the impression that the facade is an elevation drawing rather than a three-dimensional structure. De Pouilly's open iron spire was covered with slate tiles in 1859.

The interior has galleries over the side aisles and frescoes painted by Erasmus Humbrecht in 1872. Stained glass side windows made by the Oidtmann workshop of Linnich, Germany, in 1929 depict the life of Louis IX, King of France, patron saint of the cathedral. Over the years, the cathedral has been renovated several times, including following Hurricane Katrina in 2005. In 1964, Pope Paul VI designated the cathedral a minor basilica, with the title Basilica St. Louis King of France, but the building remains known as St. Louis Cathedral.

St. Anthony's Garden, behind the cathedral, is on the site of the original cemetery and is therefore one of the earliest designed spaces in the community. The fifteen-foot-high marble obelisk topped by a burial urn was moved here in 1914 from its original site at the Quarantine Station, seventy miles downriver from New Orleans, along with the remains of nineteen sailors who died of yellow fever during the epidemic of 1857. Renovations from the early 1940s have been attributed to landscape architect William Wiedorn and architect Richard Koch. Following Katrina, the space was redesigned by French landscape architect Louis Benech, using an eighteenth-century garden vocabulary and plant selections taken from written exchanges between the colony and the Jardin des Plantes in Paris.

1.3   The Cabildo
1795 – 1799, Gilberto Guillemard. Chartres St. at St. Peter St.

The Cabildo and the Presbytère (**1.4**), designed by the French-born military architect-engineer Guillemard (1746 – 1808) as a pair flanking St. Louis Cathedral, housed the administrative units of the Spanish government. Almost identical in design, the two buildings are also similar to those in other Spanish colonies of the time, such as in Havana and Mexico (e.g., the

Casa Reale, 1781, Antequera, Mexico). Built on the site of the
early-eighteenth-century courthouse, barracks, and prison, all
destroyed in the fire of 1788, the Cabildo was intended to be
the city hall. Classical in design, it has an arcade supported on
piers at the ground level and a second story featuring pilasters between the arched windows. The center of the facade
is marked by a slightly projecting three-bay, two-story order,
Tuscan half columns below and Ionic above, topped by a pediment. Guillemard gave the building a flat tiled roof; the mansard
roof with its large voluted dormer windows and cupola was
added under city surveyor Louis Surgi (1815–1869) in 1847. The
exterior of the brick building is covered with stucco to match
St. Louis Cathedral, and the wrought-iron balcony railings were
made in New Orleans by Marcellino Hernandez, who emigrated
from the Canary Islands. The Cabildo, along with the earlier St.
Louis Church (later Cathedral) of 1789–1794 and the Presbytère,
introduced to New Orleans such classical elements as engaged
columns, pilasters, and a central pediment.

The Cabildo served as New Orleans's city hall from 1803 (the
Louisiana Purchase transfer took place here) to 1836. The American emblems on the pediment were added in 1821 by Italian
sculptor Pietro Cardelli. When New Orleans was divided into
three municipalities in 1836, the Cabildo served as the municipal
hall for the Creole population. After the City's reunification in
1852 and until 1910, the Supreme Court of Louisiana occupied
the building. In 1911, the Cabildo opened as the Louisiana State
Museum. Following a fire in 1988 that destroyed the third floor,

the Cabildo was restored by Koch and Wilson, Architects, matching the old heavy timber construction, at which time the buff-tan exterior color used in 1847 was replicated.

1.4 The Presbytère

1791–1813, Gilberto Guillemard; Gurlie and Guillot. Chartres St. at St. Ann St.

Begun in 1791 according to Guillemard's 1789 plans, and originally intended as the rectory for St. Louis Cathedral, the Presbytère was used as the courthouse. It was financed, as were the Cabildo and the St. Louis Cathedral, by the entrepreneur and merchant Don Andrés de Almonester y Roxas. Designed to match the Cabildo, the Presbytère is, in fact, a few feet wider and has broader arches than that structure. Only one story of the Presbytère had been constructed when Don Andrés died in 1798. The French-born architect-builders Claude Gurlie (1770–1858) and Joseph Guillot (1771–1838) completed the building in 1813. Rear wings designed by French immigrant Benjamin Buisson (1793–1874) were added in 1840, and the mansard roof in 1847; the cupola was removed after damage in a storm. Along with the Cabildo, the Presbytère was transferred to the Louisiana State Museum in 1911, itself becoming a museum piece.

1.5 Pontalba Buildings

1849–1851, James Gallier Sr., Henry Howard. St. Peter and St. Ann sts. between Chartres and Decatur sts.

The Baroness Micaela Almonester de Pontalba, who inherited from her father, Don Andrés de Almonester y Roxas, the land and deteriorated structures on which the Pontalba Buildings

Food, Cuisine, and Food Culture

Nestled in a region of rich agricultural and maritime resources settled by many immigrant groups from the eighteenth century to the present, New Orleans has earned a reputation for its distinctive multicultural cuisine. Early settlers learned what to plant and where to find sustenance from native communities, and the value of settlers who had agricultural experience became evident as the city grew. Many early farmers were Germans, drawn to the region by John Law's ill-fated "Mississippi Bubble" in the 1720s. When this financial scheme failed, many could not return, and they remained in agricultural regions west of the community, growing foodstuffs that were brought to the colony through Lake Pontchartrain and Bayou St. John via Native American trading routes. By the mid-1790s, deliveries of produce, seafood, and other materials to the rear portion of the Vieux Carré were facilitated by the Carondelet Canal.

Enslaved and free immigrants, first from Africa and later from Haiti and other Caribbean islands, brought agricultural expertise (notably with rice and sugarcane) as well as distinctive plants (such as okra) that contributed significantly to the region's cuisine. As other groups arrived in the nineteenth century—including Germans, Irish, and Italians—their cooking traditions merged with existing practices. Such cultural additions continued through the twentieth century and into the present, as more recent arrivals from Southeast Asia (notably Vietnam) and Central America have added their distinctive flavors to the mix.

now stand, commissioned Gallier to design two rows of houses. The rows, one on the downriver side (commonly known as the Lower Pontalba) and the other on the upriver side (Upper Pontalba) of Jackson Square, were planned to accommodate sixteen houses with ground-floor stores. The buildings were financed as well as supervised by the baroness, who, after disputes with Gallier, replaced him with Henry Howard in 1849. Exactly who designed the Pontalba Buildings remains a matter of debate.

Restaurants, modest as well as grand, representing the city's diverse communities, proliferated from the nineteenth century to the present. Like corner grocery stores, neighborhood establishments have remained common, serving fare to residents and workers. Often their menus reflect both domestic activities (red or navy beans and rice with pork chops on Monday) and religious customs (fried fish on Friday), with standard fare served on other days. Local sandwich specialties include po' boys (made on long baguettes, filled with fried seafood, meatballs, or roast beef, usually "dressed" with mayonnaise, lettuce and tomatoes) and muffalettas (round loaves with a variety of Italian cold cuts, cheeses, and olive salad).

More elaborate meals are found in the old-line traditional Creole mainstays dating from the nineteenth and early twentieth centuries (including Arnaud's, Antoine's, Galatoire's) as well as restaurant dynasties now in their second and third generations (such as Dooky Chase and the Brennan family), known for signature dishes of gumbo, oysters, shrimp, crabmeat, and local fish. Newer restaurants continue to appear with dizzying regularity, often with reinterpretations of this classic fare, offering a wealth of dining options.

On tables and menus throughout the city, it is clear that, in multicultural communities, food is one of the few things that binds all people together.

Architect and historian Samuel Wilson Jr. believed Gallier was responsible for the plans, and the extant Gallier plans correspond with the as-built conditions. However, Gallier never claimed credit for the elevations and Howard did in his short autobiography. The builder was Samuel Stewart.

The houses in each row have three stories and are constructed of pressed red brick from Baltimore; New England granite was used for the square piers on the first story, and the slate roof tiles came from England. Pediments mark the ends and the center of each row and serve as a unifying element. Each house has an attic space, with horizontal windows just below the narrow cornice, which accommodated the residents' enslaved workers. The three-story cast-iron galleries, fabricated in New York, are possibly the first in New Orleans that serve as an integral part of the design rather than a later attachment. The galleries, embellished with the monogram "AP" for their patron, shaded pedestrians below and provided outdoor space for the apartments upstairs. To the rear, each house had a service wing and small courtyard. The buildings' occupants were primarily merchants and professionals, most of whom were newcomers to the city, and their servants.

Following the Civil War, the Vieux Carré saw a marked decline, and by the time the Louisiana State Museum acquired the Lower Pontalba in 1927 and the City of New Orleans the Upper Pontalba in 1930, the structures were shabby tenements. Both buildings were remodeled into apartments in 1935–1936 with Works Progress Administration (WPA) funds. A restoration in the 1950s by Koch and Wilson, Architects, returned the buildings to residential use. Over the years, the Pontalba Buildings have housed a number of significant authors, including Sherwood Anderson, William Faulkner, and Katherine Anne Porter. The Louisiana State Museum's 1850 House in the Lower Pontalba showcases the original configuration of the second- and third-floor residential spaces.

1.6   The French Market

1813–present. Bounded by Decatur, N. Peters, St. Ann, and Barracks sts.

For most of the eighteenth century, a public market was held out-of-doors on the levee near the Place d'Armes (Jackson Square), in what became known as the French Market. According to a May 21, 1779, ordinance, the City decided that "in view of the great abuses committed in the sales of provisions which are exposed to the elements," a covered market was essential for reasons of health. Consequently, the Spanish built a market of wood that was roofed but open along the sides. In 1813, the first of a series of more permanent structures was built on this waterfront site. The oldest section, formerly the meat market (Halle des Boucheries), is the 302-foot-long arcaded structure of plastered brick on Decatur between St. Ann and Dumaine streets, designed by city surveyor Jacques Tanesse (c. 1775–1824) and built by Gurlie and Guillot. Its Doric colonnade was added in the 1930s to unify the structure with the similarly colonnaded vegetable market (Marché aux Legumes), on Decatur from St. Philip to Ursuline streets, designed by city surveyor Joseph Pilié (c. 1789–1846) in 1823. From 1936 to 1938, the market was extensively remodeled by Samuel Stone Jr. and his son Frank M. Stone with Public Works Administration (PWA) funding. Extensions to the market toward Barracks Street, dating from 1938, the 1970s, and 1991, essentially follow the earlier design. Latrobe Park (mid-1970s, Cashio Cochran, landscape architects), which sits along Decatur Street near the market and is named for Benjamin Henry Latrobe, is the site of a Wallace Fountain given to the people of New Orleans by the people of Paris to mark the 1984 Louisiana World Exposition.

1.7   Joan of Arc Monument
1880, Emmanuel Fremiet. Place de France, Decatur St.

The dazzling gilded thirteen-foot-high equestrian statue of Joan of Arc, clad in armor and holding a lance (a copy of the original statue of 1874 in the Place des Pyramides in Paris), was a gift to the City from France in 1964 during the presidency of Charles de Gaulle. Originally installed in front of the International Trade Mart (**5.2**) and the Rivergate Convention Center (1968, Curtis and Davis; demolished 1995), *Joan* was moved when the present casino was constructed at that site. This new location in the heart of the Vieux Carré in a pocket park gives the work the greater visibility it deserves.

1.8   **The Moonwalk and Woldenberg Riverfront Park**
       1976, Cashio Cochran, landscape architects; 1990, Cashio Cochran Torre/Design Consortium. Canal to St. Philip St.

For the city's early settlers, the levee provided a scenic setting for public promenades, with the added advantage of cool breezes from the river. The English traveler Francis Bailey, who visited New Orleans in 1797, described it as "a handsome raised gravel walk planted with orange trees," which "in the summer time served for a mall, and in an evening was always a fashionable resort for beaux and belles of the place." "I have enjoyed many an evening's promenade here," he continued, "admiring the serenity of the climate and the majestic appearance of this noble river."

In the nineteenth century, this land was increasingly occupied by wharves, industrial buildings, sugar sheds, warehouses, and railroad tracks. Esplanade Avenue and Canal Street replaced the levee as the site for casual perambulation. In the last quarter of the twentieth century, much of the levee fronting the Vieux Carré was returned to public use, the result of a public workshop convened in July 1972 by Cashio Cochran Sullivan and Wayne Collier, director of the Vieux Carré Commission. Improvements to Jackson Square were first (1976) followed by a redesign of Washington Artillery Park, and, on the levee, a wooden walkway with shade trees and benches overlooking the river, named the Moonwalk in honor of then-mayor (1970–1978) Maurice E. "Moon" Landrieu. Additional streetscape improvements (also by Cashio Cochran) were made to the adjacent French Market (**1.6**). In 1990, the twelve-acre Woldenberg Riverfront Park, with lawn, trees, and public art, was built upriver, extending over the river with lightweight soil on the concrete foundations that formerly supported warehouses.

1.9   The Arsenal

1839, James H. Dakin. 615 St. Peter St.

Built on the site of the 1769 Spanish Arsenal, this Greek Revival structure is one of Dakin's earliest works in the city. Designed to house the state armory, the narrow, vertical building of brick covered in plaster has a severe facade consisting essentially of four giant Tuscan pilasters raised on huge granite blocks, with the central two piers in antis. Adding to the image of strength and security, iron grilles cover the narrow windows, the massive iron door is studded with enormous rivets, and the heavy entablature presses down on the supports. Ornament is minimal, but the low-relief sculpture of exploding cannonballs on the parapet and cannons and flags in the cast-iron panels above the entablature emphasize the arsenal's military purpose.

The building housed the Orleans Artillery until the Civil War. During the war, Confederate troops stored supplies in the building until it came under Union control and served as a military prison. Following the war it had several uses until 1914, when it became one component of the Louisiana State Museum.

This old arsenal is one example of the beautifully austere versions of Classical Revival and Gothic Revival that Dakin introduced to Louisiana. Dakin, who had been a partner in the New York office of Town and Davis (later Town, Davis and Dakin) and then established his own practice in 1833, moved to New Orleans in 1835 to join his brother, architect Charles B. Dakin (1811–1839). Charles soon left for Mobile, Alabama, to run that branch of the firm. James designed numerous buildings in Louisiana, including the castlelike Old Louisiana State Capitol (1847–1852) in Baton Rouge. Though Dakin reputedly had a difficult personality, architect James Gallier Sr. described him as a genius in his autobiography—high praise indeed from a person who tended to be rather critical.

1.10   Le Petit Salon (Victor David House)
1838. 620 St. Peter St.

French immigrant and hardware merchant Victor David and his Creole wife, Anne Carmelite Rabassa, hired builders Samuel

Stewart and David Sidle to construct their four-story, side-hall house. Built of brick and raised on a full basement, the house has an exterior staircase (a rare feature in the Vieux Carré) that leads to the principal entrance on the second floor. The handsome Greek Revival entrance is framed by pilasters set between foliate ornamented jambs and supporting an anthemion-decorated lintel—details copied from Minard Lefever's pattern book, *Beauties of Modern Architecture* (1833). Each floor is marked by a narrow balcony with an iron railing, each in a different pattern; the one on the fourth floor is of crossed arrows. Horizontal windows covered with foliate-patterned cast-iron grilles provide light for the attic. Crowning the house is a strongly projecting cornice. In 1925, the house was purchased by Le Petit Salon, a women's literary and arts organization, whose first president and vice president were, respectively, author Grace King and journalist Dorothy Dix. The group hired Armstrong and Koch (the firm that preceded Koch and Wilson) to restore the house, one of the first steps in the rejuvenation of the Vieux Carré.

1.11   Pharmacy Museum (Dufilho's Pharmacy)
1823; 1837, J. N. B. de Pouilly. 514–516 Chartres St.

Louis J. Dufilho Jr., one of the first licensed pharmacists (1816) in the nation (Louisiana passed a law in 1804 requiring a licensing examination for pharmacists), acquired the site on which the building now stands in 1822. The present building is either a remodeling of his apothecary shop and residence built in 1823, or a new structure of 1837. Dufilho's apothecary shop and residence is in the style of a typical Creole-American town house. The three-story building is brick covered with plaster. Three large round-arched openings in the lower facade are matched by a similarly shaped carriage entrance at one side. An entresol between the first and second stories is lighted by the upper portion of the window arches. A botanical garden in the courtyard supplied Dufilho's medicinal herbs. Dufilho sold the building and its contents in 1855 and it subsequently changed hands and uses several times. In 1937, then-mayor Robert S, Maestri purchased the building and donated it to the City, which restored it and opened it as a pharmacy museum in 1950. Since 1987, a non-profit organization has operated the museum.

The courtyard has recently been replanted with medicinal herbs.

1.12   Napoleon House (Girod House)
1814, attributed to Jean-Hyacinthe Laclotte. 500–506 Chartes St.

J.-H. Laclotte (1766–c. 1829), from Bordeaux, studied at the Ecole des Beaux-Arts in Paris before arriving in New Orleans in 1806. He built this three-story residence for Nicholas Girod, mayor of New Orleans from 1812 to 1815. The ground story of the plastered brick building was used for business purposes and, in typical French fashion, opened directly onto the street by means of casement doors; the principal living spaces, with higher ceilings, occupied the second floor. The house was innovative in New Orleans, however, for its use of tall proportions. Curved-arched dormers and an octagonal cupola mark the hipped roof. A carriageway led from St. Louis Street into a two-story wing, dating from 1795. It is believed that Girod, one of the leaders in the plot to rescue Napoleon, wanted his house to serve as a refuge for the emperor after his escape from Elba, but Napoleon was subsequently sent to St. Helena, where he died in 1821, thus dashing Girod's hopes. However, it is claimed that Napoleon's physician, Dr. Francesco Antommarchi, maintained an office here about 1838, where he treated the poor without charge. By 1860, the building was an auction house, and in 1914 it became a bar. Today it is a popular bar and restaurant. The original courtyard has long been divided by a masonry wall.

**1.13   Williams Research Center, The Historic New Orleans
Collection (Second City Criminal Court and Third
District Police Station)**
*1915, E. A. Christy; 1993 renovated, Jahnke Architects. 410
Chartres St.*

Edgar A. Christy (1880–1959), architect for the City of New
Orleans from 1904 to 1923 and supervising architect of the
Orleans Parish School Board from the creation of the post in
1911 until his retirement in 1940, gave this building's Beaux-Arts
classical facade a rich variety of textures and decorative details.
Each of the two stories features three large round-arched
windows in the center of the facade. The distribution of weight
is effectively realized with a terra-cotta-faced first level set into
exaggerated stone joints. The second story, of brick, repeats the
round arches, but window crowns, decorative garlands, and a
roofline balustrade make the overall treatment much lighter. In
a 1993 renovation to create a research center for The Historic
New Orleans Collection (THNOC), the twenty-four-foot-high
former courtroom on the second floor was converted into a
public reading room. The building's restrained classicism makes
a nice foil for the grandiosity of the nearby Supreme Court
building (**1.14**). THNOC expanded into the adjacent building
at 400 Chartres built in 1825 by François Marie Perilliat and
restored in 2012 by Koch and Wilson, Architects.

1.14 Louisiana Supreme Court and Orleans Parish Civil District Court (Louisiana Supreme Court and Fourth Circuit Court of Appeals)
1907–1909, Frederick W. Brown and A. Ten Eyck Brown, with P. Thornton Marye; 1990s–2004 renovated, Lyons and Hudson Architects. 400 Royal St.

The Atlanta-based architects who won the design competition for the court building produced a Beaux-Arts classical showpiece inspired by late-nineteenth-century City Beautiful ideals. The symmetrical exterior has semicircular end walls that enclose courtrooms. White Georgia marble sheathes the first two floors; the upper two floors and the entablature are faced with glazed white terra-cotta. Ornamentation is rich and abundant, including marble brackets, terra-cotta pilasters, garlanded cartouches, upper-floor windows separated by two-story-high Ionic columns, and an ornate terra-cotta balustrade that surrounds the low-pitched roof. A grand staircase leads to the Royal Street entrance lobby, which is surrounded by twelve columns supporting the thirty-foot-high ceiling. The single-height Chartres Street lobby features a magnificent curving double staircase. The courthouse was controversial when built, denounced not only for causing the demolition of an entire block of nineteenth-century buildings but also for being too large and out of scale with the Vieux Carré. Its dazzling marble and glazed terra-cotta exterior has been criticized as flashy and thus incompatible with the muted tones and soft textures of the Quarter's brick and stucco buildings. In the 1950s, at the suggestion of architect Richard Koch, magnolia trees were planted around the building in an effort to hide it. In 1958, the

Supreme Court moved to a new courthouse (since demolished) in the Civic Center and this building had a variety of tenants, including the Department of Wildlife and Fisheries, before being abandoned in the 1980s. Beginning in the 1990s, it was slowly renovated to serve again for courts. Some unfortunate design decisions, particularly reglazing with heavily tinted glass, detract from the building's integrity. Despite all the former objections to its physical appearance, the courthouse reinforces the Vieux Carré as a living urban organism, able to encompass buildings that reflect all eras of its existence rather than being preserved in (nineteenth-century) aspic.

1.15 Omni Royal Orleans Hotel (Royal Orleans Hotel)
1956–1960, Curtis and Davis, and Koch and Wilson, Architects.
621 St. Louis St.

Although the Royal Orleans Hotel's developers initially selected a design by the firm of Curtis and Davis, the Vieux Carré Commission considered it too contemporary in appearance and thus incompatible with the Quarter's historic character. Consequently, Koch and Wilson, a firm known for its more traditional approach to design, was hired to design the hotel's exterior, limiting Curtis and Davis to fashioning the interiors. In its general outline, height, and cornice line, the six-story hotel was modeled architecturally on J. N. B. de Pouilly's St. Louis Exchange Hotel, which previously stood on this site and where slave auctions once took place under its rotunda. Piers from that building's granite arcade are incorporated into this hotel's Chartres Street elevation. The design features pedimented dormers, cast-iron galleries, and fenestration that suggest rooms with high ceilings, although the seemingly tall windows of the second story in fact extend over two low-ceilinged floors. This is an enormous building for the Vieux Carré; it has almost twice as many rooms as the St. Louis had. A mansard roof with dormer windows for additional rooms was added in 1963. Although the Royal Orleans is as tall as the courthouse opposite (**1.14**), its unobtrusive design, timid details, and historicized appearance enabled the hotel avoid the controversies which marked that building. Most importantly, nothing had been torn down to accommodate it because the site had been vacant for many years. However, the hotel raises crucial questions about issues of historical reproduction and deceptive period appearance as well as appropriate contextual scale.

1.16 The Historic New Orleans Collection (Merieult House, Williams House)

c. 1792 and later. 533 Royal St.

The Historic New Orleans Collection (THNOC) owns a cluster of historic properties, many of which are open to the public. This complex of brick buildings, all restored, includes the combination town house and ground-level commercial space on Royal Street that was built by Jacob Copperwaite for merchant Jean François Merieult; it was extensively remodeled in 1832 by Manuel J. De Lizardi, who substituted a granite front for the original ground-floor openings. The former Merieult House accommodates galleries and museum spaces. Behind it at the rear of a courtyard is the 1889 house purchased in 1938 by Kemper and Leila Williams, which was restored as their home by Richard Koch. The Williams House, furnished in various period styles, includes Kemper Williams's former study, which is paneled with first-growth cypress from the family's lumber business in Patterson, St. Mary Parish. On one side of the courtyard is the Counting House, a former warehouse built 1794–1795 for Merieult's business and in the 1830s transformed into a grand Greek Revival room for new owners, the Lizardi Brothers banking firm. It is now used as a reception room. Across the courtyard from it is the three-story former service wing.

Around the corner at 714 Toulouse Street is a late-nineteenth-century American town house that THNOC purchased in 1980 to accommodate staff. Also on Toulouse at 722 and 726 are, respectively, a Creole town house (1788), where playwrite Tennessee Williams lived for a short time in 1939, and a c. 1830 Creole cottage. Waggonner and Ball's renovation of the Brulatour House (1816) at 520 Royal for new exhibition space opens in 2018.

1.17 Historic Louisiana State Bank

1820–1822, Benjamin Henry Latrobe. 401 Royal St.

Latrobe was asked to design this bank shortly after arriving in New Orleans in January 1819 to complete the waterworks he had designed in 1811, which his recently deceased son, Henry Latrobe, had been supervising. The bank was Latrobe's last project, for he died in 1820 from yellow fever, the same disease that had killed his son. Builder Benjamin Fox completed the building. Exterior walls are finished with an ochre-colored

stucco, lightly scored to resemble masonry, and the entrance
is flanked by two Ionic columns painted to resemble a veined
green marble. Doors and windows on the ground story are
rectangular but set within shallow arches, and a narrow iron
balcony runs below the three second-story windows. A second,
less elaborate entrance is on the Conti Street side of the building. Originally the roof was flat; the present hipped roof and
dormers were added after 1822.

The discreet facade on Royal Street blends with the urban
streetscape, giving no hint of the wonderful space within.
A shallow brick dome tops a central circular banking room,
which is flanked by smaller vaulted spaces. The only ornament
is a rosette in the center of the dome; the curved, uninterrupted
plastered surfaces of walls and vaults provide a fluid, voluptuous
series of spaces. The plan of the interior is similar to Latrobe's
demolished Bank of Pennsylvania of 1799 in Philadelphia.
A semicircular bay housing the director's office projects into
what was once the rear yard, in which were located the quarters for the enslaved workers and the carriage house, entered
through gates on Conti Street. The cashier's living quarters were
on the second floor. The building has housed many different tenants in its long history, including the Royal Turkish Bath Company

for Ladies and, for many years, an antiques shop. The building currently is an event space, appropropriatly named Latrobe's.

Several financial institutions were located near this corner of the Vieux Carré in the early nineteenth century, including the former Bank of Louisiana (**1.18**) diagonally opposite. The former Banque de la Louisiane occupied 417 Royal Street from 1805 to 1819 and the c. 1800 Vincent Rillieux House at 339 Royal Street, attributed to Barthélemy Lafon (1769–1820), was occupied by Planters' Bank from 1811 to 1820 and by the Bank of the United States from 1820 to 1836.

1.18 New Orleans 8th District Police Station (Bank of Louisiana)

1826, Bickel, Hamblet and Fox; c. 1861 alterations, James Gallier Jr. 334 Royal St.

After this massive rectangular two-story building of stucco-covered brick was damaged by fire in 1861, Gallier added a Tuscan entrance portico. He also gave the bank a more imposing appearance by replacing the Ionic capitals of the two-story engaged columns with weightier Tuscan capitals. A prominent cornice and balustrade adorned with urns on rectangular pedestals complete the ornamentation of the building. The fence and gates, based on Robert Adam's gates to Lansdowne House, London, were produced by a New York company in 1827. After the bank's assets were liquidated in 1867, the building served as the state capitol from 1869 to 1870, after which it housed an auction exchange, a concert hall, a saloon, a criminal court, and a tourist office.

1.19 Hermann-Grima House

1831, William Brand; 2016 restored, Koch and Wilson, Architects. 820 St. Louis St.

Samuel Hermann, a German Jewish immigrant merchant and commission banker, chose architect-builder William Brand (1778–1849) to design his house. Brand, who arrived in New Orleans from Virginia about 1805, produced a subtle blend of American and Creole features in this freestanding two-and-a-half story, end-gabled house. Built to the front property line, the house has a central entrance raised four steps above the sidewalk to a Federal doorway, set between slender Ionic columns with glass side panels and topped by an entablature and fanlight. On the second floor, an almost identical door

opens onto a balcony. Windows are the double-hung American type on the first floor and triple-hung on the second, and the roofline is defined by a sawtooth-band cornice. Exterior symmetry reflects the American-style central-hall plan with flanking front rooms. However, the rear second floor embraces the Creole loggia (now enclosed) between cabinets. The house is constructed of Philadelphia red brick laid in Flemish bond and painted pink with white mortar joints.

At the rear, a galleried, three-story brick service wing, which includes an open-hearth kitchen, extends along one side of the large courtyard. Paved with flagstones that came as ship ballast, the courtyard has planting beds that were raised to provide drainage and includes a replica of the original cast-iron cistern. In 1844, Judge Felix Grima and his wife, Adelaide, acquired the house and in 1850 built the adjacent stables. It is recorded that he owned fifteen enslaved workers and employed one free woman of color. His descendants sold the house in 1924 to the Christian Women's Exchange, an organization active in charity work, which was responsible for its restoration in 1965. The house, opened to the public in 1970, is associated with the James Gallier House (**1.26**).

1.20 Forstall House
c. 1845; 1858, Gallier, Turpin and Company; 2010 renovated. 920 St. Louis St.

This building's sophisticated neoclassical-influenced facade is a remodeling by James Gallier Jr. of a preexisting three-story brick building that banker Edmund J. Forstall and his wife, Clara, purchased in 1857. The first story is rusticated with round-arched windows, the two floors above are united by two-story high Corinthian pilasters, with round-arched windows at the third level, and the building is topped by a low attic above a heavy cornice. The keystones of the third-floor windows are shaped as grotesques. Small iron balconies in front of the windows add a local touch, and the entire facade is painted in shades of a creamy color. This is an unusual design for New Orleans and reflects Gallier's broad knowledge of fashionable European and American East Coast styles. In the twentieth century the building had various owners and uses but was returned to residential use in 2010 when it was renovated and converted to condominiums.

1.21   Madame John's Legacy

c. 1730; 1789 rebuilt, Robert James; 1971–1972 restored, Waggonner and Ball Architects. 632 Dumaine St.

This complex, including a house, kitchen, and *garçonnière* organized around an L-shaped courtyard, is an important example of Creole architecture. Originally freestanding and set farther back on the lot, the house was reconstructed for Spanish officer Don Manuel de Lanzos by Anglo-American builder Robert James from materials salvaged after the citywide fire of 1788. James followed the pre-fire design, incorporating the original foundations, walls, and iron hardware. The house is raised on a brick basement with heavy batten doors that lead to service rooms and a loggia at the rear, framed at each end by cabinets.

The upper floor, of brick-between-posts construction covered on the outside with wide, beaded, horizontal boards, is shaded by a six-bay gallery supported on turned, shaped colonnettes. The double-pitched roof, over Norman trusses, has two dormer windows. Rooms are arranged en suite without hallways, in the Creole fashion. A restoration in the 1990s returned the house to the original paint colors: white at first level, moss green doors, and oxblood red sides. Believed to have been built by sea captain Jean Pascal, the house was occupied by his widow until 1771. Its name is said to derive from George Washington Cable's short story "Tite Poulette," which is about a quadroon called Madame John. Artist Morris Henry Hobbs lived in the house in the early 1940s. The last owner, Stella H. Lemann, bequeathed the residence to the Louisiana State Museum in 1947, which maintains it; the house is open to the public. The elegant window and shutter details as well as the beautiful hardware match those on the contemporaneous Pitot House (**4.13**).

1.22   Miltenberger Houses

1838; 1858 galleries. 900–910 Royal St.

The cast-iron galleries added to this group of brick three-story buildings illustrate the transformation undergone by many quite plain buildings in the Vieux Carré in the mid-nineteenth century. Ornamental cast iron was manufactured by several companies in New Orleans, reaching its peak of popularity in the 1850s, when the city had become a center for cast-iron work. Complex and naturalistic patterns were preferred, such as these representing oak leaves and acorns. The houses, acquired by the Miltenberger family in 1854, were occupied by the Miltenberger brothers, who were engaged in the ironwork industry. The raised tomb for the Miltenberger family in Greenwood Cemetery (see **10.10**) is made entirely of cast iron.

Opposite at 915 Royal is one of New Orleans's three cast-iron fences with a cornstalk pattern (one surrounds the Robert Short House [**7.20**] and the other at 1206 N. White has cornstalk-decorated posts). The design of the c. 1850 fence on Royal Street represents cornstalks entwined with morning-glory vines. From this spot on Royal Street looking toward the Central Business District, a view of the fifty-one-story One Shell Square building (**6.15**) makes abundantly clear the sharp contrast between the low-rise, highly textured surfaces of the

Vieux Carré and the crisp verticality of the business district just a few blocks away.

1.23 Lafitte's Blacksmith Shop
c. 1795. 941 Bourbon St.

Although often touted as a typical Creole or Vieux Carré structure, the single-story Blacksmith Shop is inauthentic on many counts. Partial removal of the exterior stucco revealed the brick-between-posts construction. Although removal allows us to see this old construction method, it is not historically correct, for without this protective barrier, the wood frame and soft bricks would have rapidly deteriorated in the New Orleans climate. Additionally, the building has lost the roof extension that shaded the walls and has acquired dormers, and the original four-room interior has been totally altered. The building's purported history is also false; there is no evidence that the pirates Jean and Pierre Lafitte had anything to do with the building or even used it as a cover for their smuggling activities. But these tales and the building's overly quaint appearance continue to make it a highly popular bar and tourist attraction, representing, perhaps in microcosm, the Vieux Carré's mystique.

1.24 Dolliole-Masson House
c. 1795; 1981 restored, Frank W. Masson. 933 St. Philip St.

Entrepreneur Jean-Louis Dolliole (1779–1861), a free man of color, constructed this fine example of a four-bay, hipped-roofed Creole cottage with brick-between-posts construction, two rooms wide and two deep, with small cabinets at the rear, and a central chimney. A roof extension (*abat-vent*) shades the facade, and shutters cover the doors and windows. The house resembles Benjamin Henry Latrobe's description of a typical Creole cottage, written in his journal in 1819: "The roofs are high, covered with tiles or shingles, and project five feet over the footway, which is also five feet wide. The eaves therefore discharge the water into the Gutters. . . . These one stories houses are very simple in their plan. The two front rooms open into the street with french Glass doors. Those on one side are the dining and drawing rooms, the others chambers. . . . The french and continental Europaeans [sic] . . . employ the room they have, to more advantage, because they do not require so much space for passages. . . . The french stucco the fronts of their buildings and often color them." In 1981, architect Frank W. Masson (1949–2008) restored the house with as much historical accuracy as possible, including colors such as the mango yellow exterior. Dolliole built a number of houses in the Creole sections of New Orleans and contributed financially to the construction of St. Augustine Church (**2.10**).

1.25   Thierry House
1814, Arsène Lacarrière Latour and Henry B. Latrobe. 721 Governor Nicholls St.

This one-story house of plastered brick was built for Jean Baptiste Thierry, editor of the newspaper *Le Courrier de la Louisiane*. According to restoration architect Samuel Wilson Jr., Latour (c. 1770–1839) was responsible for the rear with its loggia and cabinets, and Latrobe (1792–1817) designed the Doric portico with segmental arches at the front. Wilson regarded the portico as the oldest residential use of Greek Revival in New Orleans. The facade's severity and planar undecorated surfaces are reminiscent of the contemporary work of John Soane in England. The house is set back rather than flush with the sidewalk, as are most Vieux Carré buildings. Latour and J.-H. Laclotte (see **1.12**) formed an architecture and engineering firm c. 1810 and operated a school for drawing, architecture, carpentry, interior design, and decoration.

Opposite at 716–724 Governor Nicholls, three brick buildings arranged around a central open court were built c. 1834 by Paul Preval as public stables, a carriage house, and a warehouse. Later converted to apartments, the buildings were renovated in 2015 by Harry Baker Smith Architects.

1.26 James Gallier House

1857–1860, James Gallier Jr. 1132 Royal St.

Gallier Jr. designed this two-story residence for his wife, Josephine Aglae Villavaso, and their four daughters. Constructed of stuccoed brick, rusticated and painted to resemble granite on the ground floor, the mildly Greek Revival facade is softened by a two-story, rosette-patterned cast-iron gallery. In his plan, Gallier combined the Creole carriageway leading back to a courtyard with the American preference for a staircase in the side hall rather than on the rear gallery. A double parlor divided by a screen of decorative pilasters and square columns is situated on the ground floor; four bedrooms occupy the second floor, and the dining room is in the service wing. Gallier's house possessed all the architectural amenities and fashions of the upper-middle-class lifestyle at that time, including a ventilation system, plumbing, hot and cold running water on the second floor, a copper bathtub, a cast-iron cooking range, and closets. The present exterior cistern (c. 1850) was moved here from a St. James Parish plantation. A wing for four enslaved workers, including a kitchen, is attached to the rear of the house. Gallier maintained an office in the upstairs hall, illuminated by a skylight. Architectural drawings (including indications of the garden) and house records made possible an accurate restoration of the building in 1971 by Henry Krotzer of Koch and Wilson, Architects, with interiors by Samuel Dornsife; the landscape architect was Christopher C. Friedrichs (1932–2015). It is now a house museum associated with the Herman-Grima House (**1.19**) and open to the public.

1.27 Croissant d'Or Patisserie
c. 1870; 1907 alterations. 617 Ursulines St.

In the late nineteenth century, a large number of immigrants from Sicily settled in the Vieux Carré. Angelo Brocato opened a confectionery and ice cream parlor in this stuccoed brick building in 1907 and tiled its interior in the style of those in his hometown of Palermo. Re-creating the archways of traditional ice cream parlors, he then divided the space into two salons to separate the sexes; sawdust covered the floor. The walls are entirely covered with white glazed tiles, including, just below the ceiling, a charming low-relief border of pastel-colored garlands. The exterior of the first floor has been altered. Another early-twentieth-century tiled building is Casamento's Restaurant (1919; 4330 Magazine Street), whose shiny white tiles include decorative bouquets.

1.28 Beauregard-Keyes House
1826, François E. Correjolles. 1113 Chartres St.

Auctioneer Joseph Le Carpentier purchased this lot from the Ursuline nuns and hired Baltimore-born Correjolles (1795–1864) to design his house. James Lambert was the builder. After 1833,

Writing New Orleans

In the golden moment of American literature between 1920 and World War II, many of America's best writers spent time here and made it the focus of their works. As Stella says to her sister Blanche DuBois in Tennessee Williams's *A Streetcar Named Desire*, "New Orleans isn't like other cities." The Vieux Carré's "raffish" qualities (as Williams noted) added to its bohemian atmosphere, making it especially attractive.

A central figure during this heyday was Lyle Saxon. Born in Baton Rouge, he moved first to 612 Royal Street in 1928 and then to 534 Madison Street in 1937. Saxon wrote *Fabulous New Orleans* (1928) and, as head of Louisiana's Federal Writers project, directed the WPA guides to New Orleans (1938) and Louisiana (1941). He restored several houses, and his history-based writings brought attention to local folklore and the Vieux Carré's unique architectural qualities. Later literary figures include Harnett Kane and Frances Parkinson Keyes; their romanticized novels, set in the city and region, highlighted Louisiana's history and architecture, encouraging early preservation efforts. Keyes left her mark on the Vieux Carré in the house and garden (**1.28**) at 1113 Chartres Street she purchased in 1950 and restored.

Short-story writer Sherwood Anderson lodged first at 708 Royal Street and then, from 1924 to 1926, at 540-B St. Peter Street in the Pontalba (**1.5**). His apartment became a hub for visiting writers, and as editor of the *Double Dealer*, a literary magazine published between 1921 and 1926, Anderson showcased early

the house had a succession of owners and residents, among them Confederate General P. G. T. Beauregard, who rented rooms here for eighteen months in 1866–1868. From 1944 to 1955, popular novelist Frances Parkinson Keyes leased the house, where she wrote a book about Beauregard, *Madame Castel's Lodger* (1962). She began restoration of the house with Richard Koch in 1945 and in 1955 created the Keyes Foundation, which acquired ownership at her death in 1970. Constructed works by William Faulkner, Ernest Hemingway, and Robert Penn Warren. Faulkner stayed with Anderson in 1925 before renting an apartment at 624 Pirates Alley (now Faulkner House Books), where he wrote *Soldiers' Pay*, his first novel. Truman Capote, born here in 1924, composed parts of *Other Voices, Other Rooms* (1948) at 711 Royal Street. He returned often, noting in 1981, "it's like a hometown to me."

After arriving in 1938, Tennessee Williams lived at 722 Toulouse (now part of THNOC; **1.16**), then moved to 632 St. Peter Street, where he wrote much of *Streetcar*. Although not a permanent resident, he never lost his passion for New Orleans, purchasing the house at 1014 Dumaine Street in 1962, which he owned until his death in 1983. The Monteleone Hotel's Carousel Bar and a front table at Galatoire's were among his favorite haunts. Every March, Williams is celebrated in New Orleans during a five-day literary festival.

Not all writers settled in the Vieux Carré. New Orleans–born author Grace King hosted visiting writers in her house on Coliseum Square (see **7.4**). F. Scott Fitzgerald stayed for a few weeks in 1920 at 2900 Prytania Street, and Lillian Hellman, born in New Orleans in 1907, spent half of her youth here with maiden aunts at their boarding house at 7209 St. Charles Avenue.

For these and other writers, New Orleans and its inhabitants directly or indirectly inspired and shaped their works, which have added to the city's mystique.

of plastered brick, the raised house combines the American central-hall plan with the Creole open gallery, or loggia (now enclosed), flanked by cabinets at the rear. At the front, curved granite twin staircases rise to pedimented, four-columned Tuscan portico and the double doors that open to the principal living area. For its time, this is an unusual and sophisticated design within the Vieux Carré; the newly fashionable classical elements were perhaps influenced by Correjolles's East Coast background. The side walled garden is laid out in parterres, based on an 1865 drawing in the City's Notarial Archive that shows a design from that period. The garden can be viewed from Chartres Street. The house is open to the public.

1.29   Old Ursuline Convent
1749–1752, Ignace François Broutin; 1845 church, J. N. B. de Pouilly. 1100 Chartres St.

In the late 1720s nine Ursuline nuns, one novice, and two postulants arrived in New Orleans from Rouen, France, to operate a new hospital. The nuns also opened a school and orphanage for girls. This building, their second convent, was designed in 1745 by French-born engineer Broutin (1690–1751), although construction did not begin until 1749 after their first building disintegrated. Designed in 1734 by Broutin and Alexandre de Batz, the first building's timber frame and *bousillage* (a mixture of mud and Spanish moss or animal hair) walls lacked the protective covering necessary to prevent deterioration from rain and humidity. Broutin, however, used brick for the new convent and covered its exterior with white-colored stucco.

Plantation owner Claude Joseph Villars Dubreuil, who was also responsible for the first levees in the city, funded the new building. The convent is the only structure surviving in New Orleans from the era of French colonial rule. The present facade is quite simple, articulated by a slightly projecting central pavilion with a pediment and segmental-arched casement windows, and a steep hipped roof, which curves at its edges and is pierced by small dormers. The one-story entrance portico was added in the 1890s; initially, the front entrance was on the river side of the convent. Inside is a cypress staircase with wrought-iron railings, re-used from the earlier convent.

In the 1820s, when street construction impacted the convent grounds, the nuns relocated to a new building downriver. The convent then served until 1899 as the archbishop's residence, for which Bishop Antoine Blanc commissioned a new chapel in 1845. Designed by J. N. B. de Pouilly, this features a gabled facade, given a classical effect by the addition of four pilasters and moldings around the gable. Following the hurricane of 1915, the chapel's French glass was replaced with stained glass by the Emil Frei Art Glass Company of St. Louis, and a sanctuary was added. Renamed several times over the years, for a time as Our Lady of Victory Church, it is known once again as St. Mary's Church.

In 1973, the convent was restored and now houses the Historical Archdiocesan Archives and a museum. Today, a parterre garden, thought to be the work of A. G. Seifried dating from 1955, ornaments the convent's grounds. Little is known about the original composition of a garden or of the medicinal plants that might have been grown, although plant lists from period sources exist.

1.30   Le Richelieu Hotel (Lanata Houses)
1845, J. N. B. de Pouilly. 1234 Chartres St.

These five Greek Revival houses are a type more commonly found in the Lower Garden District. Two stories high, with two-story galleries on slender piers, the houses are distinguished by an austere simplicity of form, Greek Revival shoulder molding around the windows and doors, and the height of the interior rooms, unusual within the scale of the Vieux Carré. The exteriors are brick stuccoed and scored to resemble stone. Their setback from the property line with small gardens in front makes their elegant severity easier to view. The wooden fence extending along the front of the houses is new.

Tremé

New Orleans's rapid expansion in the late eighteenth century led to growth beyond the Vieux Carré, across Rampart Street to Faubourg Tremé and downriver to Faubourg Marigny, Bywater, and Holy Cross. Tremé, bounded roughly by N. Rampart, Canal, and N. Broad streets and Esplanade Avenue, was platted in 1812 by city surveyor Jacques Tanesse on former plantations, including that of Claude Tremé. Tremé was populated mainly by free people of color, many of whom came to New Orleans from Saint-Domingue (Haiti) and Cuba. The dwellings

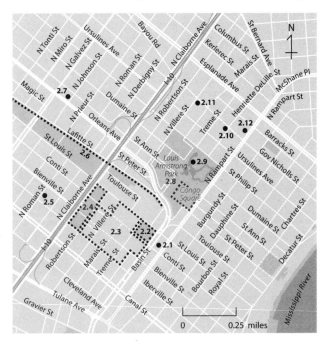

are mostly Creole cottages and shotgun houses. Front yards are infrequent and for the most part, houses front directly on the street, with steps (or stoops) for sitting outside.

2.1 Our Lady of Guadalupe Chapel (Mortuary Chapel)
1826, Gurlie and Guillot. 411 N. Rampart St.

Because it was believed that corpses laid out for burial were a source of contagion for yellow fever, the wardens of St. Louis Cathedral established a mortuary chapel outside the original city limits. Burial took place in St. Louis Cemetery No. 1 **(2.2)** behind the chapel. The triple-arched facade of this stuccoed brick building rises to a curved parapet and square belfry tower. Over time, the chapel assumed the duties of a parish church, celebrating Mass and offering baptisms, communions, and weddings. By 1873, the chapel served Italian immigrants settling in this area and was dedicated to St. Anthony of Padua. In 1903, the Dominicans took over the chapel and replaced the tower's dome with a steeple and clock. Subsequently, the Oblates of Mary Immaculate, from San Antonio, Texas, took charge of the chapel in 1918. With the expectation of a large Mexican con-gregation (which never materialized), they renamed it Our Lady of Guadalupe in honor of Mexico's patron saint. In the 1920s, architects Diboll and Owen refurbished the chapel, and the Emil Frei Art Glass Company of St. Louis created the stained glass windows. A replica of the grotto at Lourdes was added in 1924, and a shrine to St. Jude, the patron saint of hopeless causes, was installed in 1935. The chapel was enlarged and remodeled in 1952.

2.2 St. Louis Cemetery No. 1
1789. 425 Basin St.

Travel writer Edward Henry Durell (pseudonym Henry Didimus), who visited New Orleans in the mid-nineteenth century, described the local practice of burial in his book *New Orleans As I Found It* (1845): "This method of above ground tomb is adopted from necessity; and burial under ground is never attempted, except . . . for the stranger without friends or the poor without money, and they find an uncertain rest, for the water, with which the soil is always saturated, often forces the coffin and its contents out of its narrow and shallow cell, to rot with no other covering than the arch of heaven." Established in 1789 just beyond the Vieux Carré's boundary, St. Louis Cemetery No. 1 is crowded with above-ground tombs, separated only by narrow and tortuous paths. Although in-ground burial was common in New Orleans's early years, above-ground tombs reflect the city's French and Spanish heritage and high water table, and their continued use is probably a result of periodic flooding. Most of the tombs are simple rectangles in shape, taller than they are wide, with flat, curved, or gable roofs. Constructed of brick, covered with plaster and then whitewashed, sometimes tinted with color ranging from yellow ochre to red, the tombs were intended for use by generations of a family and usually contained space for more than one casket. When a new burial was necessary, the bones of the current occupant were swept to the rear of the tomb or placed in an ossuary in order to provide room for the new interment. The cemetery, like others in New Orleans, contains a few multistory tombs that accommodate several burial vaults. Called society tombs, these belonged to fraternal or benevolent societies and were intended to ensure the decent burial of their members. The high brick walls enclosing the cemetery contain wall vaults (or *fours*) on their inner surfaces, with openings covered by brick or marble slabs. These vaults were a less expensive alternative to the freestanding tomb. Sale of the vaults was a source of revenue for the City. Benjamin Henry Latrobe designed the tomb for

Governor William C. C. Claiborne (1811), who later was reburied in Metairie Cemetery (**10.11**). Latrobe and his son Henry are reputedly buried in the ground in the rear in an area, originally outside the cemetery, designated for those who were not Roman Catholic. Jean Etienne Boré, sugar refiner and first mayor of New Orleans, and Marie Laveau, a voodoo practitioner, are both interred here. On every All Saints' Day (November 1), families visit their ancestors' tombs, re-whitewash them if they are stucco-finished, and decorate them with chrysanthemums. The nonprofit preservation organization Save Our Cemeteries conducts guided tours here, using the fees to restore the tombs in this and other historic cemeteries in New Orleans.

2.3 Bienville Basin Apartments (Iberville Housing Development)

1939–1941, Herbert A. Benson, George H. Christy, and William E. Spink; 2017, HRI. 215 Treme St., and adjacent blocks

Iberville was one of three low-income housing developments built in New Orleans shortly after passage of the U.S. Housing Act of 1937 and the subsequent formation of the Housing Authority of New Orleans, which supervised all low-income housing in the city. Iberville and the St. Thomas housing development (the latter demolished in 1999 for mixed-income housing called River Garden) were planned for white residents, and the C. J. Peete Housing (demolished in 2008; rebuilt as Magnolia Gardens) for African American residents, although all three eventually accommodated mostly African American families. Built on a 22-acre site, Iberville was planned for a population of approximately 2,000 to be housed in 858 apartments in 75 brick buildings. Construction was federally funded, requiring the use of durable materials. These substantial, nicely proportioned three-story brick buildings were designed to be in scale with the city's houses, and each unit was provided with a front stoop or balcony, essential during the hot summers. However, the buildings' uniformity of design, materials, and detail in a city that consists primarily of diverse styles of wooden houses made the developments stand out conspicuously. Furthermore, the elimination of through streets produced enclaves judged to be unsafe, and like much low-income housing across the nation, the buildings and the grounds were not adequately maintained.

Iberville was located on the site of Storyville, New Orleans's

Music and New Orleans

Few buildings remain to tell the early story of jazz, the musical form that originated in New Orleans around the turn of the twentieth century. Urban renewal projects have swept away many clubs, dance halls, and saloons where jazz thrived, notably those in Storyville (see **2.3**), in the Tremé neighborhood, and in resorts along Lake Pontchartrain (see **11.1**). Today, a few buildings on the 400 block of S. Rampart Street, once an important African American commercial corridor, are left to tell the story.

Cornetist Buddy Bolden, considered the first jazz band leader, performed with his group at the three-story former Masonic/Odd Fellows Hall (later known as the Eagle Saloon) at 401 S. Rampart between 1898 and 1906. Jelly Roll Morton could be heard from 1912 to 1918 at the Iroquois Theater at 413 S. Rampart, where a teenaged Louis Armstrong once won a talent contest. In their off time, musicians often frequented The Little Gem Saloon at 448–449 S. Rampart, which closed during Prohibition in 1920. Long empty, it was saved from demolition in 2000, restored and designated a local historic landmark, and offers live performances.

notorious redlight district, where prostitution was legal until 1917. When the United States entered World War I, military authorities fearful of the spread of venereal disease pressured cities with large numbers of military personnel, including San Francisco, Boston, and Kansas City, to ban prostitution. Nevertheless, Storyville continued to operate illegally, although the area became increasingly blighted and, beginning in 1939, the large houses were razed and replaced by the Iberville Housing Development.

After Hurricane Katrina, federal housing officials decreed that most of the New Orleans housing developments would be demolished (a few buildings were retained), and new ones have been built in styles that mimic some generic nineteenth-century elements within a more suburban planning construct. This policy decision was not without national controversy,

Several houses where early jazz musicians lived survive; most are modest cottages or shotguns. King Oliver, leader of the Creole Jazz Band, once lived at 2717 Dryades Street. Buddy Bolden's residence was at 2309 First Street, trombonist Kid Ory's at 2135 Jackson Avenue, and Jelly Roll Morton's at 1441–43 Frenchmen Street. The Preservation Resource Center of New Orleans (https://prcno.org) has an app listing the homes of the jazz greats.

Flooding from Hurricane Katrina in 2005 displaced many of today's musicians, but Musicians Village (**3.13**) was built to encourage their return to the city. This small neighborhood is anchored by the Ellis Marsalis Center for Music, named for the jazz dynasty's patriarch.

Although little architectural evidence survives of jazz's origins, the music itself is as vibrant and inventive as ever and can be heard in clubs, Mardi Gras parades, funeral processions, and from ad-hoc street groups. Preservation Hall at 726 St. Peter Street in the Vieux Carré offers traditional jazz, and the New Orleans Jazz Museum in the Old Mint (**4.1**) recounts its rich history.

yet residents are enthusiastic about the new housing because it erased the negative connotations associated with these "projects." The new community at the site of Iberville, Bienville Basin, was the last of the large New Orleans developments to be reconstructed. A far higher percentage of existing structures was retained, and the design has a greater connection to the city's context as a result.

2.4   St. Louis Cemetery No. 2
1823. 300 N. Claiborne Ave.

Originally laid out as one continuous strip with a broad central avenue and narrower parallel side aisles, St. Louis Cemetery No. 2 was divided into three almost square units when Bienville and Conti streets were cut through. Although this partition diminished the monumental aspect of the central avenue, the

arrangement of straight aisles lined with tombs still gave each of the cemetery's squares a formal order. In the early nineteenth century, cemetery design in the United States was profoundly influenced by the new Père Lachaise Cemetery in Paris, which combined formal avenues and winding paths, all lined by handsome marble tombs. In New Orleans, where space was limited, cemetery planners adopted the tightly packed straight avenues of Père Lachaise rather than its spacious garden-like aspects. Although not strictly enforced, the social distinctions that existed in life were carried into death in the designation of sections for different religious faiths and ethnic groups. Many of the most sought-after tomb designers in nineteenth-century New Orleans were French immigrants, among them Paul H. Monsseaux and Prosper Foy, whose son Florville Foy followed in his father's footsteps. Some of this cemetery's most striking tombs were designed by J. N. B. de Pouilly, who probably introduced temple-fronted tombs to New Orleans, in the style of those at Père Lachaise. De Pouilly's Peniston-Duplantier tomb (1842) is a good example. De Pouilly's sketchbook (now in The Historic New Orleans Collection) reveals his interest in tomb design. Particularly noteworthy is his Gothic Revival tomb (1860) for the Caballero family, with a trefoil arch in each gable, crockets, and finials. With tombs neatly aligned along straight avenues and many surrounded by low cast-iron fences, St. Louis Cemetery No. 2 conveys the appearance of a city in miniature. Each of the cemetery's squares is surrounded by a high brick wall lined with wall vaults; de Pouilly's simple tomb is located in one of these.

2.5 St. James African Methodist Episcopal Church

1848–1851; 1903 alterations, Diboll and Owen. 222 N. Roman St.

This attractive small church, established by free people of color, was built in the mid-nineteenth century, but its present Gothic Revival appearance dates mostly from the early twentieth century. In a renovation of 1903, Diboll and Owen replaced the pediment with a parapet ornamented with a blind arcade, added an openwork bell tower with a steeple in the center of the facade and pinnacles at its corners, and resurfaced the brick facade with stucco textured and scored to resemble rusticated masonry. The ornamental pressed metal ceiling inside was added at this time. The interior is a single large space with a polygonal-shaped apse and is illuminated by tall pointed-arched windows. Much of the stained glass, added c. 1891 with funds from the Louisiana Masonic organization, includes small painted medallions featuring Masonic symbols.

The church has played an important role in the city's history. New Orleans police closed the church from 1858 to 1862 after the Reverend John M. Brown allowed slaves to attend—an act prohibited in the state charter issued to the church—and church members advocated an end to slavery. During the Civil War, the church was used as the headquarters for a company of African American Union soldiers under the command of Colonel James Lewis. In 1865, the first annual African Methodist Episcopal (AME) Church Louisiana conference was held here. A century

later, in the late 1950s and into the 1960s, St. James was a center
for civil rights activities in New Orleans.

2.6   Lafitte Greenway

2010–2015, Design Workshop. Lafitte Ave. from Basin St. to
S. Jefferson Davis Pkwy.

The Lafitte Greenway, a 3.1-mile linear park, was one of the
first revitalization projects initiated in New Orleans following
Hurricane Katrina (2005). The 54-acre site roughly follows the
paths of the former Carondelet Canal (built in the 1790s) and
later railroad rights-of-way that connected the inner city (Vieux
Carré and Central Business District) through Bayou St. John
and Lake Pontchartrain to the outside world. This corridor,
passing through several historic nineteenth- and twentieth-
century neighborhoods (notably Tremé), is today a rich mix of
residential, retail, and industrial uses that represents the city's
economic, social, political, architectural, environmental, and
cultural histories.

Planning for the Greenway began in early 2006 when a
small group of neighborhood activists and design professionals,
alarmed by the City's initiative to sell off property and street
rights-of-way for a private development of dubious public benefit, coalesced around urban design opportunities presented in
post-hurricane recovery efforts. The group organized, expanded
via social media outlets, and started annual "Walk the Corridor"
events to bring public attention to the potential this corridor
had for a unique linear parkway. Members advocated for the

greenway concept at all opportunities, developed a strategic vision that was widely distributed, and lobbied elected officials and community stakeholders in efforts to build consensus for the idea. This strategy paid off, and when federal funding became available for post–Hurricane Katrina recovery projects, this concept had evolved and secured widespread community support, making it among the first such ventures to be initiated.

After delays and false starts at the end of one political administration and the beginning of a new one, the City engaged the Austin office of Design Workshop and formal planning began in 2010; ground was broken in 2014, and the Greenway opened in 2015.

The construction budget was modest, yet the lead consultant assembled a multidisciplinary effort incorporating public input, synthesizing measurable objectives (including stormwater management and restoring the urban tree canopy), and working across a range of scales to transform this undeveloped corridor into what is now an active greenway for non-motorized access through neighborhoods in the city's central core. Extensive community engagement ensued through a series of public meetings, individual stakeholder meetings, and presentations. The resulting master plan outlines developmental stages that extend the corridor to Canal Boulevard and identifies amenities that can be added as future funding becomes available.

Much of the limited budget went to clearing up legal issues related to the site's boundaries and its environmental condition as an industrial corridor. Nevertheless, a strong design strategy was developed that draws upon its ecology and builds upon its rich layers of history while also taking into account previous land uses and community input for proposed new uses. The historic alignment of the Carondelet Canal is marked by a mile-long bosque of bald cypress trees evocative of the *Ciprière au Bois* (Cypress Forest) that once covered the site, according to an early map. Within this grove is a rain garden filled with native plants. Rust-stained bands of paving trace the location of train tracks that once traversed the site. Plantings reflect the natural vegetation patterns of south Louisiana, with swamp species that transition to bottomland hardwoods and upland species as the Greenway meets the Metairie Ridge to the north and natural level of the Mississippi River to the south. The design provides open space for formal and informal activities. Georeferencing of eighteenth-century maps identified the location of the Carondelet Walk, a historic tow path alongside the former Carondelet Canal. There are new pedestrian pathways and community gardens near the location of the Lafitte community garden, once the longest continuously operated community garden in America, associated with the Lafitte public housing development.

What began through informal small-group discussions has now grown into an active nonprofit (Friends of Lafitte Greenway) with paid staff, regular events, and ongoing efforts to expand the Greenway's impact through community partnerships and the addition of new features identified in the planning process. From the outset, the Greenway's acceptance, its success to date, and the visibility of the nonprofit organization have come through social media, probably the first such public project in the city to have employed this innovative platform for community engagement. And while this new venture may look rather sparse in terms of features and plantings, its community impact has been far more apparent because of the participatory planning process through which it was created, as well as the connection the Greenway has facilitated among diverse neighborhoods and their residents.

2.7   Carver Theater

1950, Jack Corgan; 2014 addition and renovation, Perez APC.
2101 Orleans Ave.

Built when segregation was still in effect, this Moderne movie theater served African American patrons with seating for 1,050. Dallas-based architect Corgan had established his practice in 1938 specializing in movie theaters, and this building's brick-veneered concrete-block walls are geometrically articulated solely by repeating vertical grooves and horizontal-shaped windows. The theater's boldest feature is the corner entrance, with its freestanding ticket booth (rebuilt), angled marquee, and illuminated vertical sign with the theater's name on a red background. After the theater closed in 1980, the interior was converted into offices, including a medical clinic, which closed after it was flooded by six feet of water during Hurricane Katrina. The building was renovated in 2014.

2.8 Congo Square and Louis Armstrong Park
1970s Congo Square renovations, Cashio Cochran; 1974–1979 Armstrong Park, Robin Riley and others. 701 N. Rampart St.

Armstrong Park is adjacent to Congo Square, where as early as the 1740s slaves sold their homemade wares and gathered socially, performing music on Sunday afternoons. One of the most significant sites of African American culture in the United States, the square has unfortunately lost its clear identity, being completely subsumed within Armstong Park.

Louis Armstrong Park was planned as a typical mid-twentieth-century urban renewal project, programmatically akin to New York City's Lincoln Center, on a thirty-two-acre site covering fourteen blocks of Tremé's historic urban fabric, nine of which were cleared of houses to facilitate its construction. Later named for the famous New Orleans musician, the park includes a statue of Armstrong by African American artist Elizabeth Catlett, together with later artworks of varying quality. Loosely modeled on Tivoli Gardens in Copenhagen, Denmark, Armstrong Park was picturesquely laid out with a lagoon, hillocks, and three hundred trees. From the start, the project was controversial because it ruthlessly swept away a historic neighborhood of architectural and cultural significance, including bars and clubs where jazz musicians had played and houses where they lived. When the park was completed, it was perceived as unsafe (even with a substantial fence) and was little used.

Among the structures within Armstrong Park is one of the red-and-white Mediterranean Revival pumping stations of the Sewerage and Water Board of New Orleans. In front of Congo Square is Favrot and Livaudais's Renaissance-styled Municipal Auditorium of 1929, built on land created when the Carondelet Canal and its turning basin were filled, which has sat unoccupied and deteriorating after taking on five feet of water during Hurricane Katrina. While smaller nineteenth-century buildings were moved into the park (see **2.9**), its principal new building is the Mahalia Jackson Center for the Performing Arts (1973), designed by Mathes, Bergman and Associates with Harry Baker Smith. Nearby is a collection of heirloom roses, many of which were rooted from plants in the city's older neighborhoods. The park will gain new life when (and if) the National Park Service completes the New Orleans Jazz National Historical Park within its boundaries, a long-planned initiative that has yet to be funded.

2.9   Perseverance Hall No. 4 (Loge La Perseverance)
1819–1820, Bernard Thibaud. 901 N. Rampart St.

Refugees from Saint-Domingue and Cuba made up most of the original membership of this Masonic lodge, which was chartered in 1810 and is thus the oldest lodge in Louisiana. The tall rectangular building of stuccoed brick is articulated with shallow pilasters on both stories of its narrow facade. Alterations in 1850 removed much of the interior millwork, but the main staircase, musicians' gallery, and entrance doors are original. The hall will become an educational and performance venue for the planned New Orleans Jazz National Historical Park. Moved to this site and located behind and to the right of the lodge is the Rabassa–De Pouilly House (c. 1825), a four-room cottage with raised galleries and rear cabinets, formerly the residence of J. N. B. de Pouilly.

A few blocks away at 1433 N. Rampart is the former Etoile Polaire (North Star) Lodge No. 1 F&AM, a two-story, Greek Revival, stuccoed brick building (c. 1840), constructed for a lodge chartered in 1816, which features pilasters between the windows and a dentiled entablature.

2.10   St. Augustine Church
1841–1842, J. N. B. de Pouilly. 1210 Governor Nicholls St.

Built by Ernest Godchaux and Pierre Vidal to designs of de Pouilly, this building occupies land donated by the Ursuline nuns for a church to honor their patron saint, St. Augustine of Hippo. Bishop Antoine Blanc contributed most of the funds for construction. The facade is quite spare, articulated only by shallow pilasters and, above the central door, a row of narrow rectangular wrought-iron grilles, over which there is a semicircular window and a circular opening in the pediment. These elements, combined with the flat, two-dimensional look of the facade, give the church an austere, abstract appearance that makes it seem almost modern. The asymmetry resulting from the bell tower on one side, added in 1858, reinforces that impression. Inside, Corinthian columns separate the nave from lower side aisles, and small circular windows in the clerestory help illuminate the interior. In a restoration of 1926, Weil and Bendernagel gave the brick exterior a plastered and scored finish. They also installed stained glass windows depicting saints of special significance to the French, which were manufactured in the Munich studio of the Emil Frei Art Glass Company of St. Louis.

When built, the church served a congregation of free people of color and French-speaking whites, with seating along the walls provided for enslaved congregants. In 1842, Henriette Delille, a free woman of color, founded the Sisters of the Holy Family here as the first exclusively African American order of nuns in New Orleans (and one of the first in the nation). The nuns devoted their lives to helping the elderly and the sick and to educating African American children; the Sisters' convent (**12.6**) is now in New Orleans East.

2.11   New Orleans African American Museum of Art, Culture and History (Villa Meilleur)
1828–1829, attributed to William Brand or Joseph Correjoles; 1990s restored, Williams and Associates, with Eugene D. Cizek. 1418 Governor Nicholls St.

Located on the old road to Bayou St. John and the site of the first brickyard in New Orleans, this raised house of stuccoed brick with a six-columned wooden gallery was built for the keeper of the city jail, Simon Meilleur, and his Philadelphia-born wife, Catherine Flack. A 1990s restoration preserved the original central-hall layout and exterior appearance, reconstructed the slate roof and the two roof dormers destroyed in a fire in 1911, and re-created the decorative cast-iron gallery railing. A central entrance door is framed by delicate Ionic columns, sidelights, and a fanlight. The house is surrounded by a garden of dubious historical authenticity. Numerous adjacent structures are now included in the museum's campus, including the Passebon Cottage (1843), built by free man of color and builder, Pierre Passebon, and restored post–Hurricane Katrina under the direction of Pierre-Antoine Gatier, Chief Architect of Historical Monuments, French Ministry of Culture, with funding from the Government of France.

2.12   George and Joyce Wein Jazz and Heritage Center (Tharp Sontheimer Laudumiey Mortuary)
1870s; early 20th century altered; 2014, Eskew+Dumez+Ripple and Rick Fifield Architect. 1225 N. Rampart St.

This center began as two separate town houses built in the 1870s by Cuban-immigrant Jules LeBlanc and combined into a single house in the early twentieth century. For decades the building served as a funeral home, and because many jazz funeral processions started from here, it was ideally suited for its new function as a center of activities for the New Orleans Jazz and Heritage Festival and Foundation. The two-story white-painted wooden building retains its early-twentieth-century full-height Ionic-columned porch and has a balustrade along the roofline. The rear of the building, however, was reconstructed to include a 200-seat auditorium of contemporary design.

Downriver Faubourgs/Neighborhoods

Marigny, Bywater, and Holy Cross follow the Mississippi River as it flows downstream. Parallel to them on the lake side of St. Claude Avenue are the neighborhoods of St. Roch, St. Claude, and the Lower Ninth Ward. Marigny, bounded by Esplanade and St. Claude avenues, Press Street, and the river, was laid out by Barthélemy Lafon for Bernard de Marigny in 1806 to a plan drawn up earlier that year by engineer Nicolas de Finiels, which called for twelve houses to a block and a public space called Washington Square. Initially Marigny, like Tremé, was populated mainly by free people of color. St. Roch, laid out in 1834, was named for the cemetery (**3.7**) and chapel at its core.

Bywater, between Franklin and St. Claude avenues, the Industrial Canal, and the river, initially housed mostly German, Irish, and Italian immigrants who arrived in great numbers beginning in the 1840s. In the twentieth century African Americans settled in this neighborhood of modest houses. The Beaux-Arts classical memorial arch (1919) in Macarty Square commemorates local war veterans. Press Street, originally Cotton Press Street, was the city's first thoroughfare paved with concrete, built to support the weight of wagons loaded with cotton bales. Holy Cross, once an area that housed truck farmers, dairies, and commercial gardeners, lies downriver from Bywater across the Industrial Canal. Jackson Barracks (**3.18**) forms the downriver boundary of the neighborhood and of New Orleans.

These neighborhoods have retained the intimacy and small-scale character of their nineteenth-century origins. While Marigny mostly has Creole cottages and shotgun houses, the latter are characteristic of Bywater and the less dense Holy Cross. In 2014–2015, the river edge in Bywater was converted to Crescent Park (**3.11**) and surviving rice, sugar, and cotton-press sheds have been converted for other uses, some as artists lofts. Marigny began to be gentrified from the late 1970s, as have the Bywater and St. Claude neighborhoods following Hurricane Katrina.

The neighborhoods on the lake side of Bywater and Holy Cross developed in the mid-twentieth century, primarily with the arrival of African American residents. But inland from the river and at a low elevation, these areas were inundated with water during Hurricane Katrina after the levee along the

Industrial Canal was breached by an unmoored barge. Rebuilding continues. Several streets in the Lower Ninth Ward became the focus of actor Brad Pitt's Make It Right (**3.15**) reconstruction campaign.

3.1 Circle Market (St. Bernard Market)

1932, Samuel Stone Jr.; 1966 additions; 2014 renovated, John C. Williams Architects. 1522 St. Bernard Ave.

This market occupies a corner site that as early as 1854 housed a market structure. It is an eye-catching Spanish Colonial Revival design, with a covered arcade that curves around its St. Bernard Avenue facade and continues on the S. Claiborne Avenue side. The steel-framed building is covered in white stucco and has a red tile roof, ornamental parapet, and decorative iron grilles over the windows. The market's tower and cupola are visible from I-10, which in 1966 was built above S. Claiborne Avenue. The market was one of thirty-four that the City of New Orleans controlled and operated, one for every neighborhood and more than any other city in the nation. In 1941 the City dissolved the Department of Public Markets and began to sell the buildings; this one came into private hands in 1947. A few of the market buildings survive, most adapted for different uses, but this one and St. Roch (**3.6**) still serve as markets.

3.2 Antoine Boutin House

c. 1830. 1445 Pauger St.

Integrating Creole and American forms, this house represents southern Louisiana's unique and creative solution to the blending of local traditions and new fashions and influences. One-and-a-half stories in height, the stucco-covered house, of brick-between-posts construction, is shaded by an *abat-*

vent on iron brackets, and a small single dormer with pilasters and arched top pierces the gable roof. However, the slightly recessed central entrance with fanlight and the Ionic pilasters marking the ends of the facade reveal the builder's taste for stylistic innovation. The house was built for commission merchant Antoine Boutin, but financial problems forced him to sell it to W. C. C. Claiborne II in 1845. The house is also known as the Flettrich House for a later owner.

On the opposite side of the street (1436 Pauger Street) is a fine example of earlier traditions, a stucco-covered Creole cottage of brick-between-posts construction built by Jean-Louis Dolliole for his family in 1820. Its charm also lies in its unusual outline, which exactly fits the curved configuration of the wide-angled corner site.

3.3   Sun Oak
1808; c. 1836 remodeled; 1976 restored, Eugene D. Cizek. 2020 Burgundy St.

Free woman of color Constance Rixner Bouligny, who owned investment property in New Orleans, built this house for her own residence. The brick-between-posts Creole cottage is unusually wide with seven openings across the front, including a narrow one at the end that led to an alley. The openings were all covered by French doors. In 1836, merchant Asher Moses Nathan purchased the house for his *placée*, a free woman of color whom he could not marry because of the *Code Noir* (his wife lived on the Gulf Coast). Nathan remodeled the house in Greek Revival style, including the addition of cypress panels to the facade to simulate stone and the replacement of some of the French doors with windows. He also built a two-story slave quarter and kitchen building at the rear of the house. The house was sold at auction in 1843 after Nathan's fortune suffered in the Panic of 1837. In the 1890s the house was divided into three rental properties. When architect and preservationist Cizek purchased the building in 1976 it was in poor condition. He renovated it for his own residence, painted it the red color it was in the mid-ninteenth century, and named it Sun Oak for a large tree in the rear.

3.4 Claiborne House
1855–1859, James Stewart, builder. 2111 Dauphine St.

Splendidly located facing Washington Square, a nineteenth-century urban square that retains its period cast-iron fence and basic design (refurbished in the 1970s by architect Webster Deadman), this two-story Greek Revival house was built by Stewart for W. C. C. Claiborne II, son of Louisiana's first American governor, and his Creole wife, Louise de Balathier. This block of Dauphine Street, with its varied residential types ranging from this American-influenced house to the slightly earlier Creole cottages, demonstrates the shifts in fashion occurring at the time New Orleans was beginning to expand beyond the boundaries of the Vieux Carré. Stuccoed on the exterior, the brick house has a central entrance recessed between Ionic pilasters, a narrow iron balcony across the second floor, a cornice outlined by a continuous row of dentils, and a parapet disguising the gently sloped roof. A two-story brick kitchen wing extends to the rear. Inside, the staircase was located in a separate small hall at the rear and to one side of the central hall.

3.5 Historic Sts. Peter and Paul Church
1860, Howard and Diettel. 2317 Burgundy St.

The Redemptorists, who came to New Orleans from Baltimore in 1847, commissioned Henry Howard, then in partnership with Dresden-born Albert Diettel (1824–1896), who had arrived in New Orleans in 1849, to build this church for a mainly Irish Catholic congregation. Exploiting fully the sculptural potential of brick construction, the architects employed brick hood moldings with curved profiles to outline the round-arched windows and manipulated brick into elaborate corbels and moldings and a shaped parapet. Two substantial towers, one square and the other octagonal, squeeze the facade between them. The towers are of different heights; the taller was originally even higher than at present. A fire in 1911 caused the loss of the taller tower's spire, and it was then lowered twenty-five feet in 1934 when its weight caused it to sag. The sloping courses of brick at the tower's outer corner reveal the problem, and the tower leans slightly to the left front. Inside the church, a flattened barrel vault and attached columns between the arches of the nave arcade establish a smooth rhythm toward the altar. The stained glass windows featuring religious figures were made in 1908 by Flanagan and Biedenweg of Chicago. The adjacent school, designed in 1899 by New Orleans architect Allison Owen (1869–1951) of Diboll and Owen (Collins C. Diboll, 1868–1936), repeats the narrow vertical forms of the church. The Archdiocese of New Orleans closed the church in 2001, and the building and its adjacent school are being converted (2017) into a hotel and event venue.

3.6 St. Roch Market

1875, William H. Bell; 1914 enclosed; 1937 renovated; 2013 renovated, Lee Ledbetter and Associates, and Williams Architects. 2381 St. Claude Ave.

Located on the neutral ground (median) of St. Roch Avenue, this market offered fruits, vegetables, fish, and meat sold by individual vendors from open stalls. The building's original

Public Markets

Associated with cultural foodways are traditions and venues related to the community's access to foodstuffs. Early settlers adopted the public marketplace on the bank of the Mississippi River established by Native Americans, which became the French Market (1.6). From the nineteenth-century on, this covered space—later separated into markets for seafood, meats, poultry, vegetables, fruits, and wild game—served the city.

A particularly notable account of the French Market is found in architect Benjamin Henry Latrobe's *Impressions Respecting New Orleans: Diaries and Sketches, 1818–1820,* where he describes not only the wide array of things for sale but also the multiple languages and cultures on display. This marketplace, which served as the center of the community well into the twentieth century, was renovated in the 1930s and again, with an eye more toward tourist activities, since the 1980s.

Another important public marketplace primarily for those of African descent was Congo Square (2.8), located just outside the boundary of the Vieux Carré and adjacent to the Carondelet Canal. Here, according to rules of the French *Code Noir* that governed French colonies (which curiously remained in place here for over two decades after the Louisiana Purchase in 1803), enslaved people could congregate freely on Sunday (their mandated "day off") and engage in commercial activities (related to

materials—iron frame and brick lower walls—have been somewhat modified over the years. In 1914 following a State Board of Health mandate, the market was enclosed with brick walls and windows. Iron columns with inverted bell capitals support the roof, which carries a ridge ventilator with louvered windows. The market was modernized by the WPA in 1937 and the two front bays were removed to provide more space in front. Renovated post–Hurricane Katrina to its 1937 appearance, the market now offers upscale provisions to tourists and neighborhood residents.

bartering and selling what they had grown) and entertainment (drumming and dancing). Latrobe similarly provided a particularly vivid description of activities in Congo Square, which continued here among African Americans and others throughout the nineteenth century, and additional observers' accounts highlight musical activities, "Grand and Novel Entertainment" (including balloon ascensions and, from 1859, a discussion of "Women's Rights") and various foodstuffs ("pies, roasted peanuts and cakes" from 1845).

Late-nineteenth-century immigrants, particularly Italians, imported citrus and became suppliers of fresh fruits and vegetables in public markets and neighborhood grocery stores, often located on block corners. Some of these still exist, offering specialty items recalling the generations of owners who have served their communities.

Public markets operated well into the twentieth century throughout the city. They were managed by the City until the 1940s when it sold them; suburban supermarkets made many of them obsolete. A handful of the markets remain (**3.1**, **3.6**), while others have been converted to new uses (see **8.7**). An infusion of Central American and Asian immigrants has brought new groceries that cater to these communities, offering non-native fruits, vegetables, live seafood, and other exotic delicacies.

3.7   St. Roch Cemetery and Chapel
1875 dedicated. 1725 St. Roch Ave.

The cemetery and its chapel are the only ones in the United States dedicated to St. Roch, the fourteenth-century French saint who ministered to plague sufferers. German immigrant Father Peter Thevis of Holy Trinity Church purchased the land to build the cemetery and chapel in thanks to St. Roch for saving his congregation from the devastating yellow fever epidemic of 1867 (3,107 people died in New Orleans that year). The interior

of the diminutive stuccoed brick Gothic Revival chapel is dimly lit by tall narrow windows, and its lower walls are faced with metal panels painted in imitation of wood. The cemetery, laid out like the Campo Santo dei Tedeschi, the German cemetery in Rome, is surrounded by a brick outer wall containing vaults and chapel-like niches for almost life-size sculptures of the Stations of the Cross that were installed in 1948. Two sturdy castellated Gothic Revival towers guard the cemetery's entrance. An extension to the cemetery and St. Michael's Mausoleum were added soon afterward.

Nearby at 1835 St. Roch Avenue is the cruciform Our Lady Star of the Sea Catholic Church, which faces the two-block-long St. Roch Playground.

3.8   Marigny Opera House (Holy Trinity Church)
1853, Theodore E. Giraud. 714 St. Ferdinand St.

In the 1840s, the growing number of immigrants who came to New Orleans tended to settle in neighborhoods by ethnic group and establish their own churches, where services were conducted in their native languages. Holy Trinity was one of the churches established for German Catholic immigrants in this part of Marigny, once popularly known as Little Saxony. Twin bell towers with small segmental, onion-shaped domes mark the corners of the plain plastered brick facade, which is scored to imitate stone. Entrances and windows are round-arched, and elliptical clerestory windows line the upper side walls. Inside the

church, slender box columns support the barrel vault. Closed in 1997 because of dwindling attendance, the church was afterwards deconsecrated and, in 2011, converted for use as an arts and performance venue. The sixteen rare French stained glass windows dating from the 1880s were removed by the archdiocese for installation elsewhere. Theodore E. Giraud (c. 1821–1864) came to New Orleans from Galveston in the late 1840s, where he designed several churches (most since demolished) in New Orleans and southern Louisiana before departing for Monterrey, Mexico, where he died.

3.9 Blessed Francis Xavier Seelos Catholic Church (St. Vincent de Paul Catholic Church)
1866, Daniel Mulligan. 3053 Dauphine St.

Carpenter and builder Daniel Mulligan (1821–1874) emigrated with his brother, builder Thomas Mulligan (1823–1877), from Ireland. This bright red brick church, with a tall, massive square tower marking the center of the facade, is a major landmark in a neighborhood of small one- and two-story wooden houses. The mostly French-speaking congregation was formed in 1838 and worshiped in a wooden structure until the new church was built. The entrance portal at the base of the tower is a monumental arched opening, vigorously outlined by multiple rounded moldings. Although the bell tower's upper stage was probably intended from the beginning, it was not built until 1924. Inside the church, Corinthian columns, which were added in 1923 to reinforce the superstructure, reached to colorful scenes depicting events in the life of St. Vincent de Paul, painted across the shallow-arched barrel vault c. 1907 by Italian-born New Orleans artist Achille Peretti (c. 1857–1923). In 2003 a fire destroyed much of the interior, including the murals, but not the French and American-made stained glass that fills the tall paired round-arched windows. The interior was restored but not the murals. In 2001, the church was amalgamated with three other churches to form a new parish.

3.10   New Orleans Center for the Creative Arts (NOCCA)
2000, The Mathes Group with Billes/Manning Architects; 2014 addition, John C. Williams Architects. 2800 Chartres St.

This public high school for the creative arts, known as NOCCA, incorporates recently built structures and renovated nineteenth-century brick warehouses. The new structures were designed to relate to the neighboring industrial buildings, evident in the use of corrugated metal siding. However, the intricate layout of the complex, the over-restoration of the brickwork on the original warehouses, and the reuse of some original material can make it difficult to distinguish between old and new construction. Clearly old is the large brick warehouse with segmental-arched windows and corbeled gable, as is a row of granite post-and-lintel openings retained from a warehouse by Alexander T. Wood along the St. Ferdinand Street side of the Center. The new three-story, curved metal structure that defines NOCCA's boundary along the railroad tracks of Press Street includes a second-floor terrace that provides a view of the river over the adjacent floodwall. The Center houses a 300-seat theater, a black-box theater, recording studios, art and dance studios, an art gallery, performance rooms, culinary arts space, and a restaurant. NOCCA is a nationally recogized professional training center in the visual and performing arts, serving students from over twenty Louisiana parishes.

Nearby at Press and Royal streets is the site (a plaque marks the spot) of the streetcar stop where, in 1892, Homer Plessy boarded a streetcar, bought a ticket, announced he was a Creole of color, sat in the front of the car (reserved for white riders), and was subsequently arrested. The resulting legal action culminated in the historic Supreme Court case *Plessy v. Ferguson* (1896), which legitimized "separate-but-equal" and ushered in the Jim Crow laws of the twentieth century.

3.11   Crescent Park

2014–2015, Eskew+Dumez+Ripple, Hargreaves Associates, Michael Maltzan Associates, and Adjaye/Associates. Riverfront from Marigny St. to Alvar St.

A recent addition to the city's open spaces is the twenty-acre Crescent Park, providing riverfront open space for residents of Marigny and Bywater neighborhoods and an interesting view upriver to the city. Linear planting, paths, and elements from the site's former maritime and industrial uses were incorporated into the design. Almost 1.5 miles long, the park has limited access due to its separation from residential areas by the floodwall and active rail lines, with one upriver entrance at the Mandeville Street wharf, one from downriver, and, at Piety Street, a rather severe Cor-Ten steel bridge designed by London-based architect David Adjaye.

3.12   Lombard Plantation
1825–1826; 1991–2011 restored. 3933 Chartres St.

In 1825, Marie Azelie Zeringue, wife of Joseph Guillaume Lombard, purchased the land on which this house stands from the Macarty family. The house was built by her father-in-law, French immigrant Louis Lombard. The property was a working plantation, probably raising sugarcane, and it is thought that it was worked by hired labor, including free blacks and Irish immigrants. Raised on brick piers, the one-story house has a front gallery carried on slender wooden columns, and a hipped roof with a slight uptilt along its perimeter and a small dormer. Norman trussing in the attic suspends a roof system over a large floor area with only two interior supports. The house has a Creole plan of four rooms, with a brick chimney between each pair, and a rear space between cabinets. In 1833, the Lombards sold the house, which then had a succession of owners. A bill of sale of 1864 indicates the property had a brick kitchen, a livery, a stable, and other dependencies suitable for a working plantation, and two enslaved workers (despite the Emancipation Proclamation of 1863). Over the following decades the plantation was reduced in size and the surrounding area became increasingly built up and poor. But poverty allowed the house to survive with its interior relatively untouched, including some of the stenciled designs of moons and crescents in the former dining room. In 1991, historian Frederick Starr purchased the house and some adjacent land and began a long process of restoration, with the advice of architect Eugene D. Cizek, contractor Jack Stewart, and architect Rick Fifield. The kitchen house, which burned down in 1880, was reconstructed based on an 1843 plan and the garden was reconstructed based on mid-nineteenth-century garden plans, all in the Notarial Archives.

3.13   Musicians Village

2007 and later. Bounded by N. Johnson, Alvar, N. Roman, and Mazant sts.

This post–Hurricane Katrina project conceived by New Orleans musicians Branford Marsalis and vocalist Harry Connick Jr. is a residential community planned to provide housing and encourage the return of musicians to New Orleans after Katrina. The area was heavily flooded after the levees failed in the aftermath of the hurricane's landing. The New Orleans Area Habitat for Humanity built sixty-nine single-family one-story houses, raised on concrete-block piers, with hipped or gabled roofs, front galleries or porches, and front lawns. The houses are painted in various bright pastel colors, creating a lively streetscape. This is their most notable characteristic, since architecturally they are examples of New Orleans vernacular houses. The community is anchored by the Ellis Marsalis Center for Music (2007–2008, Mathes Brierre) a two-story building at the intersection of N. Prieur and Bartholomew streets that is named for the Marsalis patriarch. The center provides class and practice rooms, a performance hall, meeting rooms, and a courtyard. Opposite is a children's playground.

Nearby at 3811 N. Galvez Street is William Frantz School (1937, E. A. Christy), a three-story building with Art Deco detailing around the entrance that was renovated and given a large

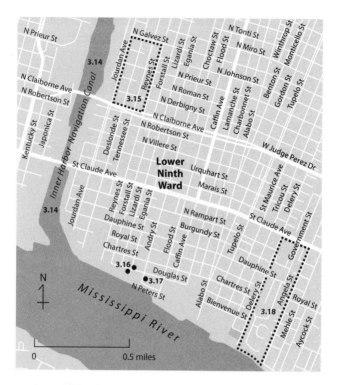

modern addition by Billes Partners in 2013. In November 1960, six-year-old Ruby Bridges attended the all-white school, one of four black students to integrate New Orleans's public schools; the other three girls went to McDonogh School No. 19 (1929, E. A. Christy; 5909 St. Claude Avenue), closed since Hurricane Katrina.

3.14 Inner Harbor Navigation Canal (Industrial Canal)
1918–1923, George G. Goethals. From the Mississippi River to Lake Pontchartrain

Built at a cost of $19 million, this 5.5-mile deepwater canal permits navigation between the Mississippi River and Lake Pontchartrain and provides a connection to the inland route of the Gulf Intracoastal Waterway and the Mississippi River–Gulf Outlet (completed in 1966, and known as MR-GO). The latter, a deep-draft route through the marshes of St. Bernard Parish, shortened the distance between the Port of New Orleans and the Gulf of Mexico from the 110 miles via the river route to 76 miles. However, the MR-GO allowed saline intrusion into freshwater marshes, creating ecological havoc. Its role in causing Hurricane Katrina flooding in St. Bernard and the Lower Ninth Ward finally led to its abandonment and closure by the U.S. Army Corps of Engineers after enormous public pressure. Work on the canal began in 1918 under the direction of engineer George G. Goethals (1858–1928), who was also the chief engineer for the Panama Canal locks and, in Louisiana, for the Plaquemine Lock (1895–1909; see **Day Trip 3**) in Iberville Parish. The canal (usually called the Industrial Canal) gives approximately 11 additional miles of waterfront to the Port of New Orleans for wharves, shipyards, and industries. Midway along the canal's eastern side, a 150-acre railroad yard provides the land-based component of this transportation complex. A 640-foot-long lock to mediate the difference in water levels between the Mississippi River and Lake Pontchartrain is located at the river entrance to the canal; a project to widen it was initiated in 1999, faced public opposition for years, but was brought back to life in 2017 despite the waning traffic using the Industrial Canal. At St. Claude Avenue, the canal passes under the drawbridge of 1919. Originally the truss bridge carried railroad tracks at its center, but these were removed for two additional vehicular lanes. The levee that borders the canal was breached in the aftermath of Katrina, devastating the blocks just downriver from it.

3.15   Make It Right Houses

2005 and later. Roughly bounded by N. Claiborne and Jourdain aves. and Reynes and N. Galvez sts.

Actor Brad Pitt established the Make It Right Foundation in 2007 to provide houses for people of the Lower Ninth Ward who lost their homes after the levee failed and Hurricane Katrina's storm surge flooded this neighborhood with twelve feet of water. Approximately one hundred houses have been built, mostly along four streets parallel to the flood protection wall and the Industrial Canal. Some of the new houses are inventive and colorful reinterpretations of traditional New Orleans residential types, such as the shotgun house, but others follow more traditional forms. Prominent architects from the region, the nation, and elsewhere in the world, who participated in the rebuilding effort, are responsible for the more creative designs. Although there are still some vacant lots between these houses, the contrast with the mostly empty streets a few blocks downriver is striking and speaks to the devastation the area experienced. However, the lack of a coherent urban program has demonstrated that high profile individual buildings do not constitute a successful urban neighborhood.

3.16 Doullut Steamboat Houses
1903 and 1913, Milton P. Doullut. 400 and 503 Egania St.

These two almost identical houses were built by river pilot, civil engineer, and shipbuilder Captain Milton P. Doullut and his wife, Mary—one house for themselves (number 400) and the other for their son, Paul, who helped construct them. Doullut's profession explains the nautical details of these octagonal buildings, which include porthole-type openings; broad galleries reminiscent of riverboat decks, draped with double strands of wooden balls strung on steel wires; an enclosed belvedere resembling a pilothouse; and twin metal smokestack chimneys. Asian influences are seen in the tiered effect of the three stories, the concave roof, and deep eaves. The houses are remarkably similar to the Kinkaku, or Golden Pavilion, in the Japanese Village at the 1904 Louisiana Purchase Exhibition in St. Louis and are also reminiscent of Longwood, erected in 1860 in Natchez, Mississippi, which Doullut had probably seen. Equally delightful is Doullut's smorgasbord of building materials, including white glazed brick for the lower exterior walls, pressed tin anthemion cresting along the roof overhang, green roof tiles at number 503, stained glass windows, and, inside the houses, glazed brick walls on the ground floor and pressed metal walls and ceilings upstairs. Each house has a central-hall plan with two rooms on each side.

3.17   Holy Cross Project/Global Green Complex
2006–2015, Workshop/apd, with John C. Williams Architects; D.I.R.T. Studio, landscape. Andry St., between Douglass and N. Peters sts.

This project arose from a national design competition sponsored by the nonprofit organization Global Green International following Hurricane Katrina. It occupies part of a block abutting the Mississippi River and currently consists of five houses and a fourteen-unit apartment building. A goal of the project was to act as a catalyst for rebuilding sustainably. The houses, based on the New Orleans shotgun form, have galleries and porches, with solar panels fitted on their shed roofs. The project had difficulty with construction costs, similar to the Make It Right Houses (**3.15**), and the New York City–based designers struggled to understand the local conditions. But the sustainable design goals have been achieved and the buildings are LEED Platinum certified.

3.18   Jackson Barracks
1834–1835, Frederick Wilkinson. 6424 St. Claude Ave.

Now the headquarters for Louisiana's National Guard, Jackson Barracks was begun during Andrew Jackson's presidency to house a federal garrison. Then known as the New Orleans Barracks, the complex was renamed in 1866 to honor the hero of the Battle of New Orleans. The barracks, which now extends one mile inland from its original site on the Mississippi River, in-

GEN. PERSHING REVIEWING TROOPS
JACKSON BARRACKS. 2-16-1920

cludes more than sixty buildings, a museum, and several Air National Guard airplanes. Captain Frederick Wilkinson (1812–1841), then only twenty-one years old, designed the original scheme: a rectangular parade ground facing the river, measuring 300 × 900 feet, flanked on each of its long sides by three buildings and, at its head, by a group of four buildings arranged in a square formation. All of these red brick structures, designed to house the troops and officers, have two-story galleries with full-height white-painted Doric columns. A description of the barracks published in *Architectural Art and Its Allies* in November 1910 noted that the quarters for the enlisted men were "heated by open fireplaces, and lighted and ventilated by large windows," but observed that during the long hot summers "the majority of the men sleep on the veranda." The officers' quarters were better equipped than those of the troops and included piped-in water.

The simplicity and proportions of these buildings, with their symmetrical layout and scale in relation to the parade ground (now a lawn), combine to form one of Louisiana's most serene and magnificent spaces. Although many new buildings were added to the barracks in succeeding years, they were fortunately placed farther inland and did not disrupt Wilkinson's scheme.

Shortly after completing the barracks, Wilkinson designed Cypress Grove Cemetery Gate and Lodge (**10.10**); he was later appointed deputy U.S. surveyor. The barracks have seen constant use as a debarkation point: for U.S. troops and Indians during the second Seminole War, for troops for the Mexican

War, for Confederate and Union forces in the Civil War, and during World Wars I and II.

In 2005, Hurricane Katrina severely damaged the barracks, inundating the site with four feet of water at the river's edge and around twenty feet at the St. Claude Avenue end. Many of the buildings have since been restored.

Esplanade Avenue to City Park

Esplanade Avenue's closely spaced houses, tall and narrow with side halls, and often built up to their property line, give the street a distinctive and sophisticated urban character. By the 1850s, when the Vieux Carré was becoming shabby, Creoles—often free people of color—began to build houses along Esplanade Avenue. Many adopted the American town house plan: three bays wide to incorporate a side hall, a service wing to the rear, a rear or side garden, and Greek Revival embellishments, most notably around the entrance portal. Houses on the blocks from the Mississippi River to N. Rampart Street display these features best. By the early twentieth century, Esplanade Avenue was built all the way to Bayou St. John, beyond which lay City Park. Midway along Esplanade, in the 2200 block, is a small triangular park, Gayarré Place (dedicated to New Orleans historian Charles Gayarré), marking the point where Bayou Road crosses the avenue. A statue of the Goddess of History stands on a tall square pedestal of red terra-cotta decorated with arches, cherubs, and various leafy ornaments. The pedestal was originally displayed at the Cotton Centennial Exposition of 1884 in Audubon Park as a demonstration of the versatility of terra-cotta.

Esplanade's architectural integrity was compromised by construction in 1966–1968 of the Claiborne Avenue elevated expressway (I-10), which cut across the avenue and other connecting streets, bifurcated the historic Tremé neighborhood (causing several blocks of houses to be demolished or become derelict), eliminated double rows of live oak trees, and effectively destroyed the African American commercial corridor along lower Claiborne Avenue. Efforts are now underway to study and address the expressway's removal.

Bayou St. John is about four miles long and, since it empties into Lake Pontchartrain, was a Native American trade route.

Jean-Baptiste Le Moyne, Sieur de Bienville, referred to it as the "back door" entrance to New Orleans and named it for his patron saint, John the Baptist. In the eighteenth and early nineteenth centuries the bayou was an important transportation route linking Lake Pontchartrain with the Vieux Carré, via the Carondelet Canal (1790s), and then to the Gulf of Mexico. In addition, this area was a popular site for pedestrian activities (the "Carondelet Walk") and nineteenth-century pleasure gardens (commercial amusement parks on private property). Today, the bayou is a placid waterway picturesquely lined with houses on both banks, leading toward City Park.

4.1   Old U.S. Mint (Louisiana State Museum)
1835–1838, William Strickland; 1981 renovated, E. Eean McNaughton Architects. 400 Esplanade Ave.

As a center for foreign trade and for gold, especially after gold deposits were discovered in nearby Alabama, New Orleans was selected as the site for a mint during the presidency of Andrew Jackson. Benjamin F. Fox and John Mitchell constructed the three-story, E-plan brick building—set on the site of Fort St. Charles (San Carlos) of 1792—according to plans by the noted Philadelphia architect William Strickland. Although not an inspiring design, the Greek Revival building looks secure and functional. Its most architecturally developed feature is the projecting portico with four Ionic columns flanked by Doric piers. Each corner of the building is defined by a gray granite pilaster. The present exterior surface of red-tinted stucco scored to resemble granite blocks follows the original finish. Although the walls are three feet thick at ground level, Strickland may not have been fully attentive to the soft conditions of the soil on which the Mint was to be built (he never visited the site), and structural reinforcements were necessary within a year of its completion. James Gallier Sr. inserted iron rods to stabilize the groin vaults, and in the 1850s, General P. G. T. Beauregard improved the building's fireproofing, replaced the slate roof with one of corrugated galvanized iron (then a new building material), and added iron balconies. Approximately $300 million in coins were manufactured here before the Mint closed in 1909. The building then served various functions, including use as a federal prison from 1932 to 1943. Following renovations in 1981, it reopened as a museum and archive. Its focus is currently New Orleans jazz, and a fine performance space has been created on the third floor by Eskew+Dumez+Ripple. The Old Mint was designated a National Historic Landmark in 1975.

4.2 Lucy Cheatam Houses
1861–1862. 529–533 Esplanade Ave.

These two houses were built by free woman of color Lucy Cheatam on land bequeathed by white cotton factor John Hagan to their two sons. In many ways a typical example of Esplanade Avenue's two-story, side-hall houses, these are smaller and have a more human scale than many others on this street. They also differ in being set back behind front gardens. Constructed of brick, plastered and scored, the houses have facades shaded by two-story cast-iron galleries, one ornamented with a pattern of grapes and the other of flowers; number 529 has anthemion cresting. Entrance doors are surrounded by Greek key architraves, and the square-headed windows are finished with molded lintels. The building contract specified marble mantels and wallpaper, the latter very modish at the time, for the parlors. Two-story brick service wings extend from the rear of the houses.

4.3 Johnson House
1879, William Fitzner. 547 Esplanade Ave.

Designed by the German-born architect William Fitzner (1845–1914) for lawyer Charles A. Johnson, this two-story Italianate town house with an attic is an impressive example of the side-hall residences in these blocks of Esplanade next to the Vieux Carré. Edging its property line, the front-plastered

brick house with a hexagonal bay on the right side is entered by way of six steps that rise to the recessed entrance vestibule, framed by pilasters, which has a coved ceiling decorated with rosettes. The windows are segmental arched and surrounded by heavy moldings. The second story opens onto a small cast-iron balcony, and a large bracketed cornice defines the roofline. A lower two-story service wing at the rear is visible on the Chartres Street side of this corner house, as is the row of ground-level ventilation openings covered with cast-iron grilles. Peter Middlemiss (1826–1887) was the builder for Fitzner's design.

4.4 Gauche-Stream House

1856; 1937 restored, Richard Koch; 1969 restored, Koch and Wilson, Architects. 704 Esplanade Ave.

Crockery merchant John Gauche supervised the construction of his large, square house. Exceptionally fine cast ironwork adds a light and delicate touch to the weighty qualities of the stuccoed brick house. Putti (or miniature figures, possibly representing Bacchus) cavort among the grapevines adorning the second-story cast-iron balcony; at eaves level, a projecting cornice supported on paired iron brackets is edged with a cast-iron frieze with anthemion cresting. The building's finest feature, and one unusual for New Orleans, is the light gray granite pedimented Doric portico; its severity makes a splendid foil for the lacy cast-iron decoration. The house is set back slightly from the property line and enclosed by a cast-iron fence and granite gateposts. To the rear, a lower two-story service wing faces the carriage entrance on Royal Street. The house has a central-hall plan, with a stairway located in a side opening to the rear, and full-length casement windows. Richard Koch restored the house for Matilda Geddings Gray after she purchased it in 1937 and Koch and Wilson undertook further restoration in 1969 for Matilda Stream when she inherited the house from her aunt.

4.5 Dufour-Baldwin House

1859, Howard and Diettel. 1707 Esplanade Ave.

Designed for lawyer and state senator Cyprien Dufour and his wife, Louise Donnet, this house cost $40,000—an extraordinary amount for the time—and the price of the lot was $12,000. Howard and Diettel designed this and the Robert Short House (**7.20**) at the same time, and the two have many features in common: a three-bay facade, stucco-covered brick construction, side bays, and Italianate details. However, the Dufour-Baldwin House exhibits more exciting and dramatic effects than the Short House. The facade is shaded by a two-story wooden gallery supported on paired columns; paired brackets and dentils mark the cornice; and a parapet adds additional height. Two large side bays have triple-arched doorways with multiple prominent moldings. At the rear of the house, a two-story galleried round bay outlines the staircase at the end of the wide interior hall. Extending from the right side of the rear facade, the lower two-story service wing also has a bowed gallery. This magnificent combination of galleries, bays, and curves evokes an opera set. The builders were Wing and Muir. The house is named for its first two owners, the second being hardware merchant and bank director Albert Baldwin, who purchased it in 1870.

4.6 Benachi House and Gardens (Benachi-Torre House)
1859. 2257 Bayou Rd.

In 1853, one year after Nicholas Benachi purchased an existing house on this enormous lot, his wife and two of his children died of yellow fever. A few years later, Benachi married Anna Marie Bidault and replaced the old house with this tall, handsome Greek Revival residence built of wood. The house features a two-story gallery supported on slender paired piers, a plain entablature, two dormers, and a central-hall plan. A detached two-story service building has a two-story gallery. The grounds, originally even bigger but reduced when Laharpe Street was cut through it on one side, is enclosed by a cast-iron fence with beautiful Gothic Revival paneled gateposts and a wide entrance gate in the shape of an ogee arch. Peter Torre bought the house in 1886; it is now a venue and event space.

4.7 Joan Mitchell Center and Fleitas House
c. 1800; 1836; 2015, Lee Ledbetter and Associates. 2275 Bayou Rd.

The oldest building in this residential artist retreat is the Fleitas House, a raised galleried house built c. 1800 nearby and moved a block to this site and remodeled in 1836. It now comprises offices, guest rooms, and a kitchen for the Joan Mitchell Center, the hub of which, an 8,000 square-foot L-shaped building of 2015 containing ten studios, is at the rear of the property. The studios, organized in a staggered arrangement, are each lit by a north-facing triangular-shaped clerestory and a controllable skylight. The Center is funded by a New York philanthropy founded in the memory of abstract painter Joan Mitchell, who died in 1992. The organization selected New Orleans as the site in the aftermath of Hurricane Katrina in order to help artists reestablish themselves. Architect Jonathan Tate converted the former restaurant at the corner of Bayou Road and N. Roche-blave Street into gallery space and several adjacent cottages into dormitories.

4.8   George W. Dunbar House
1873–1874. 2453 Esplanade Ave.

This two-story Second Empire house— a handsome example of a style that is rare in New Orleans—was built by Boston-born businessman George Washington Dunbar for one of his sons. A similar house constructed next door for his other son was demolished in 1974. The two-story raised wooden building has a three-bay facade with a side-hall entrance, and a large semi-hexagonal bay on one side. The concave mansard roof covered with patterned tiles is pierced by one large dormer window on the front and four along the house's N. Dorgenois Street side—all with segmental-arched windows—and iron cresting crowns the roof.

4.9   Hannon House
c. 1902. 2809 Esplanade Ave.

Irish real-estate speculator W. James Hannon built this exu-berant Queen Anne raised wooden house, which appears to incorporate every variety of wood trim available at the time: turned columns, spindlework, brackets, bargeboard, and quoins. A double flight of stairs (added in 1946 when the house was raised) rises to a richly decorated central gabled portico and a deep, shady gallery. One side of the gallery ends in an angled corner; the other side, sweeping in a wide curve around that end of the house, is topped by a squat octagonal spire with a multicolored roof. The owners boasted that the 12 × 86–foot central hall was the largest and longest in town. The gazebo in the side garden is a modern but sympathetic addition.

4.10   Luling Mansion
1865–1866, Gallier and Esterbrook. 1438 Leda Ct.

Luling Mansion originally faced Esplanade Avenue behind a deep front garden, which was sold and subdivided for houses in the early twentieth century. This Italianate house, the largest and most elaborate of James Gallier Jr.'s residential designs, was built for German immigrant and cotton merchant Florence A. Luling. Raised on a terrace, the three-story mansion of plastered brick is surrounded by a dry moat and, on the second and third levels, by galleries with low balustrades. The hipped roof extends well beyond the walls to shade the upper balcony and is finished with a parapet cornice and a square belvedere. All the windows are round arched, which contributes to the impression that the mansion belongs in Renaissance Italy. A granite staircase rises from the rusticated first floor to the second-level entrance. The house was originally flanked by pavilions (removed by 1924), which accommodated a conservatory and a bowling alley and were linked to the house by bridges across the moat. There were extensive gardens refelecting period styles of lavish plantings. After Luling's two young sons drowned in nearby Bayou St. John and he suffered financial setbacks in the Reconstruction economy, he sold his mansion and thirty acres in 1871 to the Louisiana Jockey Club for use as a clubhouse and moved to England. The house is now subdivided into apartments.

4.11 St. Louis Cemetery No. 3
1854 established. 3421 Esplanade Avenue

This cemetery was laid out following the yellow fever epidemic of 1853, which killed 10 percent of the city's population. First established with three main avenues and four narrower parallel aisles, the cemetery was enlarged and improved in 1865 by French-born surveyor Jules A. D'Hémécourt (1819–1880). By widening the central aisle and adding cross aisles, he provided grand vistas along the continuous rows of aboveground tombs. The uniform size and gable roofs of the tombs give this cemetery, more than any other in New Orleans, the appearance of city streets in miniature. Near the entrance is the monument that James Gallier Jr. designed in 1866 for his father, James Gallier Sr., who died at sea along with his wife, Catherine. It is a vertical composition of stacked pedestals surmounted by a large urn. Among the society tombs, those for the Slavonian Benevolent Society (1876) and the Hellenic Orthodox Community

(1928) are particularly impressive; much simpler is the multivault tomb of the Little Sisters of the Poor, which was donated by philanthropist Margaret Haughery (**7.3**). Francis Lurges fabricated the elaborate iron entrance gates.

4.12   Holy Rosary Rectory (Evariste Blanc House)
c. 1834. 1342 Moss St.

As the water link between New Orleans and Lake Pontchartrain, Bayou St. John had some of the city's earliest habitations along its banks. Although this structure was built later than some, such as the Pitot House (**4.13**), it has much in common with earlier examples. However, its emphasis on height, its Greek Revival elements, and its central-hall plan clearly reveal the impact of American ideas on Creole forms. Fronted by a two-story gallery supported on heavy Tuscan columns at ground level and turned wood columns above, the stuccoed brick house has a hipped roof and widow's walk. The central front door is set between Ionic columns and sidelights and is topped by a fanlight; the same design is repeated on the floor above. The house was donated to the Catholic Church in 1905 by Evariste Blanc's descendants, the Denegre family.

4.13   Pitot House
1799; 1805, Louis Hilaire Boutté. 1440 Moss St.

Merchant and shipowner Don Bartholemé Bosque, from Palma, Majorca, began construction of this beautiful house and sold it unfinished in 1800. In 1805, Marie Tronquet, the widow of Vincent Rillieux and great-grandmother of Edgar Degas, purchased the residence and Boutté (1754–1808) completed it. The ground floor is constructed of stuccoed brick and the upper of brick-between-posts covered with stucco. Front and side galleries are supported on brick Tuscan columns at ground level and slender wooden colonnettes above. The house has a double-pitched hipped roof. The plan consists of three rooms across the front, without corridors, with a loggia between two smaller cabinets at the rear of the second level. Stairs in the rear loggia link the two floors. An original set of stairs within the side gallery was intended for guests. Some scholars describe this house type as French West Indies because it is similar to contemporary houses on the Caribbean islands; however, others believe that French Canadians brought the type and style with them before 1700. In 1810, commission merchant James (Jacques) Pitot, who came to New Orleans from Saint-Domingue in 1796 after the slave uprisings, purchased the house for his family. He later became New Orleans's first elected mayor. Behind the house Pitot had two cabins for his six enslaved workers, a kitchen, a barn, stables, privies, a vegetable garden, and farm animals. In 1904, Mother Francis Cabrini purchased the house and used it as a convent, then rented it out. In 1964, when the sisters planned to demolish the building in order to build a school on the property, the Louisiana Landmarks Society acquired and moved the timber-framed structure two hundred feet from its original location, now occupied by the neighboring school. Koch and Wilson, Architects, were hired to restore it to the Pitot time period, and it was opened as a house museum in 1972. Although none of the dependency buildings survive, garden areas have been developed over time, recently (2006-2007, Lake Douglas, landscape architect) with native plants, flowering shrubs, herbs, and vegetables representative of local nineteenth-century gardens.

Nearby at 1300 Moss Street is a similar house, known as the Spanish Custom House, built after 1807 by Robert Alexander for Captain Elie Beauregard. That residence probably acquired its nickname during the Spanish era, when it was the home of Spanish custom officer Luis Blanc. This house, which also features a double-height living space from the early twentieth century, was recently restored by Waggonner and Ball Architects.

4.14 New Orleans City Park and Botanical Garden

1850, 1890s; 1933, Bennett, Parsons and Frost. Bounded by City Park and Orleans aves., and Wisner and Robert E. Lee blvds.

City Park's origins date to 1850, when eighty-five acres of swampy land adjacent to Bayou St. John were donated by John McDonogh to settle his tax debts with the City of New Orleans. The City gained clear title to the property in 1858 and a contract was executed in 1872 with John Bogart and John Y. Cuyler, staff engineers in Frederick Law Olmsted's office, for a park plan. Their scheme was rejected however, and there were few improvements until the 1890s, when the area was properly drained and additional land acquired. At that time, civil engineer George H. Grandjean, a member of the City Park Board, devised a master plan, and a local firm of surveyors, Daney and Wadill, was hired to work out the scheme of lagoons, footpaths, and bridges, with the help of architect Paul Andry (1868–1946). Based on City Beautiful concepts, the plan inspired several donors to fund structures, pavilions, and conveniences. The largest and most splendid building was the Isaac Delgado Museum of Art (**4.15**) of 1911, named for its benefactor and now known as the New Orleans Museum of Art. Other structures, all designed by New Orleans–based architects, included the Peristyle, a rectangular dance pavilion with rounded ends surrounded by an Ionic colonnade, conceived in 1907 by Paul Andry and Albert Bendernagel (1904–1961); Emile Weil's circular Popp Bandstand (1917), a replica of the Temple of Love at the Petit Trianon, Versailles, funded by lumberman John F. Popp; a refreshment

The Urban Landscape: Plants and Their Uses

Early-eighteenth-century explorers commented on the lushness and variety of plant material they encountered as well as the opportunities they saw for agricultural production. But the largely cypress swamps and marshlands they found had to be cleared before any development could take place, and clearing these low-lying areas proved difficult. In addition, heavy rains, periodic flooding, and tropical storms interfered with settlement activities.

European settlers' experiments with crops—indigo, tobacco, rice, and mulberry trees (for silk worms)—met with limited success, but by the beginning of the nineteenth century cotton and sugarcane proved successful (see **3.12, 6.14**), and these crops fueled the region's economy in the first half of the nineteenth century.

There is evidence of plants being cultivated for medicinal purposes by nuns at the Ursuline Convent (**1.29**) early in the settlement's history. Some of what they grew was imported from France, but native plants were among many grown, reflecting horticultural and medicinal practices learned from Native Americans.

As the community stabilized and matured, attention turned to more sophisticated patterns of architecture, interior furnishings, and exterior design. Advertisements for ornamental plants regularly appeared in local newspapers from the 1820s, and with these we can trace plant availability, introductions ("Exotics from Mexico, Brazil, New Holland, the Indies and China" according

pavilion known as the Casino, with triangular arches, created in 1913 by Nolan and Torre; a Beaux-Arts classical bridge (1923), given by Felix Dreyfous; a brick pigeon house (1928), perhaps by Dreyfous's son, architect F. Julius Dreyfous; and a mechanical carousel (1910) in a pavilion built in 1906. The entrance to the park from City Park Avenue is marked by a pair of pylons with engaged Ionic columns, built in 1913. Alexander Doyle's bronze to one advertisement from 1850), and other characteristics of horticultural commerce, including businesses, proprietors, and inventories.

From the mid-nineteenth century on, gardening almanacs were published locally, and surviving nursery catalogs and advertising broadsides list inventories of regionally available plants. Depictions of nineteenth-century gardens exist in the City's Notarial Archives, documenting properties for sale. These show gardens as functional (producing food for the table) and ornamental, complex and simple, designed and vernacular, sometimes with details of plants and garden features.

Several written accounts of New Orleans gardens appeared in contemporary national periodicals, offering first-hand observations of the city's horticultural richness. One author (1845) describes "a tolerable display of Flora's beauties . . . conjuring up a spring-like appearance in the gloomy season of winter." This effusive account is balanced by another (1851), in which the author notes that "there is little attention here . . . to gardening" and while "nature has done much to adorn the scene, art has done little or nothing."

One might make the same observations today: plants grow here with little attention, contributing to the urban landscape's lush, mysterious, and exotic character. Domestic gardens, now as in the past, are more about the interest of the individual homeowner (see **4.13**, **7.16**) and less about manicured spaces consciously designed by professionals (see **10.12**).

equestrian statue of General P. G. T. Beauregard (unveiled in 1915) that stood in front of the entrance has been removed, one of four monuments in New Orleans related to the Confederate cause taken down from public sites in 2017.

In 1929, the Chicago firm of Bennett, Parsons and Frost was hired to draw up a new plan for the park, which by then had increased to thirteen hundred acres. Work could proceed only after the receipt of federal funding, first from the PWA and then the WPA. The park underwent a spectacular transformation that cost $13 million, of which the City Park Board paid only 5 percent. From 1934 to 1940, fourteen thousand men, using mostly hand tools, laid out golf courses on the east side of the park (supervised by landscape architect William Wiedorn), dug more than sixty acres of lagoons, and built eight new bridges, a stadium, fountains, and cast-concrete benches. Wiedorn (1896–1988) had worked in Boston (in the Olmsted Brothers office), Cleveland, and Florida before moving to New Orleans to supervise construction of the golf courses. He remained in the city and maintained a modest practice. Mexican-born sculptor Enrique Alferez, assisted by a team of sculptors, created both freestanding and architectural sculpture in a stylized Art Deco manner that suited the architectural forms. Particularly note-worthy is the Popp Fountain (corner of Marconi Boulevard and Zachary Taylor Drive), with waterspouts in the shape of leaping dolphins (recast in bronze in 1998), surrounded by a circle of twenty-six columns. The fountain's site was developed by Olmsted Brothers; Wiedorn was the local project supervisor. The firm of Weiss, Dreyfous and Seiferth managed these federal projects.

Wiedorn and architect Richard Koch laid out the Botanical Garden and its structures in the 1930s. The garden was restored in the 1980s, and a multi-activity pavilion by Trapolin Architects was added in 1994. Particularly noteworthy in the garden are original benches, ornamental gates, and a sundial by Enrique Alferez, together with recent additions.

After 1965, the park acquired land on the lake side of Harrison Avenue in compensation for the intrusion of I-610. Now encompassing over sixteen hundred acres, City Park is one of America's largest municipal parks and it contains one of the largest collections of mature live oak trees on public land. The carefully contrived irregular landscape, the plant-ings, the more than eighty species of trees, and the sensitively placed pavilions and sculptures give the park, despite its flat terrain, the romantic ambience favored by nineteenth-century urban planners. Flooding in 2005 in the aftermath of Hurri-cane Katrina caused extensive damage, but new plantings and building repairs have restored this place to its former beauty. Among recent additions to City Park are Big Lake, a reconfiguration of the lagoon from the WPA era (2011, Cashio Cochran, landscape architects); the relocation of tennis courts to create a large passive green space; and a refurbishment of the Botanical Garden completed in 2007. Much of the funding for these post-Katrina improvements has come from national sources.

4.15   New Orleans Museum of Art (Isaac Delgado Museum of Art)
1911, Samuel A. Marx for Lebenbaum and Marx; 1971 addition, August Perez and Associates with Arthur Feitel; 1993 addition, Eskew Filson Architects and Billes/Manning Architects. Collins Diboll Cir.

In 1910, sugar broker and philanthropist Isaac Delgado gave $150,000 and his art collection to create a museum of art, and chose a site on a circle at the end of tree-lined Lelong Avenue. Samuel Marx of Chicago won the design competition in 1910, and the building was constructed under the supervision of Richard Koch. According to Marx, the design was "inspired by the Greek, sufficiently modified to give a subtropical appearance." The cream-colored Bedford, Indiana, limestone facade features a recessed Ionic portico with six columns set between pavilion-like wings, which are covered by pyramidal roofs of green tile and surrounded by a low parapet of stylized anthemia. The three-part composition, with a center marked by columns, bears some resemblance to the garden facade of the Petit Trianon at the Palace of Versailles, but the columns at the museum stand in front of a recessed portico, which creates a greater play of light and shadow across the building. Panels inset high on the wings replicate scenes from a Parthenon frieze. The building has the typical Beaux-Arts museum plan of gallery rooms set around a central two-story skylit sculpture hall, surrounded on three sides by a balcony supported on Ionic columns.

In 1971, August Perez and Associates with Arthur Feitel added three wings to the museum, followed in 1993 by a more sympathetic extension to the rear, which was adapted by Eskew Filson Architects and Billes/Manning Architects from a design by Clark and Menefee of Charleston, South Carolina, the winning result of an international design competition. This later addition of glass block and concrete panels made it possible to view the museum's original exterior walls and their classical decoration from inside the building.

4.16 Sydney and Walda Besthoff Sculpture Garden
2003, Lee Ledbetter and Associates and Sawyer/Berson. Collins Diboll Cir.

New Orleans–based Lee Ledbetter and Associates and Sawyer/Berson of New York City designed this sculpture garden, which opened in 2003 adjacent to the art museum. Covering five acres, the garden has more than sixty works set picturesquely among groves of trees, native plantings, a lagoon, and three bridges. Among the many internationally renowned artists whose works enhance the oak and pine setting are Augustus Saint-Gaudens, Henry Moore, Isamu Noguchi, and Louise Bourgeois. With the collection continually growing, garden expansion is being planned on an opposite site behind the museum.

Canal Street

Canal Street, 171 feet wide, extends 3.5 miles from the Mississippi River to the cemeteries on Metairie Ridge. As the city's premier commercial boulevard, lower Canal—the blocks that separate the Vieux Carré from the Central Business District (originally the Faubourg St. Mary)—flourished even as other main streets in the nation withered. Its commercial and popular success can be attributed in part to its location, adjacent to both business and entertainment destinations. In the early nineteenth century, the street had become a boundary between the French-speaking Creoles in the Vieux Carré and the English-speaking Anglo-Americans in Faubourg St. Mary and is commonly believed to be the origin of the term "neutral ground" to describe all the landscaped medians that run down the center of New Orleans's broad boulevards. A proposal in 1807 to construct a canal along the street to connect the Mississippi River with the Carondelet Canal (known as the Old Basin Canal) was not implemented but did give the street its name. Although most of lower Canal's first buildings were residences, by the 1840s they were being replaced by handsome commercial buildings that made the street a showplace of nineteenth- and twentieth-century commercial facades. The introduction of streetcars along Canal in 1861 encouraged the thoroughfare's outward growth from Basin Street; this stretch, known as upper Canal, developed with a mix of residential, institutional, and commercial structures.

In his book, *God's Own Junkyard* (1964), architect and critic Peter Blake decried what he saw as the crass commercialism and shopfront signage of lower Canal. In response, architect Robert Venturi, author of *Complexity and Contradiction in Architecture* (1966), reprinted Blake's photograph of Canal Street and declared that "the seemingly chaotic juxtapositions of the honkytonk elements express an intriguing kind of vitality and validity." For Venturi, the attributes Blake deplored were precisely what made the street successful. Some of the "honkytonk" is gone (though the casino at the foot of Canal, completed in 1999, possibly qualifies), and department stores have been converted to sedate hotels, but Canal Street remains one of the city's busiest and most vibrant public spaces. The reinstatement of streetcars (which had been replaced by buses

S Murat St **5.17** ●

0   0.25 miles

Canal St

I-10

N

5.16 ●   David St

S Carrollton Ave   N Carrollton Ave

N Scott St

Tulane Ave / US-61

Mid-City

Orleans Ave

Canal St

Bienville St

S Jefferson Davis Pkwy

Bayou St John

Banks St

N Gayoso St

S Dupre St **5.15** ●   N Dupre St

S Broad St / US-90   N Broad St / US-90

S Dorgenois St   N Dorgenois St

S Rocheblave St   N Tonti St

Canal St

5.14 ●

S Galvez St   N Galvez St

Orleans Ave

Poydras St

Tulane Ave

5.13

N Prieur St

N Roman St

N Derbigny St

N Claibrone Ave

I-10

S Claiborne Ave

Tremé

5.12

Canal St

● Marais St

Lasalle St   Treme St

Poydras St

5.11

Loyola Ave   Elk Pl   Basin St

● **5.10**

N Rampart St

Burgundy St

S Rampart St

5.7 ● ● **5.9**

O'Keefe Ave   Dauphine St

Baronne St   **5.6** ● ● **5.8**

Bourbon St

Carondelet St

5.5 ●   Royal St   **Vieux**

St Charles Ave   Chartres St   **Carré**

Camp St   Decatur St

Magazine St   Poydras St

● **5.4**

Canal St

N Peters St

Tchoupitoulas St

5.2 ● ● **5.1**

S Peters St

Convention   ● **5.3**

Ctr Blvd

Mississippi River

100

in 1964), together with the addition of new lateral streetcar lines at the riverfront, Rampart Street, Elk Place, and Carrollton guarantees the boulevard's continued appeal, and the new lines increase the Canal line's capacity and link neighborhhods together.

5.1 Aquarium of the Americas

1987–1990, Bienville Group (Billes/Manning Architects; Concordia Architects; Eskew, Vogt, Salvato and Filson; Hewitt-Washington and Associates; and The Mathes Group). 1 Canal St.

The centerpiece of the aquarium complex is a 145-foot-high turquoise glass drum with a diagonally cut roofline, which is set amid lower wings faced with white and pastel-colored tiles. Around the Aquarium are brick-paved plazas that extend to the river and to Woldenberg Riverfront Park (**1.8**). In the Aquarium's dimly lit interior, visitors proceed past the exhibits, the most engaging of which is a clear acrylic barrel-vaulted tunnel that surrounds the observer with 132,000 gallons of water inhabited by fish. The glass drum houses a tropical rainforest. A second-phase expansion included an IMAX film theater and exhibition gallery. The Aquarium's location was controversial. Critics rightly saw that by attracting more tourists to an already over-crowded Vieux Carré, the Aquarium would dilute the quarter's residential and business character and encourage the tendency to view it as an amusement park. It is unfortunate that the de-velopers succeeded in locating the Aquarium on the edge of the Vieux Carré, a part of downtown that does not need additional tourist venues, rather than in an area that would have benefited from the revitalization this popular attraction could create.

5.2 International Trade Mart Building (World Trade Center Building)

1964–1967, Edward Durell Stone. 2 Canal St.

The International Trade Mart Building (ITM) is a thirty-three-story cruciform structure prominently situated beside the Mississippi River at the foot of Canal Street. The building's original purpose was to serve as the locus of international trade for the Port of New Orleans and to promote and expand growth by accommodating the functions of two New Orleans's nonprofit trade organizations: the International Trade Mart and

International House. Initial plans for the project were made in 1957 and the following year the Arkansas-born, internationally renowned New York City–based architect Stone was invited to New Orleans and promptly commissioned to produce a modern design (which both organizations wanted). Stone's first design was a nineteen-story rectangular building, but various delays, which included securing full possession of the desired site, prevented construction. By then it was clear that Stone's scheme was too small for what was needed and he was asked to submit a new proposal. This second cruciform-shaped design carried a symbolism that the first did not: the building's four wings face the cardinal directions to signify the ITM's reach to the four corners of the world, a symbolic gesture that is not immediately obvious. Construction began in 1964.

The ITM building, a cityscape icon, is carried on spiral piles driven up to two hundred feet into the ground to find anchorage in stable clay strata. Its reinforced-concrete frame is sheathed in alternating vertical bands of precast exposed aggregate concrete panels and aluminum-framed windows. Closely spaced horizontal aluminum louvers shade the windows from direct sun and add texture to the building's surface. The dark-tinted glass walls that enclose the building's ground floor distinguish it from the lighter-colored upper floors so that from a distance the tower appears to hover above the ground, a signature feature of the International Style. A deep canopy wrapping and shading the ground floor is echoed in the horizontal extension of the rooftop observation deck and the circular uppermost three floors. The top floor accommodated a cocktail lounge (closed 2001), which rotated 360 degrees every 55 minutes to provide dramatic views of the city, the river, and the port. The entrance lobby is a handsome space, with an abundance of light, terrazzo floors, and walls of white Italian marble; the building's circulation systems are in a central core, with ten high-speed elevators.

Stone's ambitious plan for urban plazas and landscaping around the trade center were altered. Initially, an equestrian statue of Joan of Arc (1.7), a gift from France in 1964, stood in front of the ITM building, but was removed in the 1990s to a site in the Vieux Carré to make way for the casino that replaced Curtis and Davis's award-winning Rivergate (demolished 2004), a trade exhibition facility that opened in 1968 as a complement to the ITM building. From 1985 until 2009 (when it was vacated), the ITM was known as the World Trade Center Building. After years of litigation, it was ruled in 2017 that the structure will be converted for mixed-use occupancy, including residences and a hotel.

5.3   Spanish Plaza

1976 and later. Between 2 Canal St. and the Mississippi River

Spanish Plaza is located on the river side of the International Trade Mart (5.2), its entrance marked by Spanish sculptor Juan de Avalos's fifteen-foot-high bronze statue of Bernardo de Galvez, governor of Louisiana during the American Revolution.

This open space is decorated with heraldic tiles representing 48 Spanish cities (the original tiles were a bicentennial gift of Spain in 1976; they were replaced with new ones in 2002). Other elements include a malfunctioning fountain, structures that mark the plaza's entrances, restaurants, and other tourist-oriented uses. While Spanish Plaza is the site of the ceremonial meeting of the Mardi Gras krewes of Rex and Zulu on Lundi Gras (a tradition dating from the late nineteenth century), the location, disconnected from downriver open spaces by the ferry terminal, has become less of a public gathering area and more a forecourt to the adjacent upriver commercial Riverwalk, an urban shopping mall developed after the 1984 Louisiana World Exposition and recently rebranded as an outlet mall. Plans are being developed (2017, Dana Brown and Associates, landscape architects) to redesign the plaza to commemorate the tricentennial anniversary of the city's founding and connect it with downriver attractions through the redesign (Manning Architects) of the adjacent ferry terminal and open spaces.

5.4   U.S. Custom House

1848–1850, Alexander Thompson Wood; 1850–1881, multiple architects; 1990s restored, Waggonner and Ball Architects. 423 Canal Street.

The size and splendor of the Custom House testify to the importance of New Orleans as a nineteenth-century port. Occupying an entire trapazoidal block and at least three hundred feet on each side, the four-story Custom House was at the time the second-largest building in the United States after the U.S. Capitol. James Gallier Sr., James H. Dakin, and J. N. B. de Pouilly all submitted designs in a competition of 1845, but Alexander Wood (1806–1854), who had moved to New Orleans from New

York c. 1831, received the commission in 1848. According to Gallier's autobiography, Wood was in Washington during the design competition and "attended assiduously upon the secretary, having free access to all the plans and models that had been sent in, and from them concocted a design in accordance with the taste and ideas of the secretary, who . . . appointed Wood to be the architect . . . to the astonishment of all who knew anything of Wood's previous history." It is impossible to know if Gallier's reference to Wood's "history" alluded to his design skills or to the fact that he had recently been released from prison for the manslaughter in 1835 of his builder-foreman, George Clarkson.

The Custom House sits on a horizontal grillage of cypress planking, rather than vertical piles. Above it is a continuous series of inverted brick arches which help distribute the building's weight. The building is faced with Quincy, Massachusetts, granite; its upper three stories are raised over a massive rusticated base articulated with arched niches. At the center of each facade are engaged porticoes with lotus-blossom capitals on fluted columns supporting a pediment. The building's intimidating scale, the powerful and complex relationship between walls and windows, the stylized rustication, sense of enclosure, and Egyptian Revival exterior detailing inspired Dakin to describe it as fit only for a "Mausoleum or Tomb for an Egyptian king." Mark Twain thought it looked like a "state prison."

Inside, stairs from the groin-vaulted ground floor lead to the Central Business Room (known as the Marble Hall), a Greek Revival space measuring 125 by 95 feet and which is three stories (55 feet) in height with fourteen freestanding Italian white marble Corinthian columns, one of the city's grandest spaces. Column capitals display the heads of Mercury, the Roman god of commerce, and Luna, the moon goddess, whose crescent shape represents the Crescent City, a nickname by which New Orleans is known. Because the Custom House lacked a roof for years during its long building campaign, the columns and capitals are somewhat weathered from exposure. Although a dome had been planned, it was omitted because of a three-foot settlement of the building during construction, although some subsidence would have been expected for such a heavy structure on New Orleans's soft, moisture-laden soils. The hall was finally covered and illuminated by skylights with operable windows. It was in this hall that ship captains declared their cargo, a practice that continued through the building's long history until Hurricane Katrina in 2005.

Problems posed by subsidence, political infighting, and the Civil War delayed the building's completion. In 1850, Wood was removed as architect, and a series of supervising architects took over, among them James H. Dakin, from 1850 to 1851, who proposed a range of major changes that were rejected. He was followed by Lewis E. Reynolds, then General P. G. T. Beauregard (from 1853 to 1860) and Thomas K. Wharton (from 1861 to 1862). English-born Wharton (1814–1862), who immigrated with his parents to America in 1829 and trained as an architect in New York, had worked on the Custom House as a draftsman in 1848, recording his experiences in his journal. Although the building was partially occupied in 1856, it was still incomplete by the time of the Civil War, during which it served as a prison for Confederate soldiers while the city was under Union control. The Custom House was finally finished in 1881 under Alfred B. Mullett, Supervising Architect of the U.S. Treasury Department. Among the various modifications made to the Custom House over this protracted construction campaign was the employment of a cast-iron cornice instead of stone in order to reduce the building's weight.

Following a number of unsympathetic renovations, beginning in 1914 when the vast post office space on the lake side of the first floor was subdivided, through 1978 when most of the vaulted ceiling was hidden above acoustical tile, the building was restored beginning in the 1990s by Waggonner and Ball Architects. It required additional rehabilitation after Hurricane Katrina collapsed a roof and caused substantial water damage to the interior. The customs service has returned to its old home, but currently the ground floor accommodates mixed uses. The Audubon Institute Insectarium, entered directly from Canal Street, occupies the river side of the first floor.

5.5   Commercial Building (Merchants' Mutual Insurance Co.)
1859, William A. Freret Jr. 622 Canal St.

Freret's design for this cast-iron facade, fabricated by the New Orleans foundry of Bennett and Lurges, is a splendid example of the exuberant effects this new material made possible. The

individual elements—the round-arched openings, curved bands
of foliate ornament, spiral columns between the windows on
the second story, fluted columns above, and, at the third level,
a row of bull's-eye windows separated by prominent scrolling,
leaflike brackets—offer a dense and organic effect. The parapet
is ornamented with designs relevant to an insurance company
in New Orleans: fireplug, hose, pipe, anchor, cotton bales, bar-
rels, prow of a vessel, and furled sails. The entire facade can be
understood as a sign, designed to attract attention to itself and
clients to the business. An arcade on four fluted Corinthian columns, only two of which remain, defined the ground-level story.
Mid-nineteenth-century commercial facades, of which this is a
particularly fine example, combined historical forms with showy
details to compete for attention. Some evidence of this is also
apparent in the adjacent buildings—626, 630, and 634 Canal—
which, with Freret's building, make a particularly harmonious
group. William A. Freret Jr. (1833–1911) was Supervising Architect of the U.S. Treasury Department from 1887 to 1888.

Nearby at 111 Exchange Place is another cast-iron facade
designed in 1866 by James Gallier Jr. and Richard Esterbrook

(1813–1906) and cast by the New Orleans firm of Bennett and Lurges for the Bank of America as a commercial rental venture. The five-story Venetian Renaissance–styled facade, which features fluted Corinthian columns and arched windows, awaits rehabilitation.

5.6 Boston Club (Dr. William Newton Mercer House)
1844 James Gallier Sr. 824 Canal St.

When physician William Mercer, an army surgeon in the War of 1812, had this stucco-covered brick house built, Canal Street was still a fashionable residential address. The three-story, side-hall house has an angled side bay and an attic ventilated by narrow horizontal windows covered with iron grilles. The importance of the second story as the main living area is emphasized by its extra height and is also expressed in the tall windows with pediments and the continuous iron balcony that fronts them. Marble was used for the entrance piers, sills, and entablature. Uneven subsidence has caused the front door lintel to slant downward on one side. Mercer was a generous philanthropist who funded St. Anna's Orphan Asylum (**7.7**) and St. Elizabeth's Home of Industry (**8.6**). The Boston Club, a social club for men, was organized in 1841. Named for a popular card game (not the city of Boston), the club has occupied the building since 1884.

5.7 Walgreens Drugstore
1938, Weiss, Dreyfous and Seiferth. 900 Canal St.

Pharmacist Charles Walgreen established his drugstore chain in Chicago in 1901. The smooth, streamlined exterior of this steel-framed store suits the corner site it occupies and conveys

a fresh, healthy image. A low, round tower wrapped by blue and red neon signage (added c. 1949) marks the corner entrance. Inside, retail departments and a one-hundred-foot-long lunch counter originally occupied the ground floor, the second floor housed a restaurant and kitchen, and the third floor was used for storage. In 1997, Walgreens proposed demolishing the drugstore in order to build a larger structure, but local preservation organizations prevented this; the distinctive neon sign has since been landmarked. The similarly designed neon sign on the CVS Pharmacy (formerly the Gus Mayer department store) nearby at 800 Canal is a 2010 addition to the 1940 building.

5.8   Ritz-Carlton Hotel (Maison Blanche Building)

1908–1909, Stone Brothers Architects; 2000 renovated, Robert Coleman and Partners and John Williams and Associates. 901–921 Canal St.

Originally planned as a complex combining a hotel, theater, and shopping arcade fronting on Canal Street, the Maison Blanche department store located in this building was a favorite among New Orleanians. On its Dauphine Street side, the U-shaped composition provided natural light for the offices on the upper floors, allowing a continuous facade on the Canal Street side. Striving to compete with all the other facades on this commercial street, the building features oversized columns and exuberantly interpreted classical detailing in glazed white terra-cotta. Appropriately, this commercial structure is far more floridly ornamented than the contemporaneous terra-cotta-faced Louisiana Supreme Court building (**1.14**). The terra-cotta

was manufactured by the Atlantic Terra Cotta Company of New York. Samuel Stone Jr. (1869–1933) collaborated with his architect brothers, Guy and Grover, on this large commission. The renovated building reopened as a hotel in 2000.

5.9 Kress Building

1912–1913, Emile Weil. 923 Canal St.

The Kress Company rarely employed a non-company architect to design its stores, but because of New Orleans's distance from New York and the particular circumstances of the site, Kress turned to local architect Emile Weil for its first store in the city. The four upper floors of this five-level building have a continuous vertical screen of sash windows with cast-iron mullions and spandrels set within a decorative terra-cotta frame. The Kress Company authorized the cream-colored terra-cotta facade, a material used only for its most important locations. The facade's composition and its ornamentation—stylized sunburst and geometric decorations, accented in blue, orange, and green—show the influence of Louis Sullivan. The Kress name is inscribed at the top of the building. A curved metal canopy marks the entrance, which was originally set deep within a long arcade lined with large plate-glass display windows, a characteristic of Kress stores. Inside, a spacious center court was covered by coffered skylights and surrounded by a mezzanine supported on Corinthian columns. The satisfying proportions and ornamentation of the facade more than hold their own next door to the ostentatious Maison Blanche Building (**5.8**). With the conversion of that building into a hotel, the Kress Building's ground floor became the hotel's porte-cochere entrance.

5.10   Saenger Theater

1926–1927, Emile Weil; 2013 renovated, Martinez and Johnson Architecture and Ace Theatrical Group. 1111 Canal St.

In 1911, brothers Julian and A. D. Saenger formed the Saenger Amusement Company, which eventually operated 320 theaters in eleven southern states and the Caribbean. Weil designed several theaters for the Saengers, including those in Cuba, Costa Rica, Texas, Arkansas, and the Saengers' home town of Shreveport. The New Orleans' Saenger, which accommodated almost 4,000 people, was, when built, one of the largest theaters in the South. Although the brick exterior of the reinforced-concrete structure is embellished with decorative niches, and the entrance marquee is framed by a triumphal arch motif, the glamorous interior still comes as a surprise. Weil designed a lobby embellished with black and gold marble, mirrors and crystal chandeliers, and a domed ceiling supported on elaborate Composite capitals. This lobby was for white patrons; "colored" patrons entered the theater on its Basin Street side, where stairs led directly to the balcony. The theater's highpoint is the auditorium, where, according to *Southern Architect and Building News*, Weil created the fantasy of "an Italian garden; a Persian court; in a Spanish patio." The auditorium walls were fashioned as building facades in plaster, wood, and marble, with an architectural vista of towers and rooftops lined with classical statues in front of a painted backdrop of exotic plants and birds. To complete the illusion of an outdoor setting, images of slowly moving clouds were projected across a domed ceiling painted deep blue and perforated by hundreds of twinkling pinpoint lights. John Eberson pioneered the atmospheric setting at the Majestic Theater in Houston (1923); Weil, however, credited Chicago's Capitol Theater as his source. Since the Saenger was designed and built for motion pictures as well as live theater, the auditorium had raked seating and a balcony. On the opening night, moviegoers watched the silent film *Blonde or Brunette*, accompanied by an 80-piece orchestra and the 778-pipe Morton Mighty Wonder Organ. Flooded in Hurricane Katrina, the theater underwent a complete renovation. The stagehouse was greatly enlarged, and now the Saenger is a venue for various concerts and theatrical events, including major Broadway productions.

5.11 New Orleans BioInnovation Center
2007–2011, Eskew+Dumas+Ripple. 1441 Canal St.

This building was designed as a center and incubator for biotechnology startups. The four-story L-shaped building's glass facade is shaded by a slatted sunscreen that draws on regional vernacular forms in its design. Inside the building there are balconies on every floor, communal spaces to encourage interaction among the tenants, a conference center, and a landscaped courtyard. The building is a LEED Gold facility, the first in Louisiana. Stormwater is collected in a crushed stone sub-base beneath the parking lot and water from air-conditioning condensation is channeled into a water feature in the courtyard.

5.12 Marais Apartments (Texaco Building)
1951–1955, Claude E. Hooton; 2015 renovated, HRI and Rick Fifield Architect. 1501 Canal St.

Rising seventeen stories, this International Style building's steel frame has a curtain wall of glass, turquoise enamel-coated steel, and aluminum—materials and colors made fashionable by New York City's Lever House (1952). The building was constructed for the Texaco Company when the post–World War II oil boom made New Orleans a center for oil and gas industry companies. The building's steel frame allowed for flexible interior space

with a minimum of internal supports. After Texaco moved to Poydras Street in the 1980s, the building served different tenants. Eventually, it sat vacant for several years until it was rehabilitated into apartments for the elderly and the handsome original curtain wall was restored. Claude E. Hooton (1905–1993), born in Mansfield, Louisiana, practiced in both New Orleans and Houston. During his relatively brief stay in his home state, he also worked as associated architect on the former Pan-American Life Insurance Building (**5.14**).

5.13   University Medical Center (UMC) of New Orleans
        2015, Blitch Knevel Architects/NBBJ, a joint venture. 2000 Canal St.

This expansive complex, which includes both the UMC and the adjacent Veterans Administration (VA) Hospital, is a result of post–Hurricane Katrina "urban renewal" that effectively destroyed a working-class neighborhood of modest houses, many of which had been renovated by owners after the storm. Properties were seized through eminent domain, while the preservation community fought to have structures moved rather than being razed. Results were mixed; some structures were moved and languished in new locations, while others were destroyed. The argument for creating a vast medical complex here near the city's Central Business District was economic and occurred at the state level, leaving the city with little input. To date, the rosy economic predictions and anticipated occupants of the complex have not materialized.

5.14   Southeast Louisiana Veterans Health Care System (Pan-American Life Insurance Company)
1951, Skidmore Owings and Merrill, with Claude E. Hooton; 2016 renovated, Eskew+Dumez+Ripple, Rozas Ward Architects, and Woodward Design Group. 2400 Canal St.

This rectangular steel-framed concrete and glass building marked Skidmore, Owings and Merrill's first use of a wrap-around sunscreen and was possibly the first large-scale use of that feature in the United States. Interior spaces are shielded from the sun on all four sides by tiers of thirteen-foot-high aluminum louvers set into the aluminum-edged, cantilevered concrete floor slabs. Because the main wing is oriented with the long sides facing northeast and southwest, the fins, thirty inches deep, are at right angles to the walls. The building was also engineered to be fully air-conditioned. The aluminum-louvered facade was described at the time as "light and lacy" and a modern reinterpretation of New Orleans's balconies. The building is elevated on a podium-like basement, giving it a classical presence, an impression enhanced by the broad and ceremonial flight of stairs that originally led to the central entrance (which have been replaced by two narrow out-of-scale staircases). The entrance level is recessed, giving the impression that the upper four floors hover over their base. A cafeteria-auditorium and an executive dining room were located on the second floor to face an interior courtyard (landscaped by Ralph Ellis Gunn of Houston and now altered), and a one-story service wing extends to the rear. SOM's associate architect for this project was Claude E. Hooton. After standing vacant since 2000 (the building was used as an annex to City Hall after Pan-American moved into its new SOM-designed high-rise at 601 Poydras Street in 1980), it was renovated as administrative spaces for the adjacent new VA Hospital complex.

Opposite at 2425 Canal is Curtis and Davis's Caribe Building of 1958. It is composed of two units, the larger at four stories facing Canal. The exterior screen of clay tile for sun control and privacy is set three feet in front of the building's glass walls to reduce heat transfer. The Curtis and Davis office occupied the upper floor when it was built.

5.15   Swan River Yoga Studio (Canal Branch Library)
1910–1911, Lagarde and Burk; 2010 renovated, Errol Barron/ Michael Toups Architects. 2940 Canal St.

Built with funds from Andrew Carnegie, this Arts and Crafts for-mer library is two stories in height with a pair of stairs flanking a ground level entrance and rising to the principal floor. Closed in 1958, the building subsequently had several tenants before it was inundated by four feet of water in Hurricane Katrina. When the building was renovated for its current use, a WPA-funded mural was uncovered and restored. Painted by local artist Edward T. Schoenberger in 1941 for the library's reading room, the fifty-foot-long mural, *The History of Printing*, depicts artists from stone carvers to printers working a press.

5.16 Mid-City Public Library (Automotive Life Insurance Building)
1963, Curtis and Davis. 4140 Canal St.

Converted for use as a branch library in 2016, the former insurance company's headquarters was designed with a facade of gray solar glass and side walls of white marble, surrounded by a groin-vaulted arcade supported on precast concrete cross-shaped columns. Each vault defines a twelve-foot-square bay, a module that underlies the entire plan. The vaults are not structural, consisting instead of plaster on a steel skeleton beneath a flat roof. The architects decided that local experience with new concrete construction methods was inadequate, although a few years later they experimented with thin-shell concrete construction on the Rivergate (see **5.2**). The building's pavilion form masks rather than expresses the two-story interior. Entrance is across a shallow moatlike pool, through the portico to a central hall that leads past an enclosed garden to what was originally a two-story reception area at the center of the building. All the office spaces were laid out on two floors on both sides of this central corridor. When first opened, the building was a huge success, particularly because of its appearance at night when it glowed like a lantern in its dark, then-residential neighborhood. Nathaniel Curtis and Arthur Q. Davis established their firm in 1946 with the intention to design solely in a modern idiom; this building achieves that goal in its adherence to contemporary architectural forms, if not entirely in the structural system and materials used.

5.17 William J. Kane House (William Cowley House)
1918, H. Jordan MacKenzie. 4506 Canal St.

H. Jordan MacKenzie (1870–1956), who arrived in New Orleans from California in 1904 and departed for Texas in 1917, designed several houses in the city that were influenced by Arts and Crafts or Secessionist forms. The bright blue tile roofs he introduced to New Orleans earned him the nickname "Blue Roof" MacKenzie. Among his houses with this feature was the one he built for himself in 1909 at 6339 West End Boulevard, where he lived for two years. Unfortunately, most of his houses have been altered. Although this house's roof is of green tiles, the low, broad residence set on a raised basement and built of red brick with concrete details reveals MacKenzie's interest in expressive forms, textures, and colors. The coffered entrance porch, reached by a double set of stairs, is supported on overscaled columns with capitals that look as if they are oozing from their hefty shafts. The house is sheltered by a sweeping roof with deep unsupported overhangs that adds a Prairie Style flavor. The house, built for contractor William H. Kane, was shortly after acquired by steamship agent and broker William Cowley.

Central Business District

The abrupt and startling difference in scale between the low-rise Vieux Carré and the towering buildings of the business district on the opposite side of Canal Street highlights the contrasting histories of these two areas of New Orleans. What is now known as the Central Business District (CBD) began

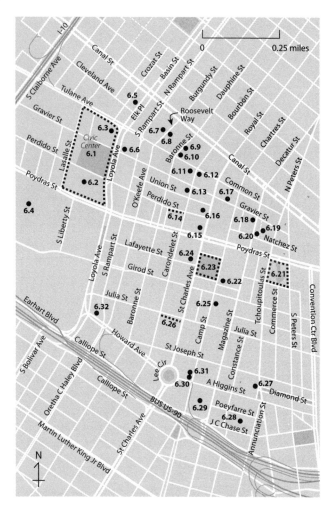

as Faubourg St. Mary, laid out by Carlos Trudeau in 1788 and inhabited by Anglo-Americans who flocked to New Orleans after the Louisiana Purchase in 1803. The Anglo-Americans and the French-speaking Creoles soon found that they disagreed about almost everything. As a result, New Orleans was divided into three municipalities in 1836; Anglo-Americans dominated this section of the city and built their own city hall and public square. This division lasted until 1852, when the city was reunified.

Warehouses and industrial structures were built along the

streets closest to the wharves by the river; inland rose a mix of commercial and residential buildings. By the early twentieth century, high-rise commercial structures had largely displaced residential property. In the mid-twentieth century, the remaining residential areas, primarily African American neighborhoods, were cleared for a new civic center (**6.1**). Further demolition took place for the Superdome (**6.4**), which resulted in vast areas of surface parking, particularly on S. Rampart Street. Following the early 1980s collapse of the oil boom that had fueled the New Orleans economy after World War II, the city increasingly turned to tourism as a source of revenue. In the late twentieth century, a convention center on the riverfront begun by Perez Associates in 1984 for the Louisiana World Exposition expanded upriver over several blocks. Simultaneously, high-rise commercial buildings began, and continue to be, converted into hotels and abandoned warehouses repurposed as apartment buildings, all bringing a new vitality to this area. Most recently new residential construction is booming in an area called South Market.

6.1   Civic Center

1954–1961. Loyola Ave., bounded by Poydras and La Salle sts. and Tulane Ave.

Conceived as an urban revitalization plan by Brooke H. Duncan (1887–1950), a civil servant who became city planning director, this project centralized the city's government, which had been housed in several scattered buildings. The seven-square-block site on eleven acres, a "blighted" and crowded African American neighborhood, was selected because of several factors: the land could be acquired cheaply; the plan would clear a section of slums considered too close to an expanding downtown business sector; traffic circulation could be expanded with the construction of Loyola Avenue; and abandoned railroad tracks could be used for new expressways. Instant urban improvement was the goal. The state and city buildings, constructed mostly of glass and beige limestone, with the clean lines and smooth surfaces popular in the 1950s, are placed—also typically for the 1950s—around an asymmetrically shaped green space (Duncan Plaza) and approached by diagonal pathways. The buildings include City Hall (1956; **6.2**), designed by Goldstein, Parham and Labouisse, with Favrot, Reed, Mathes and Bergman. The same firms, with the addition of August Perez and Associates, produced the State Supreme Court and the State Office Building, both dating from 1958 and demolished post–Hurricane Katrina, and the Civil Court (1959). The New Orleans Public Library (**6.3**) of 1958 anchors the downtown side of the complex.

Although several of these civic buildings were undistinguished, their symbolic value was great, demonstrating the city's desire to show a progressive face. However, the modern design provided the grounds for one of the critiques aimed at the complex: namely, that it made no effort to fit in with traditional New Orleans architecture—an unpopular move in this city. Others, including Mayor deLesseps "Chep" Morrison, described the project as a "dazzling complex" with "glistening" buildings. Duncan Plaza has been relandscaped several times, each without aesthetic success or public approval, if measured by use. In 1986, it was refurbished with a pavilion by architect Arthur Q. Davis, based on a slave hut from Melrose Plantation in Natchitoches. Another redesign is expected in 2018.

One block upriver from this complex and separated by the Hyatt Hotel are the fourteen-story Federal Office Building (1961, Freret and Wolf; August Perez and Associates; Mathes, Bergman and Associates) and the Union Passenger Terminal (UPT) of 1954 by Wogan and Bernard, with Jules K. de la Vergne and August Perez and Associates, which replaced the Louis Sullivan–designed station (the UPT consolidated into this new building the city's several train stations). The terminal's best features are the four brilliantly colored interior fresco murals, each measuring more than 60 × 8 feet, completed in 1954 by Conrad Albrizio (1894–1973), a social commentary on the history of Louisiana as depicted in four different time periods. The murals were restored in 2010.

6.2 City Hall

1957, Goldstein, Parham and Labouisse, with Favrot, Reed, Mathes and Bergman. 1300 Perdido St.

City Hall was placed on visual axis from downtown along the newly widened Loyola Avenue, and its facade of green-tinted glass conveyed an image of up-to-the minute modernity. Taking its cue from New York's Lever House, the eleven-story rectangular building has curtain walls of green-tinted glass between insulated spandrels. Corners, crown, and base are of limestone, and red granite surrounds the entrance. Large neon letters across the top of the facade (added later) identify the building and serve to distinguish it from neighboring civic buildings of similar design. The modular structural system allowed flexible floor plans, and each floor is cantilevered a few feet beyond the columns, permitting the air-conditioning pipes and ducts to run outside the main structural system. Metal-clad louvers on two sides block afternoon sun and control glare. The windows' green tint has faded, and although replacement panels seldom match the color exactly, they do have the unintended effect of enhancing the abstract qualities of the wall, making it appear even more like a modern painting. The green glass and aluminum glitter. Although the interior lacks any splendid spaces (a planned grand staircase to the mezzanine from the lobby was not built, and the numerous flags originally installed in this space have been removed), it does feature some cheerful painted wall mosaics, an installation of the City's Percent For Art program from the late 1980s. The basement's bomb shelter was planned to serve as the seat of government in the event of a nuclear attack.

In the early twenty-first century a former mayor proposed

that city government move to a nearby office building and the City Hall be demolished. In testimony before the City Council, Professor John P. Klingman of Tulane School of Architecture argued that, "Although in need of substantial renovation, the building has served the city well for over half a century and can continue to do so." By one vote the City Council rejected the move, but the building will remain vulnerable until it is renovated.

6.3   New Orleans Public Library

1956–1958, Curtis and Davis, with Goldstein, Parham and Labouisse, and Favrot, Reed, Mathes and Bergman. 219 Loyola Ave.

This three-story library is a steel-frame structure based on a four-foot module, with two basement levels and foundations of reinforced concrete. With the exception of the west facade, the walls are entirely of glass and covered by an aluminum screen that shields the interior from glare but permits light to enter. By day, the aluminum screen tends to dominate the building, but at night, as architect Arthur Q. Davis has stated, the library has "a transparency and a jewel-like quality" created by interior illumination shining through the screen. Librarians report that the screen has proved effective in eliminating glare while allowing vistas outside to the magnolia trees that now surround the building. The modular steel-frame structure makes it possible to open up interior spaces both horizontally and vertically, creating spatial drama. Open book stacks allow readers to browse; two glass-walled interior patios provide additional reading "rooms." The transparency and indoor-outdoor qualities of this library are hallmarks of Curtis and Davis's work at the time. The library won awards from *Progressive Architecture* magazine (1957) and the American Institute of Architects (1963).

6.4   Mercedes-Benz Superdome (Louisiana Superdome)

1971–1975, Curtis and Davis, with Nolan, Norman and Nolan; Edward B. Silverstein and Associates; and Sverdup and Parcel, consulting engineers; 2006 restored, AECOM, Trahan Architects, Sizeler Thompson Brown Architects, and Billes Architecture. 1500 Poydras St.

Designed in 1967 and constructed between 1971 and 1975, this multipurpose sports and convention arena was built on the former Illinois Central Railroad yards. The building itself covers

13 acres on a 52-acre site and can accommodate approximately 95,000 people (72,600 for a football game) and provide parking for 5,100 cars. The structural steel frame is sheathed with precast concrete panels, and the dome has a six-ring, patented Lamella roof framing system. The building's 680-foot diameter and interior height of 273 feet has no supporting posts. A system of movable stands makes it possible to change the seating arrangement and capacity as needed for different events. The decision to locate the Superdome in the heart of New Orleans rather than in the suburbs, although controversial at the time, gave the city a new economic base. Viewed from the river end of Poydras Street, which was widened in the 1960s, the structure's concave wall and dome offer a seductive and enticing silhouette beyond Poydras's sharp-edged high-rise buildings.

The shocking spectacle of desperate people trapped in the Superdome for days in 2005 during and after Hurricane Katrina cast the building in a highly negative light. Nevertheless, wind and rain damage to the roof was repaired in the weeks that followed, and the building hosted the first game of the 2006 football season. When the NFL Saints won that game, it signified that New Orleans was on the road to recovery, and the building immediately again became a positive symbol for the city.

Next to the Superdome, a multipurpose sports, concert, and convention arena faced with shimmering green tile designed by Arthur Q. Davis and Partners opened in 1999. Its octagonal form is somewhat awkward compared to the elegance of Nathaniel Curtis's elegant Superdome next door. Another arena from the Curtis and Davis firm is the approximately 9,000-seat Lakefront Arena of 1983 at the University of New Orleans. The three arenas reveal changing ideas about the function and aesthetics of sports and events venues.

6.5 Elks Building

*1917, Toledano, Wogan and Bernard; 2014 renovated,
Eskew+Dumez+Ripple. 127 Elk Place*

Built for the Fraternal Order of Elks, this three-story neoclassi-
cal revival building's seven-bay-wide stone-clad facade is richly
articulated with Corinthian pilasters and columns between
rectangular windows on the first story and columns and round-
arched windows on the second. Scrolled keystones carrying
sculpted heads top the second-floor windows and garlands
decorate the cornice. The plain third story, set back from the
main body of the building, is a later addition. The building was
sold in 1940 and subsequently became a headquarters for the
Gulf Oil Company, which left the location following the collapse
of the oil industry in the early 1980s. Since 2014, it has housed
the Tulane University School of Social Work.

6.6 Historic Pythian Temple

*1908–1909, Diboll, Owen and Goldstein; 1923 addition; 1961
rear addition, Benson and Riehl, with R. E. E. de Montluzin;
2017 renovated, Studio WTA. 234 Loyola Ave.*

Constructed for the Colored Knights of Pythias, an African
American fraternal organization, the steel-framed building is
clad in light-brown brick. Initially seven stories in height, the
two additional floors and rooftop terrace were added in 1923.

The tall round-arched windows that unite the two upper stories reiterate those of the building's most attractive feature, a stone frontispiece that covers the central three bays of the second and third stories. The frontispiece's cream-colored stone stands out against the light-brown brick walls in color and in its Renaissance-styled details. A theater/auditorium occupied the second floor. Smith Wendell (S. W.) Green, president of Liberty Independent Insurance and international officer of the Colored Knights of Pythias, played a major role in the establishment of the temple. The building housed various offices, including those of the People's Benevolent Industrial Life Insurance Company where Homer Plessy (of the U.S. Supreme Court *Plessy v. Ferguson* "separate-but-equal" case; see **3.10**) worked. The Knights of Pythias vacated the building in 1941, and it subsequently had various occupants. In 1957, it was "modernized" with an aluminum slipcover, which was removed in the 2017 renovation; damage to the decorative details of the stone frontispiece was repaired. After standing empty for several years, the building has been renovated for mixed uses, with office and retail space and mixed-income apartments.

6.7   Orpheum Theater

1918–1921, G. Albert Lansburgh, with Samuel Stone Jr.; 2014–2015 restored, Rick Fifield Architect and Eskew+Dumez+Ripple. 129 Roosevelt Way.

The Orpheum is one of New Orleans's finest example of a polychrome terra-cotta facade. G. Albert Lansburgh of New York, the architect for all the Orpheum theaters in the country, was known for his use of decorative terra-cotta, as was his local collaborator, Samuel Stone Jr., whose firm designed the Maison Blanche Building (**5.8**). Above the theater's marquee are three pedimented windows and a polychrome relief frieze depicting frolicking cherubs and fauns. The walls above the windows are faced with five vertical panels decorated with geometric and floral patterns, which are topped by a cornice punctuated with theatrical masks. The predominant color is cream, with details highlighted in pink, yellow, and pastel shades of green and blue. Built for live entertainment, the 1,500-seat auditorium was tiered, with two balconies. The theater also included an apartment where children could be supervised during the show. In 1933, the Orpheum was converted into a movie palace, and in 1993 it became the home of the New Orleans Philharmonic Orchestra. Flooded and abandoned following Hurricane Katrina, it has since been renovated into a venue for convention and musical events. With wonderful acoustics, it is again the home of the Louisiana Philharmonic Orchestra.

6.8   Roosevelt Hotel (Grunewald Hotel)
1893; 1907–1908 addition, Toledano and Wogan; 2009 restored, Steven J. Finegan Architects. 130 Roosevelt Way

Built and named for Bavarian immigrant businessman Louis Grunewald, in 1908 the hotel was substantially enlarged with a 14-story, 400-room addition. The hotel's principal facade with its rusticated base and tiers of bay windows is elaborately trimmed with Renaissance-inspired decoration in terra-cotta panels of floral and geometric motifs, garlands, and cartouches. The Roosevelt Way arched entrance is partially hidden by a modern canopy; the equally, though differently, ornate entrance on the hotel's Baronne Street side has an intricate metal and glass canopy that is suggestive of Art Nouveau. The hotel's signature space is the broad lobby that runs the length of the building; it glistens with marble, gilding, chandeliers, and a multicolored floor. From the 1930s, the hotel became a favored venue for New Orleanians. The Blue Room, a supper club, hosted such entertainers as Louis Armstrong, Ella Fitzgerald, Frank Sinatra, and Bette Midler. The room has been restored, as has the Sazerac Bar, where the Sazerac cocktail was first concocted. The bar also contains a four-panel mural (1938) by New Orleans artist Paul Ninas (1932–1964). Huey P. Long established his campaign headquarters in the hotel in the 1930s and moved in after he was elected Louisiana's governor. In 1923, the hotel was renamed for President Theodore R. Roosevelt (a wildlife enthusiast who had visited Louisiana in 1902 and 1915), then renamed the Fairmont in 1965. During Hurricane Katrina, the hotel's basement, which contained the electrical and mechanical equipment, was flooded with twelve feet of water. Following a complete restoration, the hotel regained its former illustrious name.

6.9   Immaculate Conception Church
1851–1857, Fr. John M. Cambiaso, with Theodore E. Giraud; 1928–1930 reconstructed, Wogan and Bernard. 132 Baronne St.

The present church is a reconstruction of the original, which was damaged first by pile driving for the Père Marquette Building (**6.10**) next door and then by dynamite blasting for a nearby bank. Although the church was rebuilt on a framework of steel and reinforced concrete, much of the original material was re-used, including the bricks (which were all numbered for accurate placement), the interior cast-iron columns, and the cast-iron pews. The only significant change was the addition of the two slender towers that were in Cambiaso's original design, which had not been built because of weight and soil problems. Exterior walls are of dark reddish-brown brick trimmed with white stone and red terra-cotta.

This Jesuit church is a highly original composition, blending Western and Eastern forms before this idea caught on elsewhere. The twin towers, tripartite facade, and triple entrance are typical of Christian churches, but many of the elements and ornamentation are identified with Middle Eastern or Moorish architecture (the church was described by contemporaries as Saracenic). These include horseshoe-shaped arches with polychrome voussoirs, interlaced arches, panels on both sides of the central door with patterns formed from Kufic script, and onion domes on the towers. The eight-pointed "rose" window in the upper facade symbolizes Mary as the morning star. Cambiaso, born in Lyons, France, taught in Africa and Spain before he arrived in New Orleans in the late 1840s, which would explain the source of these features. Moreover, St. Ignatius Loyola, the founder of the Society of Jesus, was Spanish, and possibly Cambiaso wanted his design to reflect the order's origins. The blend of East and West may also be intended to evoke the Holy Land.

In a renovation in the 1870s, James Freret added the Moorish-inspired elements on the interior: the horseshoe-arched arcade, the carved column capitals, and the spectacular gilded bronze altarpiece with three onion domes. Most of the stained glass, made in the studio of Hucher and Rathouis in Le Mans, France, depicts scenes and events in the early history

of the Society of Jesus; the six apse windows have Marian
themes. Later (c. 1900) windows came from the Franz Mayer
Studio of Munich. This church is said to be the first in the nation
named Immaculate Conception, following the proclamation
of the doctrine of the Immaculate Conception by Pope Pius IX
in 1854. To the left of the church is the rectory, which has been
attributed to James Freret, even though he died in 1897 and
the date 1899 is inscribed on the parapet. No documentary
evidence confirms the 1899 date or Freret's authorship, but the
building's polychrome masonry and Moorish features make the
attribution plausible. James Freret (1838–1897) was a cousin of
architect William A. Freret Jr., and the first New Orleans architect to study at the Ecole des Beaux-Arts in Paris.

6.10   Renaissance New Orleans Pere Marquette Hotel (Père
        Marquette Building)
        *1924, Scott Jay and William E. Spink; 2001 renovated, Lee
        Ledbetter and Associates. 817 Common St.*

This former office building was designed soon after the Chicago
Tribune Tower competition of 1922, for which the winning
entry, along with the earlier Woolworth Tower in New York,
made Gothic detailing for skyscrapers popular. Although the
design follows a tripartite definition of base, shaft, and top, in
the manner of Louis Sullivan's high-rises, its continuous vertical
piers, Tudor arches, and Gothic pinnacles and tracery emphasize
the height of the eighteen-story building, as was intended. The
ground floor is faced with polished red granite, while off-white

glazed tile from the American Terra Cotta Company in Illinois is used two stories above it. The middle section consists of pinkish-colored brick piers and green spandrels which, in 1999 when the conversion of the structure into a hotel commenced, were painted to match the tile—a reversal of the architects' intention to emphasize verticality and structure through subtle combinations of materials and color. The tower has a Gothic-patterned, glazed-tile cornice. An entrance and a lobby for the hotel were completed in 2001, with marble floors and detailing in ceramic tile, wood, and chrome that re-create a 1920s ambience.

6.11   The Maritime (Hennen Building)

1893–1895, Sully and Toledano; 1920s additions, Emile Weil; 2013 renovated, Marcel Wisznia. 202–211 Carondelet St.

When this ten-story commercial building, New Orleans's first skyscraper, was constructed, visitors paid ten cents to view the city from its roof. Commissioned by the controversial Louisiana State Lottery Company investor John Morris and named for his father-in-law, Supreme Court judge Alfred Hennen, the building is believed to be the first in the city with a steel frame. Its weight is supported on concrete and iron rafts set on spreading brick pyramids, which in turn rest on cypress pilings.

Thomas Sully (1855–1939) employed Louis Sullivan's tripartite system for organizing the facade, crowning the building with a bold projecting cornice. The yellow brick exterior walls, now painted a dark cream color, were originally painted deep russet and pale maroon; the decorative frieze beneath the eaves has Sullivan-inspired foliate ornamentation. Just a few years after the building was constructed, architectural tastes shifted to a preference for light colors and more classical ornament, as seen, for example, in the Maison Blanche Building (**5.8**). The Hennen Building's two-story base, with tall, round-arched openings, is among the alterations made by Emile Weil in the early 1920s, along with the addition of a floor above the cornice and an extension on the Carondelet Street side of the building, which omits the dramatic Chicago windows of Sully's design. Albert Toledano (1860–1923) was in partnership with Sully from 1888 to 1893. By the early twentieth century, a considerable number of architects, including Sully, maintained offices in the Hennen Building. It was renovated in 2013 and now accommodates commercial and office space, with apartments above. All of its original operable windows were replaced with fixed glass.

6.12 200 Carondelet Apartments (National American Bank)
1928–1929, Moise Goldstein. 200 Carondelet St.

Erected for the Bankers Trust Company, the twenty-three-story, steel-frame building is constructed of concrete and hollow tile. A polished black granite base gives way to a cream-colored limestone skin, interrupted at four levels by shallow setbacks. At each setback, the parapets are emphasized by geometric sculptured panels of cast concrete. A six-story, off-center octagonal tower with fluted buttresses screens a water tower and is topped by an elaborate finned bronze lantern. Goldstein described his design as an "American vertical style" with a "science fiction theme"; it was clearly influenced by contemporary Art Deco skyscrapers in New York City. In a renovation of the 1980s, the double hung windows were replaced by smooth sheets of bronze-tinted reflective glass that upset the balance of solid and void. Interior finishes are sumptuous, mixing traditional with modern. A tall, rather severe entrance leads to a marble-clad lobby, whose bronze elevator doors are decorated with stylized plant designs, and a vast columned banking hall with walnut paneling and an elaborate plaster ceiling. Check-

Building New Orleans

New Orleans's geology and semitropical climate have, perhaps more than anything else, determined the shape and materials of its architecture. By raising buildings off the ground, early settlers met the challenges of flood control and improved air circulation. Deep galleries (the term gallery, from the French word *galerie*, refers to what are called porches or verandas elsewhere) shaded a building's walls and provided an outdoor living or sleeping space that might capture a breeze. The alignment of windows (often extending to the floor) and doors provided for cross ventilation and high ceilings and steep roofs could draw up the heat.

New Orleans and its region lacks building stone, so wood from regional cypress and pine forests provided the primary building materials. The city's earliest buildings were of timber-frame construction, with the spaces between the timbers filled with *bousillage*, a mixture of mud and Spanish moss or animal hair. As soon as brickyards were established in the late 1730s, brick was placed between the posts (*briquette-entre-poteaux*). Whether the infill was *bousillage* or brick, the walls required a covering of stucco or boards to prevent their deterioration from rain and humidity, as at the first Ursuline Convent (**1.29**).

In the 1830s granite from New England became common for ground-floor piers on commercial buildings (see **1.5**, **1.15**) and until the late nineteenth century, few buildings (**6.18**) were faced in stone. Architects and builders experimented with different

writing stations with bronze grilles cover the steam radiators. The original air-conditioning system of 1929, perhaps the earliest in the state, is still operable.

6.13   Historic Hibernia National Bank
1920–1921, Favrot and Livaudais, with Alfred C. Bossom; 2013 renovated, HRI. 313 Carondelet St.

The twenty-three-story Hibernia Bank was New Orleans's tallest building (see **page iv**) until the 1960s and remains one of methods to prevent subsidence. While the Custom House (**5.4**), built 1848–1850, is carried on horizontal cypress planking, engineers perfected methods of sinking piles deep into the ground beginning in the late nineteenth century to carry increasingly tall skyscrapers (**6.13**, **6.15**).

From the city's beginnings, skilled African American brick- and stonemasons, plasterers, and carpenters—free and enslaved—built much of New Orleans; their legacy remains as these historic techniques have been passed on to subsequent generations of craftspeople.

Decorative iron elements are a quintessential feature here. Free people of color dominated the ironwork industry at first, making delicate wrought-iron balconies and fences. Sometimes a fence might incorporate both wrought and cast iron, as at the Beauregard-Keyes House (**1.28**). Cast-iron production boomed with the demand for machinery needed for the region's sugar mills, and New Orleans also became a center for cast-iron architectural and garden ornaments. The former Leeds Iron Foundry (**6.27**), established in 1825, exhibited its iron products—columns, window tracery, and hood moldings—on its warehouse, where they remain to this day.

The variety of buildings materials, from wood to stucco, stone, and iron, gives the city its rich texture and its distinctive architectural character.

the most handsome buildings in the Central Business District. Utilizing a U-shaped plan, with fourteen-story wings facing Union and Gravier streets, the steel-framed bank is sheathed in Indiana limestone. The design is obviously borrowed from McKim, Mead and White's Municipal Building (1916) in New York City, even to the tempietto at the top, although the Hibernia's tempietto also served as a beacon for ships on the Mississippi River. Corinthian pilasters enrich the exterior walls, and four engaged Corinthian columns mark the main entrance.

Charles A. Favrot and Louis A. Livaudais, who formed the firm of Favrot and Livaudais in 1895, were assisted by Alfred C. Bossom of New York City. Bossom, who specialized in the design of high-rise banks, advised on the engineering aspects of the Hibernia and on the interior.

The building has a tall ground story articulated with Corinthian columns and pilasters to make a bold and prosperous statement at street level. Above this, paired rectangular windows mark each story, and the building finishes firmly with a prominent cornice. To support the Hibernia's weight, 3,153 wooden piles were sunk to a depth of 52 feet, reaching a stable layer of prehistoric oyster shells. Bossom designed the marble banking room, giving it 24 fluted, 30-foot-high travertine Corinthian columns to support the coffered and gilded ceiling, and metal-grille tellers' cages decorated with replicas of ancient and modern coins. The boardroom was wood-paneled with carved details. A brochure published by the bank in 1921 stated that the building was in the "Renaissance style" and noted that seven high-speed elevators made the tower "only a half-minute distance from the ground floor." In 2013, the building was renovated for offices and apartments.

Diagonally opposite at 226 Carondelet is the bank's predecessor, a steel-framed twelve-story building designed by Daniel H. Burnham of Chicago. Opened in 1904, the building was sold in 1920 and, after several subsequent owners, is now a Hampton Inn.

6.14   Factors Row

1858, Lewis E. Reynolds; 2016 restored, Trapolin-Peer Architects. 802–822 Perdido St.

A rare pre–Civil War survivor in the business district, this row of seven four-story Italianate structures was constructed by speculative builders Samuel Jamison and James McIntosh and designed by Lewis E. Reynolds (1816–1879), who moved to New Orleans from Norwich, New York, in 1843. The buildings housed cotton traders, including Michel Musson, uncle of Impressionist artist Edgar Degas, who used the interior as the setting for his painting *A Cotton Office in New Orleans* (1873), in the collection of the Musée des Beaux-Arts, Pau, France. All the exterior ornament for the brick buildings is cast iron, from the ground-level arcade and the differently shaped moldings over each

floor of windows to the scrolled brackets, cornice, and parapet. Originally the row was painted white with gilded trim and had a second-floor balcony. Next door (826–828 Perdido Street), the 1869 Santini-Providence Building was designed by Henry Thiberge (1837–1882) for the New Orleans Real Estate and Auction Exchange. This three-story, stucco-finished brick building has a facade animated by large arched windows surrounded by heavy moldings, paired windows on the third floor surmounted by smaller circular openings, an overhanging bracketed cornice, and a decorated parapet.

6.15   One Shell Square

1972, Skidmore, Owings and Merrill. Poydras St. at St. Charles Ave.

In 1972, at 51 stories and 697 feet, the Shell Oil Company's office tower became the tallest building in Louisiana, a distinction it retains. Smoothly sheathed in off-white Italian travertine and bronze-tinted glass, the reinforced-concrete and steel tower is supported on an 8-foot-thick concrete mat over 500 octagonal concrete piles, 18 inches in diameter and driven 210 feet

into the ground. The reflective glass windows with dual panes eliminate the need for fins to shade the interior. Midway up a ziggurat-style stepped podium at the corner of St. Charles Avenue and Poydras Street is an orderly row of live oak trees, stunted because of limited room for root growth, that provide minimal shade and depth of color to counter the dazzling travertine. The podium, its steps, and the surrounding sidewalk are all covered with the same travertine to coordinate with the building. Thus, the petroleum company's presence is forcefully asserted on the block as well as on the city's skyline. One Shell Square is similar but not identical to SOM's One Shell Plaza in Houston (1968–1971). Although it employs the same materials and the facade is similarly expressed, Houston's facade undulates and has a smaller podium.

6.16 Hilton Hotel/New Orleans St. Charles Avenue (Masonic Temple)

1926, Samuel Stone Jr.; 2000–2001 renovated, Lyons and Hudson Architects. 333 St. Charles Ave.

The third Masonic temple to occupy the site, this nineteen-story structure is steel-framed with a limestone exterior. Sam Stone's design emphasizes verticality with its double-height triple-arched entrance and strong pilasters that rise without interruption to the top of the building and finish as round arches over the deepset windows. Upon completion, the Masonic Temple was the tallest building in New Orleans until construction of the Hibernia Bank Building (**6.13**) nearby. Ornament is spare and mostly Gothic inspired, including the lettering over the entrance that describes the building's function. Offices occupied the St. Charles front, with spaces for the Masons behind, including a triple-height theater on the fifteenth floor. The handsome elevator lobby has mottled-brown polished stone walls and a Guastavino tile vaulted ceiling. The building was sold in 1992 and converted to a hotel, which closed after Hurricane Katrina and was then purchased for the Hilton Hotel chain.

6.17   Whitney National Bank Safe Deposit Vault
1888, Sully and Toledano. 619 Gravier St.

Dark-colored buildings were favored in the 1880s, when Thomas Sully designed this sturdy two-story, steel-frame bank. Fashioned from Missouri granite cut into immense rusticated blocks and grand-scale polished columns, the bank reveals Sully's flair for exploiting the tactile qualities of materials. Described when built as Egyptian in style (presumably because of its powerful forms), the bank, in fact, has no identifiable style. Here Sully has created something quite original with his use of outsize details, miniaturized turret-like forms at each end of the roofline, and column capitals that resemble upturned elephant feet. Bronze grilles over the windows and above the doors add to the impregnable appearance. The buildings of Philadelphia architect Frank Furness seem to have influenced those of Sully, who probably saw them before leaving the Northeast and arriving in New Orleans in 1881. The bank has a twelve-foot-deep underground vault, and an elliptical coffered dome originally covered the interior. George Q. Whitney established the bank in 1883 with his brother Charles and his mother, Marie Louise Morgan Whitney. This building became the safe deposit vault when the Whitney's new building at 228 St. Charles Avenue was completed in 1911.

Around the corner at 201 Camp Street is Sully's contemporaneous former New Orleans National Bank (1884–1888), a Romanesque Revival building with a rugged first story of dark red rock-faced stone and red brick for the upper three stories. The polished granite column that marks the building's corner entrance has a capital decorated with allegorical heads, and similar heads ornament the upper floors.

6.18   Commercial Building (New Orleans Canal and Banking Company; Bank of Louisiana)

1843, James H. Dakin. 301–307 Magazine St.

This finely proportioned three-story corner building faced with light gray granite originally housed a bank and five stores. Archival drawings indicate that the superb granite Doric portico with fluted columns and a frieze of triglyphs and metopes, as well as the frame of the window directly above it, came from the previous structure on this site, a bank built in 1832 by architects J. Reynolds and J. M. Zacherie. Beginning in the 1830s, granite facings, a fashion said to have originated in Boston, became popular in New Orleans. Here, where subsidence problems usually confine the use of granite to piers at ground level, this building is unusual.

6.19   Board of Trade and Board of Trade Plaza (New Orleans Produce Exchange)

1883 Produce Exchange, James Freret; 1968 Board of Trade Plaza, Koch and Wilson, Architects. 316 Magazine St.

Formerly known as the Produce Exchange and located behind a section of Banks Arcade (**6.20**), the Board of Trade was renamed in 1889 after its merger with other associations. Freret designed a sumptuous facade for this one-story building of stuccoed brick, with full-height windows set between paired pilasters, a cornice encrusted with oversized dentils, and an entrance surmounted by cresting that curls at its edges like a pie shell. Later, the shallow dome that covers the former trading room was painted with scenes of New Orleans's economic activities. The plaza in front of the building is not much larger than a courtyard. It was developed in 1968 on the site of the hotel that occupied the central section of Banks Arcade, which was acquired by the Board of Trade in 1889 for use as an annex and demolished in 1967. This allowed an unobstructed view of the Produce Exchange facade for the first time. In their scheme for the plaza, Koch and Wilson salvaged cast-iron columns and arches from the hotel to form a loggia along one side and a blind arcade on the opposite wall. They enclosed the plaza with an iron fence, designed formal planting beds, and installed a Spanish fountain to create this little oasis in the heart of the business district.

6.20   St. James Hotel (Banks Arcade)

1833, Charles F. Zimpel; 1941 restored, Emilio Levy; 1999 renovated, Trapolin Architects. 330 Magazine St.

Only about one-third of this formerly block-long row of three-story brick commercial and office structures survives today. The storefronts were separated by identical granite piers on the

Magazine Street facade, but the shops were entered from the rear, where a three-story-high, glass-covered pedestrian arcade, extending from Gravier to Natchez streets, was attached to the building behind. Over the years, Banks Arcade (so named because it was built for businessman Thomas Banks) housed a newspaper office, a hotel, an exchange, a restaurant, a barber shop, a bar, and a coffeehouse, where meetings were held in 1835 that led to the Texas Revolution; in the central section was a hotel. Bad investments and financial difficulties forced Banks to sell the arcade in 1843. A two-story, cast-iron gallery was added to the corner unit after the Civil War and was extended across the rest of the facade in the twentieth century. This surviving section of the row of buildings was renovated for use as a hotel in 1999.

6.21   Piazza d'Italia

1975–1978, August Perez and Associates, and Charles Moore for Urban Innovations Group; 2003 restored, Hewitt-Washington and Associates; 2017 renovated, Torre Design Consortium. Bounded by Poydras, Tchoupitoulas, Lafayette, and Commerce sts.

Conceived as the centerpiece of a retail development and a site for festivals, especially for people of Italian heritage, the Piazza d'Italia originally included a temple-shaped pergola, a triumphal arch of painted stucco over a steel frame, a campanile (now demolished), and a set of curved colonnades as a backdrop to a pool surrounding an "island" in the shape of Italy.

The pastel-colored columns of the colonnade each represent different classical orders. Water streams down the columns from the stainless-steel capitals of the front four colonnades into the pool and flows around the eighty-foot-long contoured island. Cartouches, one in the shape of Charles Moore's head (added during construction without his knowledge) are set into the Doric colonnade and spout water. At night, neon lighting outlines the arches and columns. In an early scheme, the city of Rome was highlighted on the island of Italy, but following a review of the project by New Orleans's Italian community, which was to a large extent of Sicilian origin, the island of Sicily was given proper prominence. The historical allusions and playfulness of the ensemble were considered an ultimate expression of Postmodernism. The Piazza nonetheless had critics, many of whom felt it was too frivolous and did not respect the city's traditional architecture.

Soon after completion the Piazza was beset by problems. Because the surrounding area remained undeveloped, few people frequented it, and the absence of pedestrian traffic combined with the Piazza's lack of shade and its rough cobblestone paving made the space uninviting. As well, the inexpensive materials of construction were easily degraded by New Orleans's harsh climate; proposed renovations to adjacent buildings did not happen; and the City neglected its responsibility for maintenance and operation of the water system. By the late 1980s, the Piazza had disintegrated; the Postmodern icon became another piece of neglected urban fabric and the first Postmodern ruin. The campanile had been stripped to a rusting metal framework (it was eventually demolished), the triumphal arch was clumsily repainted in different colors, and the nooks and crannies formed by the arches and columns provided a refuge for the homeless. Now restored, even in a form less theatrical than originally intended, the Piazza is a colorful and cheerful oasis in the dense city grid, leased from the City and maintained by the adjacent Loew's Hotel. However, it is fenced and gated and open to the pubic only sporadically.

6.22   John Minor Wisdom U.S. Court of Appeals (Fifth Circuit Court of Appeals, U.S. Post Office and Federal Courthouse)
1911–1915, James Gamble Rogers for Hale and Rogers. 600 Camp St.

In his use of Beaux-Arts classicism for this three-story courthouse, Rogers was following Supervising Architect of the Treasury James Knox Taylor's design guidelines for government architecture. Rogers won the courthouse competition of 1907 with a design that resembles an Italian Renaissance palazzo, producing two separate facades for the freestanding building. On the upriver long side, Rogers created arched openings along a rusticated ground floor and borrowed from Antonio da Sangallo's Palazzo Farnese (1541) for the alternating triangular and segmental pediments over the second-floor windows. Third-floor windows are square-headed, and the building is finished with a balustrade. More dramatic are the structure's short sides, where two-story Ionic colonnades screen the second and third floors. Heavy, rusticated Doric portals are a feature of the corner pavilions; on the roof of each is a copper globe surrounded by four female figures, Daniel Chester French's allegorical sculptures representing History, Horticulture, Commerce, and Industry. The building, faced with Georgia marble, is organized around two interior courtyards, now roofed over, and includes three double-height courtrooms on the second floor. Rogers's wide-ranging stylistic vocabulary is demonstrated in his more reticent design for the H. Sophie Newcomb Memorial College (**9.3**). The building has suffered from an unsympathetic renovation that included replacing all of the original glazing with heavily tinted fixed glass, creating a gloomy interior rather than the original light-filled spaces. Inside, the generous double-height post office workspace on the first floor has been compromised with a low generic suspended ceiling.

6.23   Lafayette Square

1788. Bounded by St. Charles Ave., and Camp and N. and S. Maestri sts.

Originally named Place Gravier, the square was renamed for the Marquis de Lafayette in 1824, following his visit to New Orleans during his triumphal 1824–1825 visit to the United States. The square, formerly fenced like Washington and Jackson squares, served as the public open space for Anglo-Americans, their equivalent of the Creoles' Place d'Armes (now Jackson Square). It also became a focus for commemorative statues, among them Joel T. Hart's bronze statue of Henry Clay (1860), a bronze of Benjamin Franklin (1926), and Attilio Piccirilli's sentimental bronze (1898) of two children reaching up to a bust of John McDonogh (1780–1850), commemorating his 1850 bequest of $750,000 to the public school system of New Orleans (he gave a like amount to Baltimore). Attilio immigrated to the United States with his father and five brothers in 1880. All were sculptors/marble cutters, and the brothers carved the Lincoln Memorial in Washington, D.C., under the direction of Daniel Chester French. With Gallier Hall (formerly City Hall) on one side, the square became the site of political demonstrations and annual celebrations for school children honoring McDonogh. Today it is the site of public festivals and grandstands set up for carnival parades.

6.24 Gallier Hall (Old City Hall)

1845–1851, James Gallier Sr.; 2016 renovated, Markdesign/ Mark Reynolds Architect. 545 St. Charles Ave.

In his autobiography, Gallier noted that this building's "style of architecture is Grecian Ionic, and the portico is considered as a very chaste and highly finished example of that style." Although the portico was inspired by the north porch of the Erechtheum on the Acropolis in Athens, the building's axial orientation and dominant single portico give it a Roman presence. The building is raised on a dark gray granite podium, and the upper walls and columns are faced with white New York marble. Rather than rising from the podium, the portico's columns are placed midway from the base of the stairs, so that to reach the entrance, one has to pass between the columns while still climbing in the area of dark granite—a formidable experience. The principal floor is bisected by a wide central hall with pilasters along each wall and a ceiling of recessed panels. Rooms on either side have square-headed windows and are decorated with plaster cornices and ceiling medallions. New York artist Robert E. Launitz was responsible for the pediment sculpture of Justice flanked by Liberty and Commerce. When New Orleans was divided into three municipalities in 1836, Gallier Hall served as the city hall for the Anglo-American municipality. Upon reunification of New Orleans in 1852, the building functioned as its city hall until 1957, when the new structure (**6.2**) at 1300 Perdido Street was completed. That same year Gallier Hall was renamed in honor of its architect. The building, undergoing renovation for the city's tricentennial (2018), is now used for city functions and rented for other events.

6.25   St. Patrick's Church

1838–1840, James H. Dakin and Charles B. Dakin; 1839–1840, James Gallier Sr. 722 Camp St.

St. Patrick's was constructed for the English-speaking Catholics, primarily Irish, who lived in Faubourg St. Mary. The single, square tower in the center of the facade reveals the influence of British prototypes, in contrast to the two towers of the French-inspired St. Louis Cathedral (**1.2**). Building specifications described the church as having been modeled on the English cathedrals of York Minster and Exeter, the latter for the vaulted ceiling. Although the church was designed and begun

Historic Preservation

Tourism in New Orleans is big business: around 10.45 million visitors visited the city in 2016. Maintaining historical authenticity while welcoming so many guests, especially to the Vieux Carré, is an enormous challenge.

The Vieux Carré was an early focus of preservation efforts in the city. From the 1920s onward, writers, artists, and a few influential socialites advocated for public policies to protect its unique historic buildings and its residential character, often buying buildings themselves to renovate and occupy.

The Vieux Carré Association, formed in 1926, evolved in 1936 into the Vieux Carré Commission (VCC), with the charge of maintaining the neighborhood's architecture by setting guidelines for renovations and new building designs. The VCC and the Quarter's residents have achieved notable successes, including helping defeat the Robert Moses–planned elevated expressway bordering the Mississippi River in front of Jackson Square in 1969. Retaining permanent residents despite increasing numbers of tourists, part-time residents, and commercial ventures is foremost among the challenges facing the Vieux Carré.

During the economic boom following World War II, politicians and real estate interests prioritized spending on urban renewal and interstate highways. In response, citizens formed numerous organizations with the goal of protecting historic areas and preventing demolitions.

The Louisiana Landmarks Society, founded in 1950, primarily focuses on identifying and advocating for threatened historic buildings, and purchased, relocated, and renovated the Pitot

by James H. Dakin and his brother Charles B., Gallier replaced them in 1839 when the foundations began to fail, eliminating the ornamentation that the Dakin brothers had planned for the tower and altering the 85-foot-high interior by introducing an arcade of clustered Gothic columns made of iron with wood casing. However, the lightweight fan vaults fabricated of wood

House (**4.13**) on Bayou St John as its headquarters. The Preservation Resource Center (PRC), incorporated in 1974, advocates for neighborhood preservation throughout the city. In 1981 it purchased, restored, and occupied 604 Julia Street, one of thirteen then-decaying brick town houses (**6.26**) in the Central Business District. This was a first step in a revitalization of the CBD's surviving historic structures; the PRC now owns and occupies the former Leeds Foundry (**6.27**), which it also restored.

Save Our Cemeteries, a nonprofit founded in 1974 to prevent demolition of wall vaults in St. Louis Cemetery No. 2 (**2.4**), works to protect the city's unique above-ground tombs. The City's Historic District Landmarks Commission, established in 1976, regulates nineteen currently designated historic districts. New Orleans also boasts many neighborhood organizations that are instrumental in shaping development and preservation within their specific boundaries.

The Federal Historic Preservation Tax Credit program, introduced in 1976, was crucial in converting the city's historic Warehouse District into a vital arts and residential neighborhood. Louisiana's Division of Historic Preservation, in the Department of Culture, Recreation and Tourism in Baton Rouge, administers this program and National Register nominations.

More recently, the 1995 demolition of the iconic Rivergate (1968, Curtis and Davis) has awakened locals to the importance of preserving modern architecture, and Hurricane Katrina (2005) led to new interest in safeguarding the city's natural landscape as well as its buildings for future generations.

and plaster retain the character of the original design. Despite the high ceiling, the church has an intimate feeling because of its considerable width, the low spring of its vaults, and an interior color scheme of cream and gold. After the hurricane of 1915, most of the original glass was replaced with new designs by the Emil Frei Art Glass Company of St. Louis, including the stained glass between the ribs of the semicircular apse vault. French-born artist Leon D. Pomarède (1807–1892), who worked in New Orleans from 1830 to 1869, painted the murals (1841) behind the altar, which include a copy of Raphael's *Transfiguration of Christ*. The exterior, covered with stucco several years after the church was built, is now finished with cream-colored, rough-cast weatherproofing cement. Koch and Wilson, Architects, undertook the restoration following Hurricane Betsy of 1965. To the right of the church is the two-story Italianate rectory (1874), designed by Henry Howard, which has suffered major alterations.

6.26 Julia Row

1832–1833, attributed to Alexander T. Wood. 600–644 Julia St.

Known as the "Thirteen Sisters," these three-and-a-half-story red brick row houses were built by the New Orleans Building Company, with Daniel H. Twogood, builder, as speculative real estate for Anglo-Americans, who favored this type of dwelling. These side-hall houses have entrance doors set between Ionic columns and a fanlight in the Federal style. Double parlors occupied the second floor, and service wings at the rear faced small courtyards. Built to accommodate the affluent, the houses had degenerated into boardinghouses and tenements by 1900, as the wealthy relocated to the uptown suburbs. The Preservation Resource Center (PRC) purchased 604 Julia in 1976 and renovated it in the 1980s, setting off a wave of renovation of the other houses on this block and the area in general; now, all are renovated, with commercial space on the ground floor and residential above. Architect Henry Hobson Richardson lived at 640 Julia Street as a child, from 1838 to 1841.

6.27 Preservation Resource Center of New Orleans/The Leeds-Davis Building (Leeds Iron Foundry)
1852, Gallier and Turpin; 1998 renovated, Wettermark and Keiffer Architects. 923 Tchoupitoulas St.

Designed by James Gallier Jr. for Gallier and Turpin, this three-story building was the warehouse and showroom for the Leeds Iron Foundry, one part of which was located on this block and another part upriver. Established in 1825, the foundry, the second largest in the South before the Civil War, manufactured steam engines, boilers, and machinery for sugar processing and sawmills and produced the first operational submarine in the United States (CSS *Pioneer*, 1861), as well as cannons and other matériel for the Confederacy. The Gothic Revival cast-iron window tracery, hood moldings, and ground-floor clustered columns, all manufactured by the foundry, served to advertise its products. Appropriately, the Preservation Resource Center purchased this endangered building in 1998, restored it, and opened it in 2000 as its headquarters and a center for preservation activities and information.

6.28 Maginnis Cotton Mill
1882–1887; 1896 enlarged; 1912 enlarged; 1922 enlarged, Emile Weil; 1998 renovated, HRI. 1054 Constance St.

Built by Ambrose A. Maginnis and Sons, this textile manufacturing plant once employed 900 full-time workers who operated 12,000 looms to produce 21 million yards of cloth annually.

The three-story, timber-frame brick building has twelve-foot-high, double-hung cypress-framed windows. A magnificent square clock and stair tower, wider at the top than at the base, are surmounted by a steeply pitched mansard roof, supported on stepped brackets, which sheltered a water tank. The mill was enlarged in 1912 and again in 1922 by Emile Weil, but a changed economy and the increased popularity of synthetic fabrics forced it to close in 1944. In 1998, the mill was gutted and converted into apartments. An early-twentieth-century water tower, a separate 140-foot-high structure in the courtyard, was retained to house antennae for local cellular telephone service companies. The smokestack had already been shortened from its former height of 115 feet. Despite such unfortunate new additions to the exterior as the shedlike, two-story rooftop condominium structures, the Maginnis remains the largest and handsomest of several factories and warehouses that, after standing desolate for years, have been converted since the 1984 Louisiana World Exposition brought attention to their residential and commercial possibilities.

Two other nearby examples are the five-story brick Federal Fibre Mills building (1904–1907, Favrot and Livaudais; 1985 renovated, HRI) at 1107 S. Peters Street, which was the Warehouse District's first condominium project (the lobby with its closely spaced columns, is particularly noteworthy), and the five-story Fulton Bag and Cotton Company building (1909, Stone Brothers) at 100 S. Peters (now a Hampton Inn), with a seven-story tower surmounted by a pyramidal roof supported on eaves brackets. The solidity and size of these structures and their fine brickwork remind us how important New Orleans's port and

industrial enterprises were to the economy of the city. Archae-
ological excavations before the Maginnis Mill was renovated
uncovered evidence of a late-nineteenth-century brewery,
an early-nineteenth-century girls' school, and an eighteenth-
century plantation house.

6.29 National World War II Museum (D-Day Museum)
1888, William Fitzner; 2000, Lyons and Hudson Architects;
2009–2018, Voorsanger Mathes. 945 Magazine St.

The National World War II Museum began as and grew from the
D-Day Museum that was established to honor American contributions to the D-Day invasion of June 1944 in World War II. New
Orleans was proposed as its site through the advocacy of local
historian Stephen E. Ambrose (1936–2002) and others in recognition of the crucial role the city played in the event. Landing craft
employed in the invasion of France were developed and constructed in New Orleans by Andrew Higgins and were first tested
on Lake Pontchartrain. Owner of a lumber export company, a
fleet of ships, and a shipbuilding and repair operation, Higgins
had developed before the war a highly maneuverable vessel
with a shallow draft to move cypress logs out of the swamps.
These boats also proved ideal for oystermen, fur trappers, and oil
exploration crews in Louisiana who needed shallow-draft boats.
During World War II, Higgins adapted the vessel for amphibious
landing operations. The D-Day Museum was housed in a former
brewery built in 1888 to house the Weckerling Brewing Company.

The former brewery is an important building, a reminder of
the industrial nature of this area in the late nineteenth century
and of the brewing industry (see **10.2**), the latter significant in the
history of the city's large German American population. Fitzner
designed several breweries (all demolished) in the city.

For the first addition (2000) to the historic five-story brick structure, Lyons and Hudson repeated the structure's height and its industrial character, but designed a facade of tinted glass outlined by an exposed truss, giving the impression of an airplane hangar. Set at an angle, the glass wall draws pedestrians to the entrance, showcases some of the exhibits, and gives the building a contemporary appearance.

The museum's focus from a single event to the entirety of World War II and from matériel to human stories has expanded its physical presence to cover four city blocks and accommodate its growing attractions and international popularity. Among the recent additions is the U.S. Freedom Pavilion, a glass and concrete abstractly shaped structure that contains vintage aircraft, tanks, and other equipment and can be used as an event space. Exhibits in other pavilions focus on the many campaigns of the war, the people involved, and the conflict's aftermath, including the Marshall Plan. The museum also includes a restaurant and a theater. A triangular steel and fiberglass canopy hovers 150 feet above the complex, and further additions are planned, including a central parade ground for ceremonies.

6.30   Howard Memorial Library

1886–1889, H. H. Richardson and Shepley, Rutan and Coolidge; 2003 interior renovated, Barron and Toups Architects. 601 Andrew Higgins Ave.

Shortly after H. H. Richardson's death in 1886, Charles T. Howard, president of the Louisiana Lottery Company, approached Richardson's successor firm, Shepley, Rutan and Coolidge, to commission a library in memory of Howard and his wife's late son. After seeing the drawings of Richardson's unsuccessful entry for the Hoyt Library (Saginaw, Michigan) design competition, Howard purchased the plans, which the firm reworked for its new site. The library is recognizably Richardsonian in plan and appearance. Interior functions are separated: the stacks at one end of the building and the reading room, within the curved end, at the other. The off-center arched entrance, marked by a rudimentary tower, is hollowed out of the walls of roughly cut, dark red Massachusetts sandstone facing over brick, of which the library is constructed. And, characteristic of a Richardson building, intricately patterned sculpture marks transitions from wall to opening. Despite the beauty of Richardson's building, librarians complained about the poor interior lighting, owing to the three-foot-thick walls and minimal fenestration. Nonetheless, the interiors are magnificent spaces, especially the former reading room, with its oak hammer-beam ceiling, oak paneling, and vast gray sandstone fireplace which creates the aura of a gentlemen's retreat. The stacks area also has a hammer-beam ceiling. The library was named for Howard, who donated lottery funds to the library, as well as to several charities, to give his private company an air of respectability. In 1938, the library collection, having outgrown its space, was transferred to the Tulane University campus (9.2). After occupancy by several tenants, the Howard Library became part of what is now the Ogden Museum of Southern Art. The interior has been partially renovated by Barron and Toups Architects, and the Howard Library is now an event venue. The same architects also designed the glass and brick museum (2003) on Camp Street to house local developer Roger Ogden's vast collection of southern art. A walkway beneath the Confederate Memorial Hall Museum (6.31) links the Howard Library with the Ogden Museum.

6.31 Confederate Memorial Hall Museum
1890, Sully and Toledano; 1896 additions, Sully, Burton and Stone. 929 Camp St.

Lottery profits funded construction of the Memorial Hall as well as the Howard Library (6.30), and due to similarities in design, most assume the two buildings are one. Frank T. Howard, Charles Howard's son, donated $10,000 to the Confederate veterans for an archive building, described in the *Daily Picayune* as "an annex to the library a handsome iron fireproof building

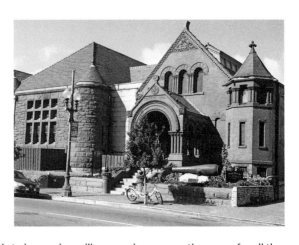

that is to be used as a library and a preservation room for all the
historical records of the confederacy at present obtainable . . .
the annex will be in keeping with the picturesque beauty of the
library itself." Indeed, the hall's form, materials, color, and decorative details echo those of the Howard Library. It is thought
that Sully and Toledano developed their design from an 1889
drawing by Allison Owen, a drawing instructor at the Tulane
Manual Training School. Sully, Burton and Stone (successor
firm to Sully and Toledano) designed the small tower and the
handsome Romanesque Revival porch for the building. The
interior is paneled with red cypress and houses one of the most
comprehensive collections anywhere of Confederate material
in displays that have not changed since the museum opened.

6.32　Plaza Tower

*1964–1969, Leonard R. Spangenberg Jr. and Associates. 1001
Howard Ave.*

Before construction began on this $18 million, 45-story tower,
opponents of the project objected because it did not conform
to the traditional architecture of New Orleans. Moreover, well
before the structure was completed, it was mired in financial
problems and scandal, including the architect's suit against the
developer, Sam Recile, for nonpayment of $600,000 in fees.
Recile and Mayor Victor Schiro similarly described the tower
as a means to "revitalize" this area of downtown New Orleans,
stimulate the economy, and "symbolize the progressive spirit
of the city." However, they miscalculated. Financial difficulties

halted construction in October 1966; the unfinished building was sold at auction in 1968 for $5.6 million, and new construction moved to the Poydras Street corridor instead. The tower, finally completed in 1969, has a latticed steel box frame, is wrapped on two sides by a lower curved section, and is finished with a broader three-story, flat-topped "hat." Early drawings of the tower reveal that its flat top was intended to accommodate a heliport; it is now littered with satellite dishes and antennae instead. The building is faced with white marble, and vertical steel columns finished with bronze-colored aluminum provide contrasting color and material. Indoor parking fits into eleven stories of the curved base. The tower is supported on 315 piles driven to a depth of 168 feet. In 1965, while the building was still under construction and only at the steel-frame stage, Hurricane Betsy, with wind forces in excess of 100 miles per hour, is said to have caused the elevator shaft to twist. At completion it was the tallest building in the city until the construction of One Shell Square (**6.15**).

Certainly unique and one of the most visually complex buildings in the city, Plaza Tower blends elements from every significant architectural movement of the twentieth century: it is an homage to constructivism, futurism, expressionism, modernism, and the work of Frank Lloyd Wright, although a jumble rather than a distillation. The curved wall, intended to echo the course of the Mississippi River, and the prowlike glass corner give it the semblance of a ship about to sail off into the future. The architect is also the designer of another unusual work in New Orleans, Unity Temple (**8.2**). The consulting engineer for the project was William J. Mouton of New Orleans. The building has been vacant for years.

Garden District and Adjacent Neighborhoods

Most of this primarily residential area of New Orleans upriver from the Central Business District comprises what was once the independent city of Lafayette and the seat of Jefferson Parish. It was annexed to New Orleans in 1852, and today consists of four distinct neighborhoods. The area now known as the Lower Garden District—bounded by Lee Circle, Erato and Annunciation streets, and Jackson and St. Charles avenues—was laid out beginning in 1807 by Barthélemy Lafon. His scheme included a circular park, the Place du Tivoli (now Lee Circle); wide, tree-lined boulevards; squares; canals; a college, which Lafon referred to as a prytaneum, for Prytania Street; and a coliseum at Coliseum Square, an irregularly shaped park. The canals, school, and coliseum were never built, but nine of Lafon's streets retain the names of the nine Greek muses. Development of Central City, from Carondelet Street to the Claiborne Canal (now Claiborne Avenue), began in the 1830s, primarily with rental property for Irish, German, and Jewish immigrants. By the early twentieth century the neighborhood was primarily African American and Dryades Street (now Oretha Castle Haley Boulevard) was an important shopping street with department stores patronized by customers not welcome in the stores on Canal Street, the shameful "separate-but-equal" legacy of Jim Crow laws.

In the nineteenth century, the Garden District referred to a much larger area of detached houses on tree-lined streets than today's more narrowly defined area, officially bounded by Magazine and Carondelet streets and Jackson and Louisiana avenues. Benjamin Buisson laid these out between 1st and Toledano streets in 1832 with four lots per square instead of twelve,

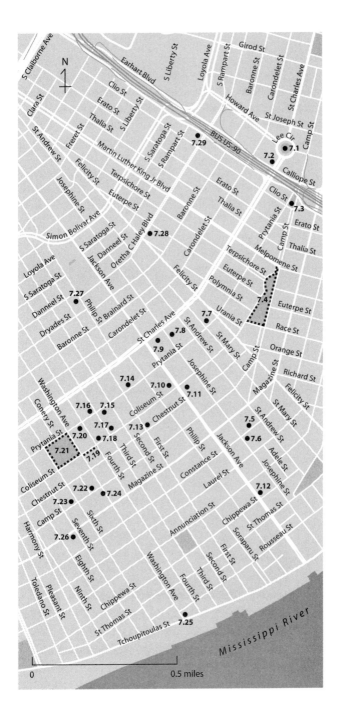

as in the Vieux Carré; in the two prosperous decades before the Civil War, fashionable architects designed mansions set in landscaped gardens for wealthy Anglo-Americans. Magazine Street separates these houses from the far more modest shotguns and cottages of the Irish Channel, given its name in the nineteenth century when many Irish immigrants lived here and worked in Garden District mansions or in industries along the riverfront. Wharves, railroad tracks, oceangoing ships, and warehouses (such as the former Amelia Cotton Press warehouse of 1882 at Tchoupitoulas and Felicity streets) line the riverfront behind the concrete floodwall that protects the city from the Mississippi River.

The ethnic mix in these neighborhoods (with the notable exception of the Garden District) has changed over the years; yet, surprisingly, the nineteenth-century character has largely remained. The houses and buildings included in this tour represent the most exceptional examples of the area's rich architectural heritage.

7.1 Lee Circle
1807, Barthélemy Lafon. Lee Cir.

In his urban plan for this area, Lafon envisioned a circular park, the Place du Tivoli, surrounded by a canal linked with the river and extending along what are now Howard and St. Charles avenues. Sadly, this imaginative scheme was never realized, and the planned park became a landscaped traffic circle. It was renamed for General Robert E. Lee in 1884, upon the dedication of New York sculptor Alexander Doyle's bronze statue of Lee atop a sixty-foot-high Doric column of white Tennessee marble. John Roy designed the monument's Georgia granite base, which has four sets of stairs aligned with compass points. The four bronze urns were added in 1930. The statue of General Lee was taken down in May 2017, one of four monuments commemorating people or events associated with the Confederate cause or white supremacy removed from public sites.

7.2 K&B Plaza (John Hancock Mutual Life Insurance Building)

1960 – 1962, Gordon Bunshaft for Skidmore, Owings and Merrill, with Nolan, Norman and Nolan. 1055 St. Charles Ave.

Constructed on the site of the demolished public library by Daniel Burnham, this seven-story office building of reinforced concrete sits on an elevated plaza, with parking space below. This was Bunshaft's first concrete-surfaced building. Vertical precast concrete louvers, three feet deep, shade the windows and balance the thick floor slabs; thin horizontal sun breaks, known as "eyebrow sunshades," provide additional shading and lateral bracing. Bunshaft described the wall as an "eggcrate wall supporting long-span beams." The precast frame eliminates support columns, leaving the cantilevered floor open. The central load-bearing core gives each floor uninterrupted, column-free space to permit partitioning as needed. The first floor was originally occupied by the John Hancock Company, and the upper floors were rented out.

On an axis with the steps to the plaza is Isamu Noguchi's rough-surfaced granite fountain, its top in the shape of a crescent to symbolize the curve of the Mississippi River. The elevated approach (U.S. 90) to the second span (1988, Modjeski and Masters) of the cantilevered bridge across the river passes next to the building, but Bunshaft's design more than holds its own. It is now known as the K&B Building, after its current owner whose former business was the regional Katz and Best-hoff drugstore chain.

The exterior plaza, and indeed the entire building, houses the extensive contemporary art collection of Sydney Besthoff. Much of the sculpture that was installed on the plaza has been donated and reinstalled at the New Orleans Museum's Sydney and Walda Besthoff Sculpture Garden (4.16) in City Park. It was when Besthoff purchased this building, and with it, the Noguchi sculpture (much to the chagrin of the sellers, it was "affixed" to the plaza), that Bestoff was inspired to start collecting art.

K&B anchors an uptown corner of Lee Circle, but the Circle has two other buildings of distinction, one old (Howard Memorial Library; 6.30) and one new, the Greater New Orleans Foundation (GNOF) of 2016 designed by Waggonner and Ball Architects at 919 St. Charles. The GNOF is a regional nonprofit that serves thirteen parishes with grants and public advocacy for community improvements and sustainability. Its new building replaced a gas station and presents a strong face to the circle's east (downtown) quadrant. The building includes ground-floor meeting rooms with expanses of windows, effectively reinforcing GNOF's mission of community engagement.

7.3 The Margaret Statue

1884, Alexander Doyle. Margaret Place at Clio St.

The Margaret Haughery statue, one of the nation's first outdoor sculptures honoring a woman, was designed by Alexander Doyle, who had just completed his statue of General Lee (see 7.1). After Irish immigrant Margaret Gaffney married Charles Haughery, they moved from Baltimore to New Orleans in the 1830s. Following the death of her daughter and husband en route to New Orleans, Margaret, penniless and illiterate, worked her way up from laundress to ownership of a dairy and bakery. She established and helped fund several asylums for orphans and the poor, and at her death in 1882 willed her fortune to eleven charitable institutions. In July 1884, thousands attended the unveiling of this white marble statue of Margaret seated on a chair with a small child at her knee, funded with small donations from those who had benefited from her philanthropy.

7.4   Coliseum Square

1807, Bathélemy Lafon; 1975–1976 renovated, Charles Caplinger, landscape architect. Bounded by Camp, Coliseum, Melpomene, and Race sts.

This elongated, grassy public space, part of Lafon's ambitious urban plan for the area, flowered as a fashionable address in the 1840s and 1850s, and many fine mid- to-late-nineteenth-century houses still surround the square. Especially notable are the Rodewald-King House (1749 Coliseum Street), built in 1849 for banker Frederick Rodewald and purchased by novelist Grace King in 1904, which has a two-story Greek Revival gallery and an Italianate segmental-arched entrance door; the Greek Revival three-story house with a two-story gallery at 1228 Race Street, designed in 1861 by Henry Howard and constructed in 1867 by builder Frederick Wing after the Civil War for wholesale grocer John T. Moore; and the E. T. Robinson House (1456 Camp Street), a two-story, side-hall town house of stuccoed brick, perhaps built by architect Thomas K. Wharton in 1859 (he lived in this neighborhood while supervising construction of the Custom House [**5.4**]).

The renovation of Coliseum Square in the mid-1970s reinforced (and rewarded) efforts by a handful of preservationists who had recently bought dilapidated nineteenth-century houses, rehabilitating them in efforts to preserve the historic architectural urban fabric as well as to voice opposition to the location here of the second span of the Mississippi River bridge, which likely would have destroyed the neighborhood. The park's design replicates pedestrian patterns from a late-nineteenth-century design, featuring a water basin with fountain and incorporating green "fingers" that extend from the "square" in three directions. Fears that architectural renovations of the 1970s and 1980s would diminish the neighborhood's unique character have proved unfounded.

7.5   St. Alphonsus Art and Cultural Center (St. Alphonsus Church)

1855–1857, Louis L. Long; 1890s portico. 2045 Constance St.

One of three churches built within a two-block radius for Catholic immigrants, St. Alphonsus served an English-speaking, mostly Irish congregation. St. Mary's Assumption Church (**7.6**) ministered to German immigrants, and the French worshiped at Notre Dame de Bon Secours, built in 1858 and demolished in 1926. All three churches were built by the Redemptorists, who had arrived in New Orleans from Baltimore in 1847. St. Alphonsus, the first of the three churches constructed, is named for St. Alphonsus Liguori, founder of the Redemptorist order. Baltimore architect Long designed the brick building, which is believed to have been built by the Irish immigrant brothers Thomas and Daniel Mulligan. In contrast to the undulating forms of St. Mary's, St. Alphonsus is crisp-edged and severely geometric, with large square twin towers and a facade animated by paired pilasters, a row of inset rectangular panels above the second-story arched windows, strongly bracketed cornices and moldings, and undecorated capitals. Spires planned for the twin towers were never built. An incongruously delicate triple-arched portico in the center of the facade was added in the 1890s. The interior is dazzling. Rear and side balconies that slope to slender column supports convey the impression of a theatrical space, an effect heightened by the splendid colorful ceiling, stained glass, and tall neo-Baroque gilded altar set in a stagelike columned sanctuary. French-born Dominique Canova (1800–1868), who settled in New Orleans in 1840, was one of the artists who frescoed the coved plaster ceiling in 1866 with images of Mary, St. Alphonsus, and other figures suspended in fluffy clouds. F. X. Zettler of Munich, Germany, manufactured the stained glass for the upper windows, depicting events from the lives of Mary and Jesus, which were installed in 1890. Services at St. Alphonsus ceased in 1979; the church reopened in 1990 as an art and cultural center focusing on the history of the Irish in New Orleans.

7.6   St. Mary's Assumption Church

1858–1860, attributed to Albert Diettel; 2015 tower restored, Koch and Wilson, Architects. 901 Josephine St.

It is said that St. Mary's German parishioners helped in the church's construction by wheeling carts of bricks from barges at the foot of Jackson Avenue. St. Mary's facade is distinguished by its beautiful brickwork and rounded forms. Tall arched openings are deeply set in the wall and outlined with prominent moldings, above which are a small rose window and a curving parapet with circular blind windows. A 142-foot-high tower, located next to the sanctuary, changes from square to variously

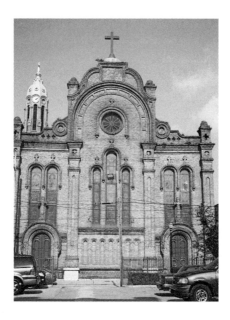

shaped octagonal stages as it rises, each transition defined by
curved arches or brackets, finally tapering to a series of miniature gilded segmental domes. Side walls are reinforced with
paired pilasters that continue above the roofline in the shape of
miniature pedestals.

The equally florid interior has a ceiling with thick-ribbed
vaults supported on fluted columns with overwrought flori-
ated capitals. Foliate pendants are suspended from each of
the arcade's arches. The multilayered, intricately hand-carved
wooden high altar was made in Germany in 1874. After the
parishioners saw the spectacular stained glass windows at
St. Alphonsus (7.5), in the 1890s they too commissioned F. X.
Zettler, who made representations of favorite German saints
and of Mary as Queen of Heaven. Following hurricane damage
in 1965, the church was restored by Nolan, Norman and Nolan,
and Koch and Wilson, Architects.

Along with the churches, the Redemptorists sponsored
Catholic schools, convents, and orphanages to serve the
neighborhood. The three-story building (1940) at 919 Josephine
Street next to the church, originally a convent, is now the Seelos
Welcome Center, named for Father Francis X. Seelos. The

former girls' grammar school (1867; now Seelos Hall) associated with St. Mary and St. Alphonsus churches stands at 2118–2122 Constance Street.

7.7   The Saint Anna (St. Anna's Orphan Asylum)

1853, Robert Little and Peter Middlemiss, builders; 2015 renovated, Studio WTA. 1823 Prytania St.

St. Anna's was incorporated in 1853 by Christian women of several denominations as an institution for the "relief of destitute females and their helpless children of all religious denominations." The asylum is one of many that were built in the nineteenth century to care for the survivors of such deadly diseases as yellow fever and cholera that regularly swept the city. William Newton Mercer, an army surgeon and philanthropist, donated the site and funded the building in memory of his recently deceased daughter Anna. Additional donations came from the entrance fees charged by Garden District resident James Robb to see his famous marble statue, *The Greek Slave* by Hiram Powers, which is now in the National Gallery of Art in Washington, D.C. The three-story brick building, positioned close to the property line, is fronted by an imposing and institutional-looking pedimented Doric portico raised on stuccoed brick piers scored to resemble stone. Although additions and alterations to the asylum were made between 1959 and 1965 by Freret and Wolf, the original facade has been retained. The building became a home for the elderly, then was renovated in 2015 as rental apartments.

7.8   The Eiffel Society (Eiffel Tower Restaurant)

1986, Concordia Architects. 2040 St. Charles Ave.

At the core of this peculiar steel-frame structure is the restaurant that was located until 1980 on the first level of the Eiffel Tower in Paris, 562 feet above the ground. Because the structure's weight was causing the tower to sag, it was dismantled and sold to New Orleans investors. The 11,000 pieces were shipped to New Orleans and reassembled as a new restaurant. The polygonal metal and glass space is enshrined within an 88-foot-high superstructure that the architects hoped would recapture the feeling of the Parisian venue, yet not imitate it. In fact, it does neither. Raised 12 feet above the ground,

with parking underneath, the building is entered by way of a 105-foot-long ramp. Despite its name, the restaurant was not a success and was subsequently reincarnated as a nightclub and event venue. Rust stains give the structure a precarious air, perhaps suitable for its primarily nocturnal use.

7.9 The Carol Condominiums
1967, August Perez and Associates. 2100 St. Charles Ave.

Although this thirteen-story apartment building occupies the full width of its block, its concrete exterior framing system of shallow pointed arches and alternating mullions sets up a crisp and lively pattern across the wide facade, moderating a sense of weight and size. The building is lifted on angled, tapered piers and the central entrance is marked by a cantilevered concrete canopy in a folded design that almost gives the impression of a billowing canvas tent. This is an elegant design for these luxury apartments.

August Perez and Associates also designed the thirteen-story former Wohl Apartments (now the Avenue Plaza Hotel) opposite at 2111 St. Charles. Completed in 1951, the modernist building's plain smooth walls are enlivened by an alternating pattern of windows and projecting frames. Next to it at 2031 St. Charles, Weiss, Dreyfous and Seiferth's twelve-story Pontchartrain Hotel is notable for the intricacy of its brickwork and Mediterranean-styled details. Completed in 1927 as a residential hotel with efficiency apartments, it was converted to a regular hotel in 1940 and renovated in 2016 by Trapolin-Peer Architects; its rooftop terrace is a prime destination. These three high-rise buildings illuminate changing tastes in twentieth-century architectural fashion.

7.10   Buckner House

1856, Lewis E. Reynolds. 1410 Jackson Ave.

The building contract for this residence, of palatial scale with galleries on all sides, specified a "two-story brick house with observatory and four pediments." Slender gallery supports with Ionic columns on the lower level and Corinthian above give a lightness and airiness to this massive house, and the two-story portico that projects beyond the facade's deep gallery adds an equally delicate note. Detailing is Greek-inspired, from the lyre-patterned iron gallery railings to the moldings outlining the entrance door. The observatory-belvedere, which also vented hot air from the house, has been reduced in size. The house has a five-bay plan, including a ballroom and a formal dining room, both with 16-foot-high ceilings, flanking the 12-foot-wide central hall; stairs are at the end of the hall. Excluding the basement, the living area encompasses about 7,600 square feet, plus a three-story service wing at the rear. Kentucky-born cotton broker Henry S. Buckner and his wife, Catherine, hired Reynolds to design the house to rival that of Buckner's business partner, Frederick Stanton, for whom the architect was constructing a palatial home, Stanton Hall, in Natchez, Mississippi. The house became the residence of Buckner's daughter, Laura, and her husband, Cartwright Eustis, in 1884. In 1923, business educator George Soulé moved his business school, Soulé College, into the house. A brick school building was constructed behind the house. When the school closed in 1983, the original house was sold and returned to residential use. Jackson Avenue was a fashionable street in the mid-nineteenth century, but only a few houses survive from this era.

7.11   Trinity Episcopal Church

1852–1854, George Purves; 1873 facade, Charles L. Hilger; later alterations and additions; 1996 restored, Jahnke Architects. 1329 Jackson Ave.

Trinity's congregation, founded in 1847, worshipped in a small wooden building until this stuccoed brick Gothic Revival church was built. Initially the church had a pair of turrets, but, considered unsafe, they were removed and the facade was plastered over in 1873 by Hilger (1830–1879). The facade is strongly articulated with a central gabled tower, a projecting gabled portico, a triple-arched window, buttresses, pinnacles, and moldings and trefoil designs. In 1883 the nave was extended by one bay and a chancel. The interior, without aisles and with tall windows, feels light and spacious. The nave is covered by a ceiling of cypress wood.

Across Coliseum Street at 1401 Jackson, Trinity Episcopal School occupies the two-story Italianate-influenced house designed by Lewis E. Reynolds in 1852 for William Perkins, renovated and expanded by Eskew+Dumez+Ripple. Les Enfants, another project on the Trinity campus, was converted in 2004 to institutional use by Waggonner and Ball Architects, linking two shotguns with a transverse room at the rear of the existing buildings.

7.12   Synagogue Apartments (Gates of Prayer Synagogue)
1865–1867, William Thiel; 2014 renovated, Terrell-Fabacher Architects. 709 Jackson Ave.

After sitting vacant for many years, this historic synagogue was transformed by Greggory Morris into twelve apartments in 2014. Constructed by builder Robert Huyghe for a mostly German Jewish congregation, Gates of Prayer was designed by Thiel (1821–1870) just before the Civil War, but it was not until 1865 that the cornerstone was laid and 1867 that the synagogue was dedicated. The building is raised on a high basement and accessed by a double iron staircase (a replica of the original). The red brick facade is exquisitely detailed in brick with pilasters, shallow niches, false gables, stringcourses, and moldings over the round-arched central entrance. The congregation vacated the building in 1920 and it was then used for a variety of purposes until abandoned. In the renovation several interior features were retained and the spiral staircase restored.

7.13 Carroll-Crawford House
1869, Samuel Jamison. 1315 First St.

Built shortly after the Civil War for cotton factor Joseph Carroll
from Virginia, this Italianate house of stuccoed brick combines
many of the architectural features that were so popular in
New Orleans just before the war. The smooth, flat facade has
segmental-arched windows and doors outlined by prominent
moldings; crowning the roofline is a cornice with oversized dentils and a central tablet. A two-story cast-iron gallery shades the
entire facade, each of its bays arched to echo the shape of the
windows behind. The contrast between the feathery ironwork
and the building's solid weightiness gives each a sharper focus.
To emphasize the central entrance, five bays wide, the gallery's
central bay projects very slightly and is supported on slender
paired columns. The house has a detached service building and
carriage house. Samuel Jamison (1808–1880), who came to New
Orleans from Ireland, had an active practice as a builder and
architect both before and after the war.

7.14 Louise S. McGehee School (Bradish and Louisa John-son House)
1872, attributed to Lewis E. Reynolds. 2343 Prytania St.

Designed to present a showy, cosmopolitan facade for New
Yorker and sugar planter Bradish Johnson and his wife, Louisa,

this house, of gray-painted brick with beige trim, rises in layers, from the tall flight of stairs to the balconied portico with Corinthian columns, the heavy cornice with paired brackets, the concave mansard roof with a prominent bull's-eye dormer window, the pedestal-shaped chimneys, and the iron cresting along the eaves of the roof. Initially attributed to James Freret, in part because the Second Empire elements were thought to be a product of his studies at the Ecole des Beaux-Arts in Paris, the house has been reattributed to Reynolds on stylistic grounds; the magnificent circular staircase has also lent support for crediting Reynolds, who wrote a handbook on stair design. However, such staircases were ubiquitous in grand mansions during this period, and designing a staircase was one of the first exercises that budding architects had to learn. This marble spiral staircase, beneath a glass dome, is reached from the entrance hall through a wide, decorated archway similar in form and effect to a theater's proscenium arch. If Reynolds did design the house, he did not take credit for it in his brief autobiography, which is included in Edwin L. Jewell's *Crescent City Illustrated* (1873). From 1873 to 1874, Reynolds was designing buildings in Galveston, one of several cities where he had worked earlier in his career. After having several owners, the house was purchased in 1929 for use as a private girls' school. The school has since expanded by acquiring several late-nineteenth-century houses in the same block bounded by Prytania, 1st., and Philip streets and St. Charles Avenue. Jahnke and Burns renovated some of them for their new academic purpose.

7.15   Gilmour-Christovich House

1853, Isaac Thayer; 1899 addition; 1985 restored, Samuel Wilson Jr. 2520 Prytania St.

For this house, built for cotton merchant Thomas C. Gilmour and his wife, Anna, New Orleans architect Thayer created a two-story Italianate-influenced design, asymmetrical in plan, with a three-bay recessed section fronted by a one-story cast-iron gallery and a two-bay projecting unit. The second story of the projecting section has a triple-arched window, and the house is finished with a modillioned cornice. After John M. and Roberta Parker, a cotton broker and his wife, purchased the house in 1882 they added a dining room extension and rear hallway and changed the staircase. In 1985 lawyer William K.

Christovich and his wife, author and preservationist Mary Louise Mossy Christovich (1928–2017), acquired the house and hired Samuel Wilson to restore it. The building, set well back on its site, allows for an unusually large front garden. The former carriage house faces Third Street and is now a residence.

7.16 Charles Briggs House

1849, James Gallier Sr. 2605 Prytania St.

Houses in the Gothic Revival style are relatively rare in New Orleans, and this one adopts the mode as lightly as a dress on a classically symmetrical body. The brick exterior, painted a cream color and scored to resemble stone, is adorned with a ground-level cast-iron gallery with Tudor arches, pointed-arched windows on the second floor with shutters shaped to match and surmounted by hood moldings, paired octagonal chimneys, and doubled pointed-arched windows on the side elevations. The octagonal side bay was added a few years after the house was constructed. Inside, the traditional double parlors are separated by Gothic-inspired clustered columns and pendant brackets. The freestanding carriage house in the side yard, now converted for residential use, is also Gothic in style but constructed of wood. Charles Briggs emigrated from England, where houses in this style were quite popular. The Briggs House is also similar to Design II, "A Cottage in the English or Rural Gothic Style," in Andrew Jackson Downing's *Cottage Residences* (1842). In 1854, a few years after the house was built, architect Thomas Wharton described the garden in his journal: "Lofty bananas fling open their rich purple pendants and reveal the fruit clusters in heavy branches. This plant groups charmingly with the more compact shrubbery, and fine examples of its introduction occur on the grounds of Mr. Briggs, whose place . . . is to my fancy the most tasteful in the entire suburb."

7.17 Walter and Emily Robinson House

c. 1859, attributed to James Gallier Jr. and to Henry Howard. 1415 Third St.

Walter G. Robinson, from Lynchburg, Virginia, made one fortune as a cotton factor and another from perique tobacco, a curly black blending variety grown only in upriver St. James Parish. He began construction of this five-bay brick house just before the Civil War. A two-story gallery across the front, sup-

ported on slender fluted columns, Doric below and Corinthian above, curves at each end to meet the facade. An arch-shaped parapet tablet at the center of the roofline emphasizes the central entrance. Midway along the hall is a curved staircase in a similarly shaped alcove and, just beyond, the hall opens onto the dining room, which projects as an octagonal bay from the side of the house. The painted ceilings (sixteen feet high) are possibly the work of Dominique Canova, who adorned the ceilings of St. Alphonsus Church (**7.5**).

The design of the house has been attributed to Henry Howard, in part because of similarities in plan to Howard's Nottoway Plantation House of 1857 (see **Day Trip 3**), but there is no conclusive evidence. Moreover, Howard never took credit for designing this splendid house in his autobiography, published in Edwin L. Jewell's *Crescent City Illustrated* (1873), whereas he did claim others in this neighborhood. Architect and historian Samuel Wilson Jr. believed that James Gallier Jr. was the designer, and certainly the curved gallery can be compared to Gallier's modeling of the curved corners of his French Opera House and his Mechanics Institute in New Orleans, both demolished. Another view is that Howard began the house before the Civil War and Gallier completed it after the war.

These huge Garden District houses required a large staff. Not atypically, approximately 30 percent of the floor area in this house provided working and living space for enslaved workers or servants. The two-story service wing extends from the left side of the house at the rear and has a two-story cast-iron gallery. To its left is the carriage house. A wrought-iron fence with anthemion ornament encloses the entire complex.

7.18 James and Ellen Eustis House

1876, William A. Freret Jr. 2627 Coliseum St.

James Eustis was elected to the U.S. Senate in the same year that his wife, Ellen (daughter of Henry S. Buckner; see **7.10**), purchased this lot, and they hired Freret to design their house. The result, perhaps the most individualistic of the nineteenth-century houses in the Garden District, reflects the period interest in exotic styles and in the three-dimensional play of forms, light and shade, textures and materials. The facade of the two-story building of painted brick is set back in three stages, each topped by an enormous projecting gable ornamented with bargeboards, pendants, and massive brackets. A single-story gallery covers only two of the stages, contributing to this theatrical composition. The side facade includes a balconied window set within a projecting gable. This extravagant exterior adorns a quite simple, conventional plan; each of the principal facade's projecting stages and its gable correspond to an interior unit of space. The central unit contains a central hall, flanked on one side by double parlors and, on the other, by the living and dining rooms. After 1884, when Eustis was appointed ambassador to France, the house was leased until purchased by architect Julius Koch and his wife, Annie, in 1903. It was restored by Julius's son, architect Richard Koch, who lived here for many years.

7.19 Freret's Folly

1861, William A. Freret Jr. 2700–2726 Coliseum St.

Not all Garden District houses were individually designed for wealthy patrons. Freret built this row of five once-identical houses as a speculative venture. Constructed at the advent of the Civil War, the two-story frame houses were financially unsuccessful, thereby acquiring their nickname. This type of town house—tall, three bays wide, with a side hall—was common in the mid-nineteenth century in many Lower Garden and Central City neighborhoods. Wooden galleries in a simplified Greek Revival style provided shade, and French windows at least ten feet high allowed cooling breezes to enter the house. Such houses

are often adorned below the parapet with paired Italianate brackets and cornices with dentils. When they are part of a row, as here, their harmonious proportions form a unified, urbane streetscape.

7.20 Robert Short House
1859, Howard and Diettel. 1448 Fourth St.

Although it is justifiably famous for its cast-iron fence (one of three nineteenth-century cornstalk fences in the city; see **1.22**), the house itself is equally splendid. The fence, patterned in morning glory vines and cornstalks, was manufactured in New Orleans by Wood, Miltenberger and Company. Henry Howard designed the Italianate house for Kentuckian Robert Short, a cotton commission merchant, at the same time as the Dufour-Baldwin House (**4.5**), and it shows the ease with which Howard could turn out magnificent stucco-covered brick houses with just enough individuality to please his clients. The house was constructed by Robert Huyghe, a builder from Baltimore. Emphasizing width as much as height, it has a suburban feel in contrast to the Dufour-Baldwin's urbanity. Two-story galleries shade the front and the curved bay on the left side; a single-story gallery wraps around the larger side bay on the right. A heavy bracketed cornice and parapet conceal the flat roof. The entrance hall extends through the house to a cross hall at the rear of the double parlors, a feature Howard employed for other houses. The double parlors to the left of the hall are separated by two columns, forming a triple arch. Interior details for door casings, plaster cornices, and the entrance door are Greek Revival. The curved staircase toward the rear of the hall was added in the early twentieth century, when some interior changes were made; Koch and Wilson, Architects, also did some work on the house in the 1960s, including remodeling the loggia. Before the house was completed, the Civil War began. Colonel Short and his wife, Margaret, fled New Orleans for Kentucky but returned after the war and reclaimed the house. General Nathaniel Banks of the Union Army occupied it during the war, in 1864 and 1865. The original grounds were subdivided in 1950 for the construction of two houses.

7.21   Lafayette Cemetery No. 1

1833, Benjamin Buisson. Bounded by Washington Ave., and Coliseum, Prytania, and Sixth sts.

Designed at the height of one of New Orleans's worst cholera epidemics, this cemetery was divided by two shell-paved avenues, carefully planned to accommodate a funeral procession, and intersecting at the center to form a cross. In 1857, the cemetery was enclosed by a high brick wall, and individual vaults were built into its inner face on the Washington Avenue side to help meet the need for additional burial space. By 1867, magnolia trees had been planted along the principal avenues. The formality of the plan and the landscaping reflect the idea of the cemetery as a garden of rest. Closely spaced above-ground tombs line the avenues and aisles in each of the four squares.

7.22   Steinberg-Fishbach House
1955–1957, Curtis and Davis. 1201 Conery St.

A steel structural frame provides the utmost freedom for interior spatial organization in this modernist house. Organized around a central courtyard, the building is composed of two levels on the bedroom side and a single thirteen-foot-high living room on the street side. Indirect light from the courtyard and the clerestory windows accentuates the interpenetration of space. The exterior also incorporates all the elements of modernist form in the way the house is cantilevered over a concrete foundation so that it appears to float above the ground, in its horizontal screenlike brick wall, the continuous band of clerestory windows, and, hovering over all, the flat roof. Circular concrete steps from sidewalk to front door are an essential part of the design. Walter J. Rooney Jr. (b. 1925), Curtis and Davis's project architect for this house, manipulated the principles of modernism to accommodate the New Orleans context and climate. The house received an Award of Excellence from *Architectural Record* in 1959.

This section of Conery Street, extending from Camp to Chestnut streets, was created in 1955, when the Baptist Theological Seminary, which occupied the entire block from Washington Avenue to Sixth Street, divided its property into lots and sold them for the construction of houses. By the time the seminary was built, this city block already had a long and illustrious history. Immediately preceding the seminary, and before moving uptown in 1917, Newcomb College was located here, occupying the former mansion (demolished) of James Robb, designed by James Gallier Jr. in 1854, and the location of one of the nineteenth-century city's most elaborate gardens. At 2828 Camp Street, the former Newcomb Pottery building (1902, Rathbone DeBuys) is now subdivided into apartments.

7.23 Shotgun Houses
c. 1890. 2901–1915 Camp St.

This row of camelback double-shotgun houses exhibits exceptionally bold detailing. The overhanging roofs at the fronts of the wood-frame buildings are supported on elaborately ornamented prefabricated brackets that could be purchased from a catalogue. French windows with shutters open onto small porches, and small gardens in front are enclosed by low iron fences. Many of the uptown streets in New Orleans have similar rows of shotgun houses that display all manner of decorative details, from fancy gallery railings to elaborate window surrounds, brackets, spindles, and arches. Other impressive rows of camelback doubles can be seen nearby on the 1200 blocks of both Eighth and Harmony streets.

7.24 Bosworth-Hammond House

1859, Thomas K. Wharton; 2007 restored. 1126 Washington Ave.

This two-story house built for Abel W. and Rachel Bosworth has an unusual bow-curved double gallery, which gives the facade a pleasing liveliness. In other respects, the house is conventional, with a central-hall plan, an entrance marked by sidelights and a transom, an L-shaped service wing in the rear facing a garden, and classical details. In reference to the house, Wharton wrote in his journal in May 1859 about the difficulties of designing in hot weather under the stings of mosquitoes, and he wistfully complained, "Why don't people bring their orders along in the winter? Drawings and specifications need cool weather." Bosworth, originally from Maine, was an ice merchant (the ice came to New Orleans by ship). Later sold to the Hammond family, the house remained in their possession until 1979, after which it slowly deteriorated until new owners restored it.

7.25 Camp Bow Wow (National Maritime Union Building)

1954–1956, Albert C. Ledner. 2731 Tchoupitoulas St.

The Maritime Union required a building with a hiring hall of column-free space, a group of offices, and natural light for the interior. New Orleans architect Ledner (1924–2017) designed a circular hall, one hundred feet in diameter, covered by a twelve-pointed star-shaped pleated roof, which he described as ridge and valley in form. The roof's twelve ridges form gables, which extend beyond the building's walls to create a highly dynamic

effect. Windows set deep within the gables illuminate the hall. The roof is composed of wood sheathing on a steel structural frame. The spaces for offices, reception, machinery, and storage that encircle the central hall are six-sided in shape. The building is now a boarding-and-care facility for dogs.

7.26 Orphanage Apartments and Commercial Building (Protestant Orphans Home)
1887–1888, Thomas Sully; 1998 renovated, John Schackai III. 3000 Magazine St.

Founded by a group of Protestant women after the yellow fever epidemic of 1853, the orphanage was first housed in a smaller building on the same site. Deadly diseases continued to take their toll during the nineteenth century, so that the city's need for orphanages did not diminish. Sully designed this large three-story building to house a boys' dormitory, infirmary, and dining hall. A girls' wing was added later. Sully blended elements of Romanesque Revival and Queen Anne styles to create a fairy-tale building, albeit a somewhat formidable one, with ornate brickwork, twin towers, turrets, and a huge, deep-balconied arch marking the entrance. However, he ornamented it with a multicolored roof incorporating rose-colored, heart-shaped tiles. For several years, a high wall enclosed the orphanage to protect local residents from diseases that, it was thought, the children might spread. The orphanage closed in 1972 and, after standing empty for some years, the building was converted into apartments and commercial spaces; it was renovated again in 1998.

7.27   Historic Dryades Street Branch Library
1914–1915, William R. Burk. 1924 Philip St.

An Andrew Carnegie grant in 1912 funded this library for African
Americans on a site at the termination of Oretha Castle Haley
Boulevard (formerly Dryades Street), a location proposed by
black civic leaders and one that gave the building a highly visible presence. Constructed of red brick with decorative details
of Bedford, Indiana, limestone, the facade imitates a triumphal
arch, with three wide, round-arched bays framed by Ionic pilasters. An elaborate classically inspired portal is set in the central
bay. The sculptural details include an open book, wreaths,
and decorative capitals. Initially, a children's reading room
was located to the left of the central entrance and an adult
reading room to the right; an auditorium was in the basement.
The library opened with 5,649 books, increasing to 13,000 by
1932. The Dryades Street Branch Library was the only public
library in the city available for African Americans until 1953
when the Nora Navra Branch at 1902 St. Bernard Avenue was
constructed. Orleans Parish libraries were desegregated in 1955,
although restrooms and water fountains remained segregated
for several years. Of the six original Carnegie-financed libraries
in New Orleans, three of the buildings survive: the Napoleon
Avenue (see **8.7**) and Algiers Point (see **page 253**) branches still
function as libraries, but the original branch on Canal Street
(**5.15**) has found a new use. The Dryades Street Library, architecturally the most handsome of the surviving group, closed in
1965 following damage from Hurricane Betsy; by then, the city's

libraries were integrated. A YMCA uses the building for activities. William R. Burk (1888–1961) was the architect for many public and institutional buildings in southern Louisiana.

7.28   Ashe Cultural Arts Center (Kaufman's Department Store)

1919, Samuel Stone Jr.; 1998 renovated, Alecha Architects.
1700–1724 Oretha Castle Haley Blvd.

German immigrant Charles A. Kaufman opened a store on this street in 1879 and expanded the business to this larger building in 1919. The department store prospered during the Jim Crow years, when black shoppers made this street a center for commercial and social activities. Until the 1960s, it was the city's second-most-important retail district after Canal Street. A Kaufman's store occupied the corner of this block before 1895, but after purchasing the adjoining property, Kaufman commissioned Stone to design a three-story building faced with fashionable white terra-cotta. Four bays wide, with huge windows on each floor, the facade is decorated with a row of terra-cotta lion heads along the cornice. Suburban shopping malls dealt a death blow to shopping streets like this one, and the store closed in the late 1960s. After standing empty for several years, the building was renovated for a community nonprofit arts organization, retail use, and apartments. On the next block, another former department store, Handelman's (1824 Oretha Castle Haley Boulevard), was designed on lines similar to Kaufman's by Weiss and Dreyfous in 1922; it closed in the late 1950s.

Nearby at 1307 Oretha Castle Haley Boulevard the former McDonogh School No. 38 (1910), a three-story Arts and Crafts design by E. A Christy, later renamed Myrtle Banks School and now Myrtle Banks Building, was adapted to house a food market and offices for arts organizations and small businesses in 2011–2013 by Eskew+Dumez+Ripple after a 2008 fire gutted the interior.

7.29   St. John the Baptist Church
1869–1872, Albert Diettel. 1139 Oretha Castle Haley Blvd.

This handsome brick church, with a golden onion-shaped spire (gilded in 1963) that is an area landmark, was built for the Irish immigrants who settled in this area. The church, replacing a smaller, wooden structure of 1851, was built by Irish contractor Thomas Mulligan to designs of Diettel, who took his inspiration from the onion-domed Hofkirche in Dresden, Germany. Diettel used paired pilasters on the facade to indicate internal space divisions and repeated the paired motif in Corinthian columns on the middle level of the tall, three-stage tower. A heavily molded and bracketed entablature wraps around the building, gently curving over the small rose window in the center of the facade. This entablature is repeated at each of the tower's setbacks in order to unify the design. The brickwork on this church is particularly fine. The cost of the building exceeded the congregation's resources, so it was not until the 1880s, after the Reverend Thomas Kenny purchased the building, that the interior was completed and the enormous stained glass windows, made in the Munich studios of Franz Mayer and F. X. Zettler, were installed. The church was struck by lightning in 1909 and repaired with a steel and concrete roof. An adjoining school, built in the 1850s, was demolished in the 1950s for the raised expressway now next door. The adjacent rectory of 1895 at the corner of Clio Street was renovated in 2016 for office space and an apartment. The two-story wooden house has been painted a bright cranberry color and its Gothic trim is painted white.

Uptown

New Orleans's expansion upriver was encouraged, beginning in 1835, by the steam-powered New Orleans and Carrollton Railroad, laid out along St. Charles Avenue and one of the nation's first such transit lines. As elsewhere, a "resort" was at the terminus in the Carrollton suburb to attract riders. The line was converted to mule power in 1867, then electrified in 1893, and the streetcars continue to carry passengers along this route. Four major streets, all running parallel to the river, define the character of Uptown.

Closest to the river, Tchoupitoulas Street developed as the industrial and warehouse corridor serving the port, evidenced in the half-mile-long brick warehouse that extends from Louisiana Avenue to General Taylor Street. The former Lane Cotton Mills (closed in 1957), established in the 1850s in a building by George Purves (d. 1883) at Valence Street and the river, was enlarged in 1881 by William Fitzner, and again in 1903 by Favrot and Livaudais; this last section has been adapted for use as a supermarket. A few blocks inland, Magazine Street grew as an eclectic mix of commercial and residential buildings. St. Charles Avenue acquired grand mansions for the affluent and became the most prestigious address in the city. By 1900, almost the entire length of St. Charles had been built up. Claiborne Avenue was developed in the early twentieth century, when more efficient pumps became available to drain the swamps that lay inland from the river. Now a major traffic route, the avenue has a wide, landscaped neutral ground that conceals a drainage canal beneath.

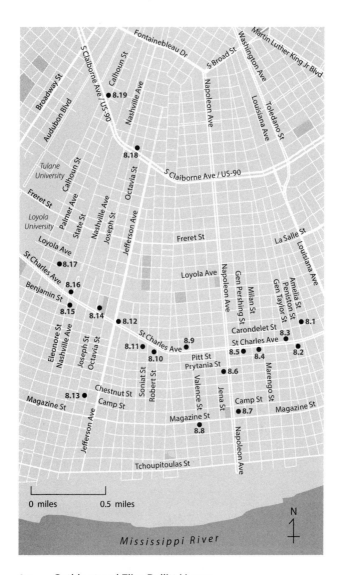

8.1 Cuthbert and Eliza Bullitt House

1868–1869, Edward Gottheil. 3627 Carondelet St.

Described as a "Swiss villa" by the *Daily Picayune* in 1868, this prettily decorated frame house raised on eight-foot-high brick piers was built for Cuthbert Bullitt and his wife, Eliza. Bullitt, from Kentucky, was a customs collector, bon vivant, and gambler who spent his winters in New Orleans as he got older (he lived to the

age of ninety-seven). It is believed that Gottheil (c. 1813–1877) brought the design from Europe. The symmetrical facade is animated with decorative cross timbers and the broad gable roof adorned with jigsaw bargeboards, and this decoration is repeated on a smaller scale on the gables over the windows. The interior details, however, are Greek Revival. Originally built on St. Charles Avenue, the house was moved here in 1883 after cigar manufacturer Simon Hernsheim purchased the St. Charles Avenue site to build his enormous mansion, now the Columns Hotel.

8.2　Unity Temple

1960–1961, Leonard R. Spangenberg Jr. 3722 St. Charles Ave.

Leonard Spangenberg (1925–2007), once a student at Frank Lloyd Wright's Taliesin Fellowship, and Ruth Murphy, a Unitarian minister, determined the plan of this church, choosing a circular design as a symbol of unity and eternity. Everything in the design is based on the circle, from the two low, intersecting domed structures to the entrance plaza, outdoor planters (one originally was a pool), catch basins, benches, lighting fixtures, staircase, pulpit, and decorative trim. The building, including its two saucerlike domes, is constructed of cast concrete. The larger dome shelters a sanctuary seating 300 people, and the smaller covers the narthex and offices. Interiors, which maintain their original condition, are illuminated by continuous bands of Plexiglas clerestory windows and circular skylights in the domes. A rectangular extension was attached to the sanctuary in 1987 but fortunately is not visible from St. Charles Avenue. Although the building is quite at odds with all the others on this conservative street, Spangenberg justified his design by claiming that new buildings were replacing old ones so quickly that any attempt at conformity was doomed. He was wrong with regard to St. Charles Avenue, but he nevertheless gave the avenue a genuinely twentieth-century design and not a nineteenth-century replica. Spangenberg also designed another of the city's unusual buildings, Plaza Tower (**6.32**).

8.3 Emlah Court Apartments
1912, Diboll, Owen and Goldstein. 3823 St. Charles Ave.

One of the first of the grand early-twentieth-century apartment buildings in New Orleans and the city's first cooperative apartment building, Emlah Court broke the tradition of single-family houses on the avenue. The five-story building is constructed of reinforced concrete, wood, and brick, and the first story is stuccoed with horizontal divisions to imitate rustication. Emlah Court offered three-bedroom apartments on each floor, with the luxury of three bathrooms and an elevator. A curved metal marquee over the entrance and curved frames on some windows suggest the influence of Art Nouveau, a rare feature for New Orleans.

8.4 John S. Wallis House

1885–1889, Sully and Toledano. 4114 St. Charles Ave.

The Shingle Style was at the height of popularity in the United States when Sully designed this house for John S. Wallis, president of the Louisiana Sugar Refining Company, probably as a wedding gift for his daughter, Louise. In his use of shingles, Sully once again introduced to the city the latest fashions in building materials and forms, and he did not do it in a halfhearted way. This house is smothered in differently shaped cypress shingles, including the front gallery piers; all the shingles are now painted white, although originally they were stained a dark natural color. Providing a striking touch of color are the checkerboard bands of blue glazed tiles and white-painted cement squares beneath the eaves of the second story. A Sully innovation is the use of lattices between each bay of the gallery, which are cut in the shape of stilted arches and impart an exotic touch. The house's widow's walk above the oversized gabled dormer blew off during Hurricane Betsy in 1965. The entrance leads into a large hall and is flanked by the library and a parlor. The former carriage house (4115 Pitt Street), also shingled, is now a residence. Sully and Toledano built an almost identical house for the Wallis family in Pass Christian, Mississippi.

Diagonally across St. Charles at number 4101 is a brick and concrete duplex that Victor Bruno (1921–2011) created in 1962 for Lester Sarpy. The two-story building's horizontal emphasis, angular intersecting volumes, and flat roofs that extend to shelter windows indicate Bruno's synthesis of modernist forms with the influence of Frank Lloyd Wright. The house marks the corner of Palm Terrace, a one-block double row of ten charming Mediterranean-styled stuccoed bungalows designed by William E. Spink (1872–c. 1951) and landscaped by Hungarian-born immigrant Sigmund Tarnok (1893–1973).

8.5   Touro Synagogue

1907–1908, Emile Weil; 1989 addition, Lyons and Hudson Architects; 1928 Sabbath School, Nathan Kohlman. 4238 St. Charles Ave.

Touro Synagogue was named for Judah P. Touro, a descendant of the Touro family of Newport, Rhode Island. A significant figure in New Orleans, he bequeathed his fortune to many charitable institutions and to Touro Hospital, formerly the Hebrew Hospital. Touro Synagogue's congregation was formed by the merger in 1881 of German and Spanish-Portuguese congregations. Emile Weil won the synagogue's design competition in 1907 with his scheme for a low-domed, Byzantine-influenced structure, a solution adopted by many synagogues because of Judiasm's Middle Eastern origins. The synagogue is constructed of beige pressed brick and ornamented with polychrome glazed terra-cotta bands and cornices; the dome is tiled in pale green interspersed with yellow and blue. The main auditorium retains its original appearance. It is covered by a shallow dome, 71 feet in diameter, and has two walls of stained glass windows in varied shades of gold and green.

The multipurpose addition (1989), next to the synagogue on St. Charles Avenue and linked to it by an arcade, echoes, in a simplified and more angular composition, the forms and decoration of the original building. It includes classrooms, a 120-seat chapel, and stained glass windows designed in the late 1980s by New Orleans artists Ida Kohlmeyer and Gene Koss. Nathan Kohlman (1883–1957) designed the Sabbath school at the rear of the Temple, which shows Moorish influences in its colorful entrance composed of three arches framed by a larger arch.

8.6 St. Elizabeth's Apartments (St. Elizabeth's Home of Industry)

c. 1864, Thomas Mulligan; 1883–1884, Albert Diettel; 2006 renovated and additions, Studio WTA. 1314 Napoleon Ave.

St. Elizabeth's Home of Industry was founded by the Daughters of Charity of St. Vincent de Paul in 1855 to teach vocational skills to orphaned girls between the ages of fourteen and eighteen. First occupying a Henry Howard–designed building at Magazine and Josephine streets, the home was relocated here in 1871. The building had formerly housed St. Joseph's Academy and at that time consisted of just the three-story central section, constructed by builder Thomas Mulligan. The brick building is shaded by a two-story gallery supported on cast-iron Corinthian columns. In 1883, a wing was added to the Prytania Street side of the building. Designed by Diettel and built by Albert Thiesen, it had a two-story-high chapel with stained glass windows on the upper floor. The wing has rusticated brickwork at ground level and on its quoined corners and is covered by a mansard roof. The following year, an identical wing was built on the Perrier Street side. In 1888, the earlier central section was given a mansard roof, an addition that gave the complex the unified appearance it has today. Although by that time mansards were no longer the height of fashion, the addition here may have been influenced by the popular mansard-roofed main building at the Cotton Centennial Exposition of 1884 in Audubon Park (**9.6**). St. Elizabeth's was funded in part by Dr. William Newton Mercer, in memory of his daughter Elizabeth; his other daughter, Anna, was commemorated at St. Anna's Orphan Asylum (**7.7**). In 1993, after standing empty for several years, St. Elizabeth's was purchased by novelist Anne Rice, who renovated it to use for charitable events and parties; she sold it in 2002 and the building was converted into apartments, as was the chapel. A row of contemporary town houses was constructed as a part of the project.

8.7 St. George's Episcopal School (McDonogh School No. 6)

1875, William A. Freret Jr. 923 Napoleon Ave.

This brick building, one of the schools funded by John McDonogh's bequest (see **6.23**), was among the first public schools "for colored children" in New Orleans. The classical entrance, added in the twentieth century, and exterior symmetry disguise the fact that Freret's design is basically Gothic Revival, apparent in the brick hood moldings and gable-end blind arcade. A feature of several of Freret's school designs was a ground-floor open play area, which in this case has been enclosed for additional classroom space. When the school board reassigned the McDonogh School No. 6 to white children in 1888, protests from the African American community, whose members then still had voting rights, caused this decision to be temporarily revoked. However, in 1926, because the school was located in a primarily white neighborhood, the board succeeded in transferring it to white students, remodeling the building for commercial and secretarial classes for girls. After the school closed in 1960, it was purchased by the Tikvat Shalom congregation and then, in 1977, by St. George's Episcopal School. A few years later, St. George's acquired the nearby former Jefferson Market (4301 Magazine Street), an E. A. Christy design of 1917, which was converted into a gymnasium in 1990.

William Freret designed several school buildings for the New Orleans public school system in the late nineteenth century.

One example nearby (1111 Milan Street) is McDonogh School No. 7 (1877), which has retained its Gothic Revival exterior. Near St. George's are two other noteworthy buildings: the Carnegie-funded Renaissance-styled library (1908; 913 Napoleon Avenue), now the Children's Resource Center Library, by Favrot and Livaudais, and, in the next block at 1025 Napoleon, the Gothic Revival St. Stephen's Church (1868–1887) designed by Thomas W. Carter, with a spire added in 1908.

8.8   Valence Street Baptist Church (Mission Baptist Church)

1885–1886, Thomas Sully. 4636 Magazine St.

Sully's versatile use of all the popular trends of his time is revealed in his admirable handling of the Stick Style for this wooden church. The frame is outlined and emphasized, giving it the skeletal attributes that are the hallmark of the style; the diagonal and horizontal arrangement of the boards on the gable further emphasizes the angular, sticklike qualities of the design. A large square tower, with small dormers set in a pyramid-shaped steeple, anchors the church to its corner site. Diamond-shaped multicolored glass fills the pointed-arched windows. In the 1930s, the church was raised to its present two-story height in order to provide more space for the growing congregation. Although this modification gave the church a much more commanding presence than was originally intended, the building retains an unpretentious character and a clarity of construction that reflect the congregation's origins. It grew from a mission opened in a house on Valence Street in 1880 by Emma Gardner, from Mississippi, following the Mississippi Baptist Convention's decision to establish more churches in New Orleans.

8.9 William Perry Brown House
1902–1907, Favrot and Livaudais. 4717 St. Charles Ave.

Cotton merchant William Brown promised his new wife, Marguerite, the best house on the avenue. Elevated on an earthen terrace, this 15,000-square-foot, two-and-a-half-story house in the Richardsonian Romanesque style is constructed of warm-hued beige limestone and has a red tile roof. The walls themselves are striking, with stones that are coursed but vary in size and surface treatment across the principal facade, whereas the gables, chimneys, and subsidiary walls are laid in random patterns. Across the front, the one-story porch, with a row of wide arches outlined by huge voussoirs and supported on squat columns, provides a deep, shadowy transition from the dazzling marble steps to the interior. The central hall led to a breakfast room at the rear, and this principal floor included a parlor, dining room, library, and billiard room. The largely classical interior decor was fashionable, and the house included hot-air heating in every room, a bath for each bedroom, electric lighting, and electric call signals for summoning servants.

8.10 Joseph and Anna Vaccaro House
1912–1913, Edward F. Sporl. 5010 St. Charles Ave.

Medieval English styles were popular when this brick house was built for Joseph Vaccaro and his wife, Anne. He was founder of the Standard Fruit and Steamship Company and an importer of

bananas and fresh produce from Central America. Edward Sporl (1881–1956) chose Tudor Revival, as evidenced in the picturesque silhouette, gable roofs, half timbering on the second floor and on the gables, prominent brick chimneys, stone trim, wraparound porch, and diamond-paned mullioned windows. The porte-cochere is more Jacobean than Tudor in its detailing. The reception and living rooms are wood-paneled and have carved stone fireplaces.

8.11 Milton H. Latter Memorial Library (Marks Isaacs House)

1906–1907, Favrot and Livaudais. 5120 St. Charles Ave.

Occupying an entire block and raised on an embankment, this stone house was constructed for Canal Street merchant Marks Isaacs. After his death, the house was sold in 1912 to lumber baron Frank B. Williams and was occupied by his son, pioneer aviator Harry Williams, who was married to silent-movie star Marguerite Clark. After Harry Williams died in a plane crash in 1936, Clark sold the house to racetrack entrepreneur Robert Eddy, who in turn sold it to Harry and Anna Latter in 1947. They donated it to the City for use as a public library in memory of their son, Milton, who was killed in World War II. Although interior changes were made for library needs, the homelike atmosphere and materials were retained, including the mahogany paneling, staircase, and dining-room mantel and ceiling murals. When built, the house possessed one of the city's first home elevators, and a ballroom occupied the third floor. A separate carriage house is at the rear of the property.

8.12 Farnsworth Apartments

1932, Weiss, Dreyfous and Seiferth. 5355 St. Charles Ave.

This small brick apartment complex, constructed for R. P. Farnsworth and Company as an investment property, was a unique addition to St. Charles Avenue in its frank expression of modernist principles. The streamlined horizontal emphasis, wraparound metal-framed windows, and flat roof were ideas new to New Orleans, not just this street. Organized in the typical U-shaped format around an entrance courtyard, the building accommodates eight two-bedroom apartments, each provided with service stairs leading from the kitchen to the basement garage and servants' entrance.

8.13 Henry G. Simon House

1960–1961, Charles Colbert for Colbert-Lowrey-Hess-Boudreaux Architects. 922 Octavia St.

Built for a young pediatrician and his family, this house is composed of four pavilions identical in size and form, connected by glazed passageways that define two interior courtyards, one for meditation and the other for recreation. Each of the pavilions serves a specific use, as specified by the clients: living, dining and food preparation, children's space, and parents' space. Each pavilion has a pyramidal roof of wood and steel. Windows on the exterior brick walls are small and high to ensure privacy, and all large glassed areas face inward to the courtyards. New Orleanian Charles Colbert (1921–2007), dean of Columbia University School of Architecture from 1960 to 1963, said of his modern design, "I have attempted to recall the earlier forms of architecture in Louisiana, maintain a reasonably constant residential scale, and repeat some of the roof forms of the immediate environs." The house was widely published in architecture journals.

8.14 Emanuel V. and Rachel Benjamin House

1916, Emile Weil. 5531 St. Charles Ave.

Weil sited this large house, built for the Benjamins, well back from the street in order to fully display its fashionable Beaux-Arts classical facade to passersby. At the time Weil was commissioned by Emanuel Benjamin, who in 1914 had purchased the Maginnis Cotton Mill (**6.28**), he was, along with the firm of Favrot and Livaudais, the architect of choice for clients seeking

to assert their social standing and wealth in a stylish house on an Uptown avenue. Both Weil and the Favrot and Livaudais firm became masters of Beaux-Arts designs derived from those of McKim, Mead and White of New York City. For this house, Weil provided a well-proportioned symmetrical facade faced in beige stone, with a wide but shallow single-story central pseudo-portico supported on paired Ionic columns in front of the slightly recessed central section. Iron railings define the portico's upper edge; this horizontal movement is repeated, in stone, in the balustrade along the roofline and in front of the house, where a low balustrade outlines a shallow front terrace. The low hipped roof has three dormers with round-headed pediments. Because there is little depth to the facade's architectural elements and thus no significant play of light and shade, the house lacks any sense of three-dimensionality. The exterior appearance is also misleading in its relationship to the interior organization; behind what would seem to be the central entrance was a wood-paneled living room, and the reception hall was located at the side of the house by the porte-cochere.

8.15 Antonio Palacios House

1867, Henry Howard. 5824 St. Charles Ave.

Cotton factor Antonio Palacios built this five-bay raised house of white-painted wood early in the development of this section of New Orleans, and at first glance, Howard's design seems to reflect an earlier era. The single central pedimented dormer and the gallery on slender Ionic columns are traditional features; only the segmental-arched windows indicate contemporary

taste. The interior has a central-hall plan, with simplified Greek Revival detailing. Set far back on its lot, the house is picturesquely veiled by the trees and foliage of its large front garden. Diagonally opposite (5705 St. Charles Avenue) is a house exemplifying Antebellum Revival: a white-painted brick replica of Tara, from the 1939 movie *Gone with the Wind*, built in 1941 for George Palmer by Andrew W. Lockett.

8.16 Nicholas Burke House

1896, Toledano and Reusch; 1907 restored, Toledano and Wogan. 5809 St. Charles Ave.

Known as the "wedding cake" house because of its tiered appearance, profuse decoration, and all-white exterior, this residence was described as "colonial" by the architects, though rarely is this style so festive. The single-story gallery of the wooden house is supported on clusters of columns with Ionic capitals draped with garlands, and garlanded friezes decorate the gallery entablature. Gallery balustrades are punctuated by finials in the shape of classical urns; window surrounds are adorned with scrolled brackets, moldings, and gooseneck gables; and the roof has elaborate dormers. The gallery is curved on the right side, which gives the symmetrical facade the deceptive appearance of asymmetry. A porte-cochere on the left side of the house and a gallery have identical decoration. Toledano was in partnership with Ferdinand Reusch (1826–1901) when the house was built. A detailed drawing of the elevation, signed but undated, identifies Toledano and Wogan (Victor Wogan, 1870–1953) as the architects; their partnership was formed in 1901 and lasted until 1914. The house was severely damaged in 1907 following an electrical fire; the extent of the restoration is unknown. The liveliness of the design was probably influenced by buildings at the World's Columbian Exposition of 1893 in Chicago, particularly the New York State Pavilion by McKim, Mead and White.

Born in Ireland, Nicholas Burke arrived in New Orleans in 1850, married Lizzie Hanton in 1857, made a fortune in the retail grocery business, was one of the founders of Hibernia National Bank, and was financial adviser to Irish-born Margaret Haughery (see **7.3**).

8.17　Curtis House

1962–1963, Nathaniel C. Curtis Jr. for Curtis and Davis; 2013 restored, Lee Ledbetter. 6161 Marquette Pl.

A focus on privacy as the main point of the design is a condition emphasized in many houses in the 1960s. In physical terms it means blank street walls and interior courts with enclosed gardens. According to the architect, who designed this house for his family, by turning its back on the street it reinterpreted the tradition of the old houses in New Orleans's Vieux Carré. Behind the white-painted nine-foot-high brick wall are three glass building units framed by slender steel columns, beams, and arches facing landscaped patios: one unit contains the living room; another the dining, kitchen, and family room; and the third, two stories in height, with its lower level depressed, seven bedrooms and four bathrooms (the Curtises had seven children). A low-ceilinged hallway (Curtis called it a gallery) runs through the house, reminiscent of a traditional central hall. Space and light flow easily from area to area, and from inside to outside in this elegant house. Architect Walter J. Rooney Jr. of the Curtis and Davis office was consulted on the landscaping. Architect Lee Ledbetter purchased and restored the house in 2013.

8.18 Lone Star Cement Corporation House (Parlongue House)
1935, Weiss, Dreyfous and Seiferth. 5521 S. Claiborne Ave.

The Lone Star Cement Corporation hired the architects to demonstrate that a well-designed, soundly constructed house could be built of concrete at moderate cost. Lone Star maintained that a concrete house—safe from termites, moisture, and decay, stable in hurricanes, and fire resistant—was ideal for the New Orleans climate. The hollow-ribbed concrete walls provided air space for insulation against heat and cold and accommodated pipes and conduits. The construction cost of the demonstration house was $10,200. Weiss, Dreyfous and Seiferth, a firm favored by Governor Huey P. Long and known for its contemporary designs, was selected by the cement company. August Perez Jr. (1907–1998), then recently hired by the firm, gave the house an appropriately modern look: a geometric composition with wraparound windows and no decoration other than polished black concrete panels between the windows and plain horizontal moldings on the wall area between the first and second stories. Lone Star insisted, for "aesthetic reasons," on a pitched roof rather than a modern flat one, but the hipped roof, with a small chimney at the center, has a low profile, so that the modern appearance of the house is not diluted. An outdoor terrace was placed on the garage roof. The interior was organized traditionally; the combination of living and dining areas created the only integration of spaces; the staircase is of cast concrete. The house, completed within three months and provided with Russel Wright furnishings from the Maison Blanche department store, was opened to sight-seers at ten cents each. Despite all the publicity and interest in the project, concrete houses never caught on in New Orleans. Recent exterior attention makes the house look new; however, a new incongruous fence detracts from the purity and simplicity of this small but distinctive building.

In 1936, the year after this demonstration model was constructed, the *Times-Picayune* commissioned Moise Gold-stein to design a "New American Home" in celebration of the newspaper's one-hundredth anniversary. Located at 1514 Henry Clay Avenue, the streamlined, white-painted brick house with modern wraparound windows and all-electric appliances had no more influence on residential design in New Orleans than did the concrete house.

8.19   Ted's Frostop
1955. 3100 Calhoun St.

A frothy, neon-lit, giant root-beer mug high atop a freestanding support quickly identifies a Frostop diner. Red, blue, green, and yellow letters spelling BURGERS, spaced across the width of the facade, advertise the signature item on the menu. Above them, a pediment-shaped metal and neon sign displays the restaurant's name at its center. The restaurant, small-scaled and unobtrusive compared with its signage, has a continuous window that wraps around the front and one side above the tile-covered lower wall. On the other side, a deep, cantilevered roof shelters what formerly was a drive-in area, where customers had to walk only a few steps to the service windows. Exterior surfaces are caramel- and khaki-colored tile. Inside, a counter and booths are arranged around the perimeter of the space. These features, with only slight variations, were found in other Frostops in southern Louisiana, most of which have since been demolished. Ted's Frostop is a rare surviving example of the kind of fast-food outlets that proliferated along America's highways in the 1950s and 1960s in response to the surge in automobile ownership. The buildings, designed to be seen at a distance, joyfully utilize brightly colored, outsize signage made possible by the availability and reasonable price of such materials as aluminum, plastic, and neon. The first Frostop opened in Springfield, Ohio, in 1926; the name and products were franchised nationwide.

The Uptown Universities and Carrollton

In the late nineteenth century, Loyola and Tulane universities (**9.1** and **9.2**) purchased large tracts of land to construct new campuses facing St. Charles Avenue just upriver of the Uptown residential area and accessible by the streetcar line. Land opposite the universities had been acquired by 1886 for Audubon Park (**9.6**) and in 1883 the U.S. government had purchased a site close to the Mississippi River for a Marine Hospital (**9.8**). These institutions and the park generated residential development in this new highly desirable neighborhood.

Carrollton was developed on former plantation land acquired by the New Orleans Canal and Banking Company and subdivided by Charles F. Zimpel in 1833. Carrollton quickly became a popular resort with a hotel and a public garden, both now buried under a levee setback, as the attraction at the terminus of the streetcar line. The town was incorporated in 1845 and annexed to New Orleans in 1874. Carrollton was reputedly named for General William Carroll, who aided Andrew Jackson in the battle to defend New Orleans in 1815 (and who later became governor of Tennessee).

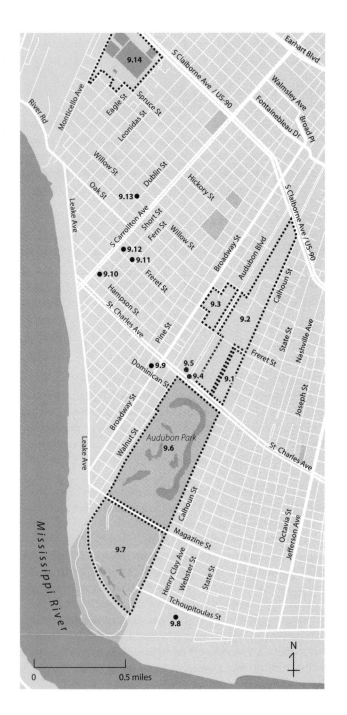

9.1 Loyola University

1909–present. 6363 St. Charles Ave.

In 1909, the Jesuits held a design competition for the new college they planned to build on this site, acquired in 1889. The competition attracted the top architecture firms in the city, including Favrot and Livaudais and Toledano and Wogan, but the Tudor Gothic Revival design by Rathbone DeBuys for DeBuys, Churchill and Labouisse won the Jesuits' favor. Although the first building completed on the new campus was the Burke Seismographic Observatory in 1909, Marquette Hall is the centerpiece of the design. A red brick structure with limestone details, reminiscent of Hampton Court Palace (1514) in England, Marquette Hall faces St. Charles Avenue across an open-ended court. It is linked to the buildings along the sides of the court by a covered arcade that has a convincing medieval atmosphere. In 1913, Rathbone DeBuys (1874–1960) designed the Holy Name of Jesus Church (completed in 1918), which is located on the upriver side of the academic court. The church is said to be modeled after Canterbury Cathedral, but its enormous square, pinnacled tower in the center of the facade is a feature of many English churches. Viewed from Audubon Park across the avenue, the tower rising above the treetops presents a scene quite evocative of an English landscape.

Subsequent buildings on the campus were arranged around courtyards in a typical collegiate manner and in styles fashionable during their decades. The Danna Student Center (1964; 2008 renovated, Kell Muñoz Architects) is a well-designed modernist box, and Monroe Hall's expansion (2015, Holabird and Root with Holly and Smith) is a stepped geometric composition in brick and glass. For a new library in 1998, The Mathes Group revived Loyola's original medieval theme in red brick.

9.2 Tulane University
1893 – present. 6823 St. Charles Ave.

Tulane University had its origins in the Medical College of Louisiana, founded in 1834, and became the University of Louisiana in 1847. The university began to prosper only after merchant Paul Tulane endowed it for white youth; it was named for him in 1884. With the purchase in 1891 of a long, narrow strip of land reaching inland from St. Charles Avenue, construction on the new campus began in 1893. The architects for the first buildings were Harrod and Andry and the successor firm of Andry and Bendernagel, whose winning entry in a design competition featured time-defying rusticated stone buildings clearly influenced by H. H. Richardson, America's most admired architect in the 1890s. Gibson Hall, the administration and classroom block facing St. Charles Avenue, was the first building completed and physically defines both the outer edge of the campus and the quadrangle behind it. Four of the quad's buildings are similar in materials and style; the most notable is the former library, Tilton Memorial Hall (1901, with a 1906 extension), by Andry and Bendernagel, which has a richly decorated triple-arched entrance, carved portraits of its benefactors on the facade, and Tiffany windows illuminating the stairs in the entrance lobby. Andry and Bendernagel's Richardson Memorial Building

(1908), of brick with limestone cladding, was constructed for the School of Medicine and now houses the School of Architecture. Its elevated porch was designed to accommodate university graduation ceremonies.

On the far side of the quad in the direction of Freret Street, and part of the initial scheme, are two orange brick structures devoted respectively to the physics and chemistry departments, dating from 1894, and the brick former refectory (now Robert C. Cudd Hall) of 1901, notable for its curving front gable in a Dutch Colonial Revival manner. The campus then expanded toward the lake, with brick buildings lightly influenced by either Richardsonian Romanesque or Dutch Colonial Revival. In the 1920s, further expansion and construction of new buildings took the campus across Freret Street. Before Freret is crossed, however, a cluster of more recent buildings, dedicated to engineering and the sciences, interrupts the historical chronology of expansion. A later arrival is the Merryl and Sam Israel Jr. Environmental Sciences Building (1999), designed by William Wilson Architects and Payette Associates, both of Boston.

Across Freret Street, the campus discards unity for modernity; buildings dating from the 1920s to the 1940s are interspersed with others from the 1950s onward in a variety of styles. Among them are the Lavin Bernick Center, a conventionally modernist expansion of 2006 by Vincent James and Associates of Minneapolis, with Studio WTA as the local partner, of Curtis and Davis's University Center of 1959. Favrot and Reed's 1,900-seat MacAlister Auditorium (1940) is a Moderne version of the Roman Pantheon, with a saucer-shaped, self-supporting dome of reinforced concrete, 110 feet in diameter, and inscribed pilasters framing the triple-door entrance, representing a kind of classical portico rendered in shallow relief.

Also on the middle campus are a number of dormitories whose style reflects the prevailing architectural influences of their times. Among them are Koch and Wilson's delicate Paterson House of 1951 and the Phelps and Irby buildings (1954) designed by a consortium of local architects. The tallest of the dormitories, the twelve-story Monroe Hall (1963, Diboll-Kessels and Koch and Wilson, Architects) had a 2004 facade redesign by John P. Klingman. Scoggin Elam and Bray designed the Willow Street Residences (1999), using a variety of sun-shading devices. The glass-walled Wall Residential College of 2005 is from a schematic design by Davis Brody Bond, with Studio WTA as the architect of record.

Beyond these structures are the red brick buildings that make up the H. Sophie Newcomb Memorial College (**9.3**), the women's college affiliated with Tulane. Academically, the two colleges are now fully integrated, but Newcomb was established as a separate institution for women students.

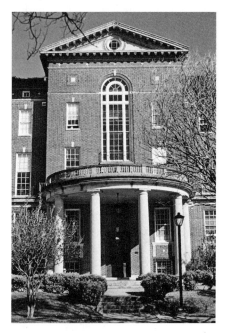

9.3   Newcomb College of Tulane University (H. Sophie
       Newcomb Memorial College)
       1917, James Gamble Rogers; later additions. 1229 Broadway

In 1886, Josephine Louise Newcomb donated $100,000 to establish a women's college in memory of her deceased daughter, Harriet Sophie Newcomb. The college was designated a coordinate college of Tulane University with its own president and administrative structure—the nation's first degree-granting coordinate college for females established within the framework of a university for males. It opened in 1887 with thirty students in a former mansion downtown but soon outgrew this space and transferred its 174 students to a larger Garden

District mansion. It was at this second location that the college earned national attention for the Newcomb Pottery (see **7.22**), a quasi-commercial venture fostered by the art program in which the students also produced metalwork, textiles, jewelry, and other handicrafts until 1940.

In 1918, Newcomb moved Uptown to a site adjacent to Tulane, into a new campus designed by Rogers, who had won the design competition in 1911. The competition program specified that the buildings be architecturally distinct from Tulane's and constructed of brick. According to the Board of Administrators' minutes of January 1912, Rogers's proposal pleased the judges because the design displayed "great dignity, memorial character, a style both American and Southern, and had the refinement, simplicity and charm fitting for a college for women in the South."

Newcomb's buildings form two open-ended courts, with Newcomb Hall, the academic and administrative building in the center, linking the quadrangles. Twelve buildings were planned, but only four were erected initially because of a lack of funds. All are built of a domestic-looking red brick with white trim and have small balconies and diffident classical details; for example, the shallow, four-columned Ionic pedimented portico of Newcomb Hall, although tall, is disproportionately small in relation to the size of the building. Although there is nothing bold or assertive about these structures (presumably the reason the judges thought the design sufficiently feminine), the ensemble is unified and harmonious. Emile Weil completed the buildings around the quadrangle, including Dixon Hall, in 1928. Subsequent buildings have followed Rogers's concept in scale and materials, while achieving a more contemporary appearance. Elleonora P. McWilliams Hall (1996, Waggonner and Ball Architects) is particularly successful, blending with the other buildings through its use of red brick. On its third story, a continuous band of windows under spreading eaves makes the building appear less weighty while giving it a contemporary look.

9.4 Audubon Place Entrance Lodge and Gates
1894, Thomas Sully. 6900 St. Charles Ave.

A rusticated Richardsonian Romanesque lodge and gates stand guard at the entrance to this private landscaped street, New Orleans's second residential park; Rosa Park, at the 5800 block of

St. Charles Avenue, was the first, in 1891. The project was developed by a St. Louis syndicate and modeled on similar successful ventures there and in northern cities. Surveyor George H. Grandjean drew up a plan in 1894 for 28 lots, each with a 100-foot frontage facing a landscaped neutral ground. The lots sold for about $5,000 each, and the minimum construction cost of a house was set at $7,000. The most unusual of the enormous houses on Audubon Place is the Flonacher residence (1926), designed by Weiss, Dreyfous and Seiferth, which is sited at the far end of the block and partially visible from Freret Street. The Spanish Colonial Revival house has a bright pink stucco exterior and is decorated with tiles from Spain. Audubon Place popularized exclusive landscaped residential streets in this area of Uptown and neighboring Carrollton, but it is the only one in the city where access is limited.

9.5   Tulane University President's House (William T. Jay House)

1907, Toledano and Wogan. 2 Audubon Pl. (6915 St. Charles Ave.)

Although the developers of Audubon Place stipulated that this house be oriented toward their street, owner William Jay, a cotton broker and vice president of the Union Lumber Company, preferred to face St. Charles Avenue. Thus, this square house was given two major entrances, ostentatious two-story Ionic porticoes with weighty entablatures and continuous balustrades that almost overwhelm the building as well as the viewer.

Both entrance doors have surrounds shaped like miniature temple fronts. To please the client, the St. Charles Avenue door led into the entrance vestibule, while behind the Audubon Place portico was a dining room. In 1917, Jay sold the house to Russian immigrant Samuel Zemurray of the United Fruit Company, who hired Edward F. Sporl to remodel the interior and enlarge the attic to accommodate a billiard room. The house is built of wood with veneering of dark brown pressed brick, originally left unpainted to contrast with the white trim but now a cream color. In 1965, the Zemurray family donated the house to Tulane for use as the president's residence. Since then the main floor interior has suffered from a series of unfortunate renovations.

9.6   Audubon Park

1898–1940s, Olmsted Brothers; later alterations. 6800 St. Charles Ave.

Established in 1886 on the site of the World's Industrial and Cotton Centennial Exposition of 1884, this major park was named in honor of naturalist and bird painter John James Audubon (1780–1851), who lived for a short time in New Orleans. Audubon Park now encompasses more than three hundred acres and stretches to the Mississippi River. The Exposition grounds were the former sugar plantation of Jean Etienne de Boré, who in 1795 developed a method for granulating sugar that could be employed on a commercial scale. Prior to the 1884 Exposition, the plantation had housed the occupying Union Army during the Civil War. The Exposition's most notable structure was Horticulture Hall, modeled on Joseph Paxton's Crystal

Palace in London of 1851, and destroyed by an early-twentieth-century hurricane.

Around the turn of the twentieth century, the Olmsted office was engaged to design the park. In an effort to give the flat site a luxuriant and southern picturesque effect, John Charles Olmsted, Frederick Law Olmsted's nephew and stepson, designed a scheme for the park that included lagoons, bridges, copses, and regional plants. The park's central section is now occupied by a refurbished "executive" golf course (replacing the original 1920s course), which restricts most public activities to the park's perimeter, where tree-lined paths attract strollers and skaters. It took many years to complete the park's landscaping; the lagoon at the St. Charles Avenue end was not finished until 1918. Two pairs of monumental stone pylons, designed by Moise Goldstein in 1921, mark the park's entrances on St. Charles Avenue. Isidore Konti (1862–1938) sculpted the attractive bronze Gumbel Fountain (1918) just inside this entrance. Emile Weil designed the oval Newman Memorial Bandstand in 1921. In 1924, the park gained an additional fifty acres following the closing of the Louisiana Sugar Experiment Station, built in 1890, and the zoo (**9.7**) was located here. In 1969, the forty-acre riverfront park, part of the original Olmsted plan, was created from landfill.

9.7   Audubon Zoo
1924; many later additions. 6500 Magazine St.

John Charles Olmsted's emphasis on using indigenous plants in his design for Audubon Park (**9.6**) heightened awareness of the beauty and unique qualities of southern Louisiana's plants and animals. Consequently, an exhibit on swamps opened here in 1913 and a flight cage for birds in 1916. These displays were followed in 1924 by Favrot and Livaudais's Odenheimer Aquarium, a circular brick structure linked to rectangular brick wings by Tuscan-columned pergolas, and a sea lion pool partially surrounded by a classical colonnade, designed by Samuel Stone Jr. The zoo officially opened in 1938, following the construction of several WPA-funded animal houses designed by Moise Goldstein beginning in 1934. These included a brick elephant house (1934) in the style of a French farmhouse, and a tropical-bird house (1936) decorated in 1939 with a low-relief sculpture of Noah's Ark by artists Hans Mangelsdorf and Alice

Fowler. Monkey Hill, New Orleans's only hill (twenty-eight feet high), is the by-product of a pile of mud left from a WPA lagoon-building project. After grass grew on the hill, it became a favorite play spot for children. In 1958, Curtis and Davis built a circular brick structure for giraffes, which now houses two camels. The zoo expanded from thirteen to fifty acres in 1978 (Cashio Cochran, landscape architects), employing what was, at the time, the innovative concept of displaying animals in settings that replicated their native habitats, and in 1980 the last cage was removed. Subsequently, the Louisiana Swamp Exhibit was added (Cashio Cochran Torre/Design Consortium), which won honors from the American Society of Landscape Architects in 1983. The zoo continues to update its facilities with periodic refurbishments but is prohibited from expanding its current boundaries.

9.8   Children's Hospital (U.S. Public Service [Marine] Hospital)

1830s and later; 1928 Main Building, James A. Wetmore, Supervising Architect of the U.S. Treasury; c. 1930 site plan, A. D. Taylor, landscape architect; 1931–1932; 2014–present, Eskew+Dumez+Ripple, with FKP Architects. Tchoupitoulas St. at Henry Clay Ave.

Surrounded by a c. 1895 high brick wall, this 17.2-acre site now occupied by the Children's Hospital has a long and illustrious history. Initially consisting of plantations, including that of Jean Etienne de Boré, the location later accommodated a sawmill and a brickworks. A cottage dating from the 1830s remains. In 1883, the land was sold to the U.S. government, which built a hospital, known as the Marine Hospital, to serve merchant seaman and local armed forces. The two-story galleried building known as the Director's House (c. 1885) belongs to this period. By the late 1920s, severe overcrowding in the existing buildings led to a construction campaign that resulted in a new hospital, the five-story Greek Revival brick Main Building, which features a monumental pedimented entrance portico and is crowned with an octagonal cupola (lit at night). In the early 1930s, landscape architect Albert D. Taylor of Ohio prepared a new site plan and the entire complex was substantially rebuilt with two-story red brick buildings that harmonized with the Main Building. The complex closed in 1981 and the federal government donated the buildings to the State of Louisiana, which used them as a psychiatric hospital for adolescents; the State closed the hospital in 2009 as a cost-saving measure. In 2014, Children's Hospital purchased the site, which is across Henry Clay from its existing facility. The Main Building will be used for office space and most of the support buildings constructed in the 1930s will be retained for the Childrens Hospital's administrative needs, including a conference center. The brick buildings are surrounded by ancient oak trees, which add to the beauty and tranquility of the site.

9.9 Greenville Hall of Loyola University (St. Mary's Dominican College)

1882, William Fitzner. 7214 St. Charles Ave.

St. Mary's, the first Catholic women's college in Louisiana, traces its roots to the arrival in 1860 of seven Dominican sisters from Cabra, Ireland, to run a girls' academy affiliated with St. John the Baptist Church (**7.29**). With increasing student enrollment and requests for boarding, the sisters purchased this site in 1865 and hired Fitzner to design a building accommodating classrooms, an administrative office, and a chapel. Thomas Mulligan constructed the building, which the *Times-Democrat* described in August 1882 as in the "style of a dwelling house," as were many women's schools and colleges in the nineteenth century. Constructed of cypress, the building is shaded by colonnaded galleries at the front and rear. A narrow gallery surrounding the central cupola provided a place for students to make astronomical observations. In this and other ways, the curriculum was advanced for its time; rhetoric, rarely taught to girls, was part of the course of study in the humanities and science, and a student literary journal was published from 1888 to 1900. In 1911, three ogee-shaped dormers were added to the third story, giving the building a Venetian flavor. St. Mary's was absorbed by Loyola University in 1984. The building is now used for administrative purposes. Adjoining Greenville Hall is Cabra Hall (1969, J. Buchanon Blitch), a dormitory with an exterior circulation gallery of arched openings, a modernist interpretation of the older building.

9.10 Historic Jefferson Parish Courthouse
1855, Henry Howard. 719 S. Carrollton Ave.

In 1855, when the town of Carrollton became the seat of Jefferson Parish, Henry Howard was hired to design the courthouse. Employing the classical temple formula then popular in America, he noted in his specifications for the building that the portico's four Ionic columns were to be based on those of the Erechtheum in Athens. However, the columns were made of brick and the bases and capitals of cast iron. The brick walls were plastered and scored to resemble masonry, and the joints were originally painted brown. A side entrance is pedimented, matched originally by side windows with pediment-shaped moldings. Frederick Wing and Robert Crozier were the builders. After Carrollton was annexed by New Orleans in 1874, the structure was remodeled for use as a public school, and this use continued, off and on, into the early twenty-first century. Vacant now for several years, the building was threatened with an uncertain future, but in 2017 it was sold at public auction to Houston developers who plan to redevelop it into senior citizen housing.

9.11 Salvatore and Maria D'Antoni House

1918, Edward F. Sporl. 7929 Freret St.

Salvatore D'Antoni, who operated a produce business, is said to have sent local architect Sporl to Chicago to see Frank Lloyd Wright's Prairie Style buildings. Their influence is evident in the house, which emphasizes horizontality with its low spreading forms, shallow-pitched roof, projecting sun-breaker cornice, and light-colored bands of stone trim. Although the front facade is symmetrical, the house conveys a picturesque aspect due to the chiaroscuro effects of multiple recessions and projections and an entrance so deeply set and heavily shaded within its porch that it seems to dissolve. The construction material—long, thin buff-colored bricks separated by wide, indented mortar bands—exaggerates the building's textural qualities and its horizontal lines. Decorative terra-cotta motifs along the cornice were inspired by the work of Louis Sullivan. The garage is a small-scale version of the main house.

9.12 Nathaniel Wilkinson House

1849–1850; 1995 addition, Trapolin Associates; René Fransen, landscape architect. 1015 S. Carrollton Ave.

English-born immigrant Nathaniel Newton Wilkinson was an exchange broker and commission merchant and an officer of the New Orleans Canal and Banking Company, which financed the Carrollton railroad and resort. He built this unusual Gothic Revival house, one of the earliest residences in Carrollton, as

a holiday home when this area was still a resort suburb. The cross-shaped, two-story brick residence resembles an English manor house in its construction materials, steeply pitched gable roofs, and such details as the Tudor-styled chimneys and diagonal-pane casement windows. These elements can be found in William Ranlett's Design III (plate 13), "The Entrance Front," in his book, *The Architect: A Series of Original Designs for Domestic and Ornamented Cottages and Villages* (1847), and it is likely that the unknown builder of Wilkinson's house, or Wilkinson himself, used this as a source. Among other similarities are a gallery supported on flattened pointed arches, a balcony with trefoil designs, bargeboards, and finials. In the nineteenth century, the exterior brick walls were stuccoed and scored. The medieval theme is carried through to the interior, with its Gothic-inspired moldings and medallions and a circular staircase in an octagonal hall. The wings of the house radiate from the hall to create rooms with windows on three sides, providing interior light and catching cool breezes. The house was originally surrounded by an eight-acre garden, now reduced to less than one acre, planted with exotic specimens that included imported tropical plants, giant bamboo, and palm trees. A 1995 wing is constructed of wood to distinguish it from the original building.

9.13 Streetcar Barn

1893. 8200 Willow St.

In 1892, the St. Charles Avenue streetcar tracks were extended along the neutral ground of S. Carrollton Avenue to a new

Streets and Neutral Grounds

As eighteenth-century plantations and land grants upriver
from the Vieux Carré were subdivided into residential lots in
the nineteenth century, wide streets often became boundaries
separating adjacent neighborhoods. These larger streets, such as
Canal, Washington, Napoleon, and Jefferson, extend from the
Mississippi River to the city's center like spokes of a wheel. The
spaces between the traffic lanes on these wide streets are called
neutral grounds (known as medians elsewhere) and range from
around a foot or so wide to over 100 feet.

By today's standards, urban conditions in New Orleans well
into the last decades of the nineteenth century were deplorable,
as in most American cities. Streets for the most part were un-
paved and appallingly bad, often with deep ruts, muck and mud,
stagnant water, open sewers, noxious wastes, household garbage,
and pestilence. This changed by the early twentieth century,
as streets were paved and as drainage technology advanced
(notably with the screw pump designed by engineer A. Baldwin

carbarn, where the Carrollton route of the New Orleans and
Carrollton Railroad would terminate with a loop through the
structure. The Berlin Iron Bridge Company of Berlin, Connecti-
cut, constructed the nine-track steel-framed carbarn (265 feet
by 128 feet), which has corrugated metal sides and a slate roof
supported on steel trusses. Adjacent buildings for storage, oil,
paint shops, and electric machinery were constructed of brick;
a few years later, a repair shed with seven tracks was built next
to the carbarn. In 1893, the railroad company converted to overhead electricity to power the streetcars, having the year before
built an electric powerhouse of brick designed by Thomas Sully
at Napoleon and Tchoupitoulas streets, to contain its boilers
and three Corliss compound steam engines. The new electric
cars, made by the St. Louis Car Company, were described in
1893 by the *Daily Picayune* as "elegantly made, and . . . furnished
inside with carved cherry wood with spring seats, and back of
woven bamboo. . . . The ceilings are of papier-maché, decorated

Wood; see **10.4**), allowing new neighborhoods to emerge in the city's center, the lowest point. Drainage canals were dug, with some submerged in the neutral grounds of major streets.

Early-twentieth-century interest in civic improvement and beautification led to street-tree plantings, with live oak (*Quercus virginiana*) being the tree of choice (see **6.15**). While their horizontal canopies give the city its characteristic year-round shady lushness, their lateral roots cause upheavals in sidewalks and exacerbate problems in streets.

Curiously, locals do not perceive neutral grounds and other linear green spaces as parts of a network of urban green infrastructure, and save for siting commemorative statues and playground equipment, city planners have generally ignored opportunities these linear spaces offer to connect neighborhoods, public facilities, and other public parks. With the success of the Lafitte Greenway (**2.6**) and increasing attention to adding bicycle lanes to city streets, this attitude is changing.

with conventional designs of brown and gold." The electrified line opened on February 1, 1893, to a performance of *The Trolley Polka*, a musical composition written for the occasion by Paul Tulane Wane. Soon dismissed were initial public fears that the electrical poles installed along the rail route would shock bystanders and that these much speedier streetcars would hit pedestrians. In 1923, the current streetcars, designed and built by the Perley A. Thomas Car Company of High Point, North Carolina, were introduced.

At 5600 Magazine Street, the Arabella streetcar barn of 1893, which began as the Mechanical Exhibits Building at the 1884 World's Fair in Audubon Park, was converted into a barn for buses when they replaced the Magazine Street streetcars. In 2001 it was acquired by a supermarket and renovated for its new use. The rear half of the structure maintains its original appearance and vehicular use. Another former streetcar barn stands at 100 Poland Avenue in the Bywater neighborhood.

9.14 Sewerage and Water Board of New Orleans
1903 begun, James Wadsworth Armstrong. 8700–9300 S. Claiborne Ave.

In 1899, two years after the city was quarantined during a yellow fever epidemic, voters passed a bond issue to finance and build a sewerage and drainage system and waterworks for the city. Construction began in 1903 to designs by Armstrong (1868–1953), who had studied engineering and architecture at the University of Illinois. The system began operating in 1907 in several parts of the city. Armstrong designed nine pumping stations and two large water-purification plants and established the exterior appearance and style of the buildings that house the pumps, boilers, and administrative offices, which the Water Board has followed in all new construction. The Water Board wanted buildings with a distinctive look, which the design achieved: red tile roofs with deep eaves, brick walls stuccoed in a cream color, and red terra-cotta outlining the round-arched openings. According to the waterworks superintendent, projecting eaves were ideal for the New Orleans climate, shading walls and saving the expense of gutters and downspouts. The buildings convey a clean, crisp image for the Water Board and were economical to construct. Engine floors in the power-houses were built well above ground level, which reduced the amount of excavation necessary for the foundations and kept the machinery above the water table. The old filter gallery, twenty-eight filters in an open water tank subdivided into 8 × 8–foot-square units and surrounded by an arcade like a medieval cloister, reinforces the Mediterranean appearance of the buildings. By 1909, New Orleans had a water-purification system, and Armstrong completed his work the following year. The Mississippi River is the source of water for New Orleans, which uses approximately 135 million gallons each day. City water is treated at this plant for east-bank residents and at another plant in Algiers, on Elmira Avenue, for west-bank residents.

Mid-City

Mid-City extends from Tremé and the Central Business District in a northwest direction toward the Metairie Ridge. Although the higher ground along the Metairie Ridge had been acquired for cemeteries as early as the mid-nineteenth century, the area's development came in the twentieth century after the New Orleans Drainage Commission's powerful new steam-powered pumps drained this below-sea-level swamp. Nevertheless, the levee breaks following Hurricane Katrina flooded the area with up to six feet of water; the area has largely recovered. Light industries and commercial companies chose to locate in Mid-City adjacent to the railroad corridor that runs through the area. Mid-City also provided land for the new institutional, educational, and medical buildings needed for a growing city. Before Interstate-10 was brought through Mid-City, Tulane Avenue (U.S. 61) was the principal automobile

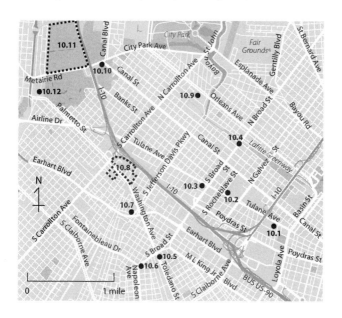

route into New Orleans from the west, but only a couple of the mid-twentieth-century motels and other traveler-related buildings survive along this formerly bustling avenue. Residential buildings in Mid-City consist primarily of shotgun houses, bungalows, and modest two-story houses.

10.1 Charity Hospital

1937–1939, Weiss, Dreyfous and Seiferth. 1532 Tulane Ave.

Until 2005, Charity Hospital was the architectural centerpiece of the city's largest medical complex, but damaged in Hurricane Katrina and then boarded up and abandoned, the building's future is uncertain. Charity's origins date to 1736, when a French sailor donated funds for a hospital for the indigent, L'Hôpital des Pauvres de la Charité. The hospital moved to this site in 1833, and a year later the Sisters of Charity arrived to nurse the sick. In 1893, they established a School for Nurses (now Delgado Community College Charity School of Nursing), one of the first in the nation. Beginning in 1928, Charity saw an infusion of money for a massive building program, first from spending promoted by Governor Huey P. Long and then federal funds. New structures were built for the Louisiana State University Medical Center School (1932; 2011 demolished) and, in 1939, a fifteen-story School of Nursing, ambulance garage, laundry, power plant, and Charity Hospital.

Governor Long's favored architecture firm, Weiss, Dreyfous

and Seiferth, designed the buildings, giving them all a similar external appearance. The twenty-story Charity Hospital, along with the nursing and medical schools, were designed like contemporary New York City skyscrapers, emphasizing verticality, with setbacks at the upper floors and carved stone Art Deco reliefs adorning the summits and entrance doors. At Charity, Enrique Alferez's decorative aluminum screen over the main entrance depicts Louisianians at work and play. The design incorporates two ducks—the sculptor's satirical reference ("de ducks were flying") to Huey Long's government, in which "deducts" from workers' pay for Long's "charitable" activities were commonplace. Identical low buildings and a forecourt form the entrance to the hospital from the street. A steel-framed building sheathed with Alabama limestone, the hospital is roughly M-shaped, organized to create projecting wings and courtyards that provide ventilation and give the interior natural light. The hospital formerly had separate facilities for African American and white patients in the east and west wings, but services were later integrated. With a capacity of 2,680 beds, Charity was the second largest hospital in the nation when it opened. The medical center buildings had some of the most modern facilities of the time and were widely published in both architecture and medical journals. The building is now vacant awaiting an adaptive reuse.

10.2 Veterans Affairs Medical Center Research Center (Dixie Brewery)

1907, Louis Lehle and Sons, with Julius Koch; 2017 renovated, Eskew+Dumez+Ripple. 2401 Tulane Ave.

With fifty breweries in 1850, New Orleans was known as the "brewing capital of the South." Prohibition in 1920 officially brought the industry to a close and most of the buildings were later demolished. Some that have survived and found new use are the Jackson (Jax) Brewery in the Vieux Carré, converted into a commercial mall in the 1980s; Weckerling Brewery, which now houses the National World War II Museum (**6.29**); and the six-story Falstaff Brewery (2600 Gravier Street), closed in 1978 and converted to apartments in 2013 by HMS Architects. Dixie Brewery, designed by a Chicago firm for Valentine Merz, the company's president, occupied a six-story, steel-framed building of red brick trimmed with white stone. A diminutive

corner turret and a tall, silver-painted mansard dome made it an area landmark. Two cylindrical storage tanks on the roof held the rice used in the brewing process, and both tanks were painted to resemble Dixie beer cans. Apart from the giant cans, Dixie had an institutional rather than an industrial appearance and it fit in well with Tulane Avenue's other buildings. During Prohibition, the brewery manufactured ice and ice cream. Emile Weil designed a four-story extension in 1919. The building was flooded following Hurricane Katrina. Subsequently, the brewery became part of the massive post-Katrina medical center redevelopment project (see **5.13**) and renovated as a research center.

10.3   Criminal Courts Building
1929–1931, Diboll and Owen. 2700 Tulane Ave.

Architect Allison Owen stated that his design for the Criminal Courts Building represented two characteristics of the law: "elegance reflected in the classical colonnade and severity reflected in . . . modern buttresses." The result does suggest that two eras have collided: a massive twelve-columned classical temple book-ended between doubled pavilions (Owen's "buttresses") of Egyptian shape and proportions and with Art Deco ornament. The building is faced with limestone and adorned with bronzed cast-iron panels between the windows that depict scenes from local history, stylized pelicans (Louisiana's state bird) in relief, and anthemia carved near the summit of the pavilions, all designed by New Orleans artist Angela Gregory (1903–1990). The courthouse entrance, at the center of the long side, is reached by way of a tall flight of granite steps passing through the colonnade. From a small marble lobby, stairs lead up to the great marble hall that extends the length of the building and gives access to seven two-story-high courtrooms. Architect Owen likened the great barrel-vaulted hall to the early-seventeenth-century Salle des Pas Perdus of the Palais de Justice in Paris; although the details differ, the overall appearance and effect are similar. Huge Art Deco chandeliers of bronze and opalescent glass illuminate the walls of veined black and cream-colored marble and the dusky pink marble floor. The hall's epic scale and luxuriant materials, as well as the noise that rebounds from the hard surfaces, are more than enough to awe both defendants and lawyers. District Attorney Jim Garrison's prosecution of Clay Shaw, who was accused and acquitted in connection with the assassination of President John F. Kennedy (a unanimous verdict took just fifty-four minutes), took place here in 1969.

10.4 Pumping Station No. 2

1899, Benjamin Morgan Harrod. N. Broad St. at St. Louis St.

The problem of flooding after heavy rains, a common occurrence in New Orleans, was solved by Albert Baldwin Wood's invention of a heavy-duty pump that could raise great quantities of water and deposit it elsewhere. Today, there are 22 pumping stations and 13 underpass stations in greater New Orleans, with 90 miles of open canals and 90 miles of subsurface canals to carry and release surplus water into lakes Pontchartrain and Borgne. The system is capable of pumping 1.5 inches of rainwater in two hours. This pumping station, located on the neutral ground of N. Broad Street over the drainage canal, was the first in a series of brick stations whose rectangular shape and walls articulated with pilasters are evocative of classical temples. The station's tall, narrow windows with keystones are covered by dark green iron shutters; rosettes decorate the entablature, and a ventilator runs along the ridge of the hipped roof. On one side, huge drainage pipes, painted green, emerge from the station's lower wall and disappear underground. The station has recently been enlarged with a sympathetic extension.

Similarly designed pumping stations are located at the junction of S. Broad Avenue and Martin Luther King Jr. Boulevard (doubled in size in 2000) and at Marconi Boulevard near Zachary Taylor Drive. Albert Baldwin Wood (1879–1956) continued to develop more efficient and powerful pumps throughout his life—notably, in 1913, the Wood screw pump, twelve feet in diameter, which was later used to drain the Zuider Zee in the Netherlands. By 1929, he had designed a pump fourteen feet in diameter; four of these were installed in the Metairie Pumping Station (Jefferson Parish) in the Metairie Relief Outfall at 17th Street. Benjamin Harrod (1837–1912), the station's designer, also was the architect for many of New Orleans's neighborhood fire stations.

10.5 Rhodes Pavilion (Rhodes Funeral Home, Tivoli Theater)

1927, Emile Weil; 1970 alterations; 2009 restored. 3933 Washington Ave.

In the late nineteenth century African American Duplain W. Rhodes established a funeral home to serve the city's African Americans. The business expanded in the twentieth century with several locations in New Orleans, and in 1969 acquired this theater that had recently closed. The building's most distinctive feature is a tall terra-cotta frieze framed by rondels that spans the central portion of the facade between two tall towerlike end wings. The low-relief frieze depicts a celebration, with dancing figures perhaps related to the Greek muses; its aesthetic source is the frieze around the Parthenon in Athens. Originally, two Doric columns visually supported the frieze, adding to the classical mood. When the theater was converted to a funeral home, the most monumental of Rhodes's locations, the interior was adapted to accommodate a chapel and a large parlor. The central recessed portion of the facade has been altered and the entire building is now painted white. In this low-lying area of the city, the building was flooded by about eight feet of water following Hurricane Katrina. Now restored, it is a multipurpose facility, available for such functions as weddings, meetings, and funerals.

10.6   Rosa F. Keller Library and Community Center
1917; 1993 addition; 2012 addition, Eskew+Dumez+Ripple.
4300 S. Broad Ave.

In 1993, the City of New Orleans acquired this 1917 Craftsman house, adapted it for use as a branch library for the Broadmoor neighborhood, and built an addition that was used as a reading room. The library, which was named for civil rights pioneer Rosa Freeman Keller, was flooded during Hurricane Katrina. Subsequently, the house was rehabilitated to serve as a community center, and a new 6,300-square-foot structure, funded by the Federal Emergency Management Agency (FEMA) recovery program, now accommodates the library, with the two buildings connected by an enclosed glass hallway. Landscaping includes a tree-lined plaza behind the building and a grassy field for children to play. Stormwater management is dramatized in the project, reflecting the recognition of its importance after Katrina in this low-lying area.

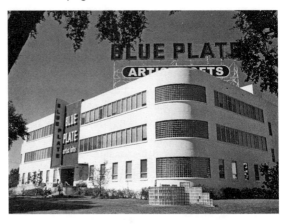

10.7 Blue Plate Artists Lofts (Blue Plate Fine Foods)
1942–1943, August Perez Jr.; 2012 rehabilitated, HRI and Woodward Design+Build. 1315 S. Jefferson Davis Pkwy.

The Blue Plate Fine Foods building was August Perez Jr.'s first major commission in New Orleans and one of the city's earliest modernist buildings. Blue Plate was named after Blue Willow chinaware, renowned for its quality, because the company liked the upscale image it conveyed, and a sign by the entrance door reproduces the Blue Willow pattern. The manufacturing process for the company's products, including mayonnaise and other sauces, determined the layout of the plant's three floors. Walls of poured concrete are reinforced with rail ties, a substitution due to a war-related scarcity of materials when the building was being constructed. The smooth white stucco-covered exterior, streamlined rounded corners, and horizontal bands of glass-block windows have a hygienic and wholesome look. An enormous blue neon sign on the roof, identifying the factory, has been amended to indicate that the building now houses artists' lofts, with the wording of the sign beside the entrance now slightly altered to reflect the building's current use. The rear of the building was near the tracks to facilitate loading the company's products. The front was set back seventy-five feet from the street to allow for a lawn and landscaping—an early instance of preserving open space on an industrial building site. In 2012 the factory was converted into apartments.

10.8 Xavier University of Louisiana
1932–present. 2 Drexel Dr.

In 1891, Katharine Drexel, the daughter of Philadelphia financier-banker Francis Drexel, founded the Sisters of the Blessed Sacrament, an order dedicated to educational and charitable work among America's minorities. St. Katharine (she was canonized in 2000) established a high school in 1915, naming it for the Spanish Jesuit missionary St. Francis Xavier, and in 1917 added a two-year normal school for training black teachers. Xavier became a four-year liberal arts university in 1925 and opened a college of pharmacy in 1927. Xavier is the only historically black Catholic university in the United States. First located at 5100 Magazine Street, a site now occupied by Xavier Preparatory High School for girls, the university moved to this location in 1932. Wogan and Bernard designed the Indiana limestone administration building with its two wings, one a science building and the other a convent for the sisters, in the Gothic style of many collegiate structures. A library (now the music building) was added in 1937.

Expansion in the 1960s added more buildings, and in the 1990s the enormous success and growth of Xavier's pharmacy and premedical programs generated further growth. Xavier now comprises multiple buildings in a multiblock area. On an unprepossessing site adjacent to a freeway overpass and a drainage canal, the campus has also grown vertically, with buildings in expressive forms and colorful materials that meet the challenge of its fragmented setting. The six-story Library and Resource Center of 1996, by Blitch Knevel Architects and

Billes/Manning Architects, was joined in 1998 by the Norman C. Francis Science Academic Complex, named for the university's recently retired president and designed by Sizeler Architects. The latter structure, a sharp-angled composition with tower, bay windows, pinnacled piers, prowlike corner, and pointed-arched entrances, has a castlelike quality that fits in with the original Collegiate Gothic building. It also features a dramatic atrium space with a projecting sculptural stair. All the new buildings have green-colored roofs, Xavier's modern signature.

A 2012 addition to the campus is Pelli Clarke Pelli's St. Katharine Drexel Chapel, a striking modern design. The octagonal chapel of cream-colored limestone has a funnel-like copper roof outlined with a band of windows that throw light down through its perforated interior surface to create an effect rather like the starry sky. Colored windows have stylized imagery and abstract patterns. A separate bell tower stands beside the walkway to the entrance.

10.9   American Can Company Apartments (American Can Company)

1906–1907, 1922 addition, Favrot and Livaudais; 2002 converted to apartments, HRI. 3700 Orleans Ave.

Favrot and Livaudais's 1922 extension to the former American Can Company, which made cans for coffee, molasses, and beer, matched their original design of 1906. The four-story factory, clearly expresses its steel frame on the exterior in the manner of Albert Kahn's early-twentieth-century industrial buildings for the automobile industry in Detroit. Like Kahn's designs, the exterior is aesthetically enriched with bands of red brick marking each floor and is lightly dotted with geometric ornamentation in brick. The factory closed in 1988 and, after standing empty for some years, was converted into apartments.

10.10 Cypress Grove Cemetery Gate and Lodge
1840, Frederick Wilkinson. 120 City Park Ave.

Established by the Firemen's Charitable Association, Cypress Grove Cemetery is located on a ridge four miles from the city center. Although graves here could be sunk six feet without reaching groundwater, the preference for above-ground tombs found elsewhere in the city persisted. The cemetery, laid out with a twenty-eight-foot-wide central avenue flanked by narrower aisles, has a monumental Egyptian Revival entrance gate, suggesting a triumphal passage from one world to the next. The stuccoed brick gate was originally topped by a lintel, making it similar in appearance to the Egyptian Revival gate at Mount Auburn Cemetery (1831) in Cambridge, Massachusetts. (Wilkinson came to New Orleans from the northeastern United States, so it is likely that he was familiar with Mount Auburn.) Two pavilions flank the gate, one a porter's lodge and the other the so-called "dead house." On a practical level, gates and gatehouses were essential for cemetery security in the nineteenth century, because grave robbery was a problem until the medical profession was able to obtain cadavers legally. One of the cemetery's finest tombs, adapted from a design in Père Lachaise Cemetery in Paris, is J. N. B. de Pouilly's monument for fireman Irad Ferry (1841), composed of a large broken column, symbolizing the extinction of life, rising from a sarcophagus-shaped marble tomb. Across the road, at 5242 Canal Boulevard, is Greenwood Cemetery, established in 1852 by the Firemen's Charitable Association, which has a cluster of magnificent tombs near its entrance. The tomb for the Benevolent Protective Order of Elks, Lodge No. 30, is a marble chamber covered by a grassy mound and surmounted by a bronze elk. The tomb is lopsided; its pedimented granite entrance with Doric columns tilts perilously forward, sinking into the soft ground because the engineer failed to include a pile foundation.

10.11 Metairie Cemetery

1872, Benjamin F. Harrod. Pontchartrain Blvd, near Metairie Rd.

In 1872, the Metairie Cemetery Association purchased the then-just-closed Metairie Course racetrack (established 1838) and converted it into a sixty-five-acre landscaped burial ground. The elliptical track formed the basis of the plan, and three smaller ellipses were laid out within it to serve as paths. Cross avenues and diagonals creating circles and triangles, live oak trees festooned with Spanish moss, and, originally, a series of lagoons created a picturesque garden of the dead in the manner of the influential Père Lachaise Cemetery in Paris. Tombs at Metairie are more spaciously laid out than in other New Orleans cemeteries and constitute some of the most spectacular and grandiose funerary architecture in the United States. They include Greek temples, Gothic extravaganzas, Islamic pavilions, a Celtic cross, and tombs embellished with stained glass windows, broken columns, and allegorical figures. The early-twentieth-century tomb of Lucien Brunswig, designed by the Weiblen Marble Company, features a pyramid, sphinx, and female figure gesturing toward the bronze door. Metairie Cemetery merged with Lake Lawn Cemetery in the 1970s; Lake Lawn's mausoleum dates to 1949.

10.12 Longue Vue House and Gardens

1939–1942 house, William and Geoffrey Platt; 1935–1939 gardens, Ellen Biddle Shipman; 1960s gardens, William Platt; 1999 Discovery Garden, Cashio Cochran Torre/Design Consortium. 7 Bamboo Rd.

Longue Vue is a re-creation of the past, a house in the classical style, built for cotton broker, banker, and philanthropist Edgar Bloom Stern and his wife, Edith Rosenwald Stern, an heir to the Sears, Roebuck fortune. It replaced another house (moved to a nearby site) after the Sterns purchased additional land and found that the eight acres of gardens designed for them by Ellen Biddle Shipman had "left the house behind," as Edith Stern put it. On Shipman's recommendation, the Sterns hired noted New

York architects William and Geoffrey Platt, sons of architect Charles A. Platt, to design a new house.

The house, like Shipman's gardens, is a carefully conceived example of nostalgic revivalism that also embraced modern structural methods and such amenities as air-conditioning and recessed lighting. Longue Vue has a Portland cement exterior over a steel frame and concrete block walls. Its two principal facades are set at 90-degree angles to each other to allow for the best views to and from the gardens. One facade, similar to that of the Beauregard-Keyes House (**1.28**) in the Vieux Carré, has a second-story portico accessed from curving exterior stairs. Flanking dependencies are linked by colonnades, which form a five-part composition in the Palladian manner.

Inside, the architects provided a circular staircase, an element that was used in some of Louisiana's grandest nineteenth-century houses, but here lit by a glass dome. The Platts designed the rooms in eighteenth- and nineteenth-century styles, incorporating original pieces, such as mantels, purchased in Europe. In contrast, the bathrooms are Moderne, Edith Stern's in powder blue tile and glass block and Edgar Stern's a dramatic Art Deco composition of Vermont black marble, black ceramic fixtures, and black-and-white marbleized wallpaper. In 1942 Longue Vue installed a central air system, the first house in the New Orleans area to do so.

For Longue Vue's eight acres of gardens, Shipman, landscape designer for such wealthy clients as the Du Ponts, Fords, and Astors, created garden "rooms" and plantings based on different themes. These included the Wild Garden, with plants indigenous to the Gulf South (Louisiana plantswoman Caroline Dorman was the consultant) and a brick *pigeonnier* modeled on a nineteenth-century structure at Uncle Sam plantation (demolished); the rose-filled Walled Garden; and a garden planted with yellow blooming plants. William Platt redesigned some areas in the late 1960s after they were damaged by Hurricane Betsy, including the Spanish Court, inspired by the Sterns' recent visit to the Generalife Gardens at the Alhambra in Granada, Spain. In 1999, a half-acre children's Discovery Garden was added by Cashio Cochran Torre/Design Consortium, replacing the cutting garden. It has since been renovated.

Hurricane Katrina left brackish water standing in the gardens for weeks and many plants subsequently died; there were also heavy losses to surrounding trees. Significant resources came from garden enthusiasts all over America to restore the garden, directed by Patricia O'Donnell, landscape architect, who had earlier renovated the Wild Garden. Today, the gardens have returned to a new version of their past glory.

At Longue Vue, the Platt brothers created a modern house that draws on historical precedent and aesthetics, and one that represents a rare blend of fashionable northeastern taste with southern atmosphere. The Sterns bequeathed Longue Vue for use as a museum of decorative arts and garden design, which opened to the public in 1968.

Lakefront

The ranch-style houses that characterize many of the twentieth-century suburbs on the Lake Pontchartrain side of New Orleans are typical of those in residential neighborhoods throughout the United States. The oldest remnants of this area's history are the fragments of the walls of the Spanish Fort, built in 1779 on the left bank of Bayou St. John where it entered Lake Pontchartrain (now Beauregard Avenue and Jay Street). For much of the nineteenth century a lakefront hotel and a pleasure garden were located here. In 1831, the New Orleans and Lake Pontchartrain Railroad, the nation's first interurban line, began to transport pleasure-seekers from the city to the hotels and restaurants along the shores of the lake. Also here are the 1855 Milneburg Lighthouse (**11.4**) and the frame New Canal Lighthouse (1890; rebuilt in 2013) at the lake end of West End Boulevard.

Suburban growth in this area began after Canal Boulevard was extended toward the lake between City Park and the New Basin Canal (now beneath West End and Pontchartrian boulevards). The neighborhood known as Lakeview was the first to develop on newly drained land. Architect H. Jordan MacKenzie built his house here at 6339 West End Boulevard in 1908–1909; the house is recognizable by its steep blue roof with a clipped gable front.

At the lake's edge the Orleans Levee Board began an extensive landfill project in 1926 (completed in 1929), pumping sand from the lake to create over 2,000 new acres along its southern shore for residential subdivisions and building a stepped seawall about eight feet above sea level along with beachfront public parks. The entire area on the lakeside of Leon C. Simon Drive and Robert E. Lee Boulevard, now residential neighborhoods, is landfill. Much of this land was given over to military installations during World War II. In 1956, the University of New Orleans (formerly Louisiana State University in New Orleans) held classes in some of these buildings until its new campus was begun in 1961. Curtis and Davis prepared a master plan and, along with several other New Orleans firms, designed the buildings.

The residential subdivisions were named for their location: Lake Vista (1936; **11.2**), West Lakeshore (1951), East Lakeshore (1955), Lake Terrace (1953), and Lake Oaks (1964). These neighborhoods were intended for middle- to upper-income white residents and the houses were individually designed. Among the noteworthy modernist houses in West Lakeshore are the Ricciuti House (1957; 7341 Beryl Street) by Ricciuti Associates, and the Valle House (1956; 423 Topaz Street) by John Rock. Lee Ledbetter and Associates designed the two-story house at 1324 Oriole Street (2003), a large structure of geometric intersecting volumes providing sufficient wall surfaces for the original owner's art collection. A levee breach of the 17th Street Canal beside West Lakeshore in the wake of Hurricane Katrina submerged much of that neighborhood and Lakeview and many houses have been replaced. Lakefront Airport (formerly Shushan Airport; **11.5**) was completed in 1934 on a separate landfill east of the Industrial Canal (**3.14**).

Just north of these subdivisions is an open space (also commonly known as the Lakefront) defined mainly by Lakeshore Drive that runs west from West End Park to the Industrial Canal between the subdivisions and Lake Pontchartrain. Between this meandering drive (roughly five miles in length that generally follows the southern edge of Lake Pontchartrain, defined by the concrete, stepped seawall from the 1930s) and the levee adjacent to the lakefront neighborhoods is a scenic lakefront linear green space popular throughout the year among locals but few tourists. The space is largely unprogrammed and has minimal amenities—a few shelters, paving and benches, picnic tables, plantings, the "Mardi Gras Fountain"—that have been added over time by different local designers and engineers.

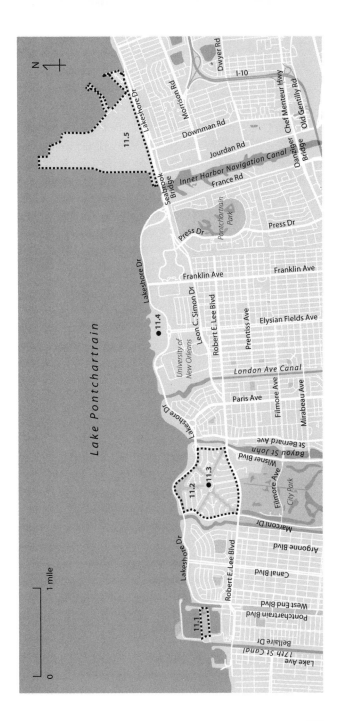

Lake Pontchartrain

1 mile

0

N

Lakeshore Dr
Morrison Rd
Dwyer Rd
I-10
Chef Menteur Hwy
Old Gentilly Rd
Danziger Bridge
Downman Rd
Jourdan Rd
Inner Harbor Navigation Canal
Seabrook Bridge
France Rd
Press Dr
Pontchartrain Park
Press Dr
Lakeshore Dr
Franklin Ave
Franklin Ave
University of New Orleans
Leon C. Simon Dr
Robert E. Lee Blvd
Prentiss Ave
Elysian Fields Ave
London Ave Canal
Lakeshore Dr
Paris Ave
Filmore Ave
Mirabeau Ave
St Bernard Ave
Bayou St John
Wisner Blvd
Filmore Ave
City Park
Marconi Dr
Lakeshore Dr
Robert E. Lee Blvd
Argonne Blvd
Canal Blvd
West End Blvd
Pontchartrain Blvd
Lake Ave
17th St Canal
Bellaire Dr

11.5
11.4
11.3
11.2
11.1

Water-related Green Spaces

Grass-covered levees and other water-related green spaces throughout New Orleans are primarily the result of infrastructure improvements, unintended and under-appreciated consequences that define the city's urban character.

The first Mississippi River levees, constructed by Bienville's military engineer in the eighteenth century, were two to three feet high. Later, a municipal ordinance set the minimum height at one foot above high-water levels, and by 1812 the levees along the Mississippi River extended upriver more than 150 miles on the east bank and more than 180 miles on the west bank.

Levees, sometimes planted with orange trees, were places from which residents viewed river activities in the late afternoon, and social spaces for promenading and romantic liaisons. An extensive account of such arrangements between European or white men and the mothers of Creole young ladies comes from Irish journalist Thomas Ashe, who described these spaces in 1806 as the "principal market for all this traffic *de coeur*."

There are several locations in the city to experience walking along linear greenspaces similar to the nineteenth-century walks adjacent to water. The newest are the Crescent Park (**3.11**) and the Lafitte Greenway (**2.6**), which roughly follows the pathway of Carondelet Walk that was adjacent to the Carondelet Canal, now gone. A similar setting is on the banks of Bayou St. John. Perhaps

11.1   West End Park
Early 20th century. Bounded by W., N., and S. Roadway sts.

West End Park is a city-owned open space near the private amusement and music venues that sprang up on the southern shore of Lake Pontchartrain at the termini of late-nineteenth-century rail lines. Such open spaces, often associated with increasingly popular rail lines (the St. Charles Avenue streetcar line and "Smokey Mary" to Lake Pontchartrain) or other transportation routes (Carondelet Walk along the Carondelet

the most obvious opportunity is the Moonwalk (**1.8**), opposite
Jackson Square, which now stretches downriver (an extension
is planned to connect with Crescent Park) and upriver to Canal
Street and Spanish Plaza (**5.3**).

In the lakefront area, a concrete bulkhead that steps down
into Lake Pontchartrain's southern shore defines about five
miles of linear green space. This park was created beginning in
the 1930s as the Orleans Parish Levee Board built subdivisions
(such as Lake Vista [**11.2**]) on landfill north of the lake's original
shoreline (roughly the present Robert E. Lee Boulevard).

From the 1830s onward, the lakefront was a venue for rec-
reation, with early jazz music halls, nightclubs, and restaurants.
Notable developments here were West End, West End Park (**11.1**),
Spanish Fort, Milneburg, and, in the mid-twentieth century,
Pontchartrain Beach (for whites) and Lincoln Beach (for blacks).
"Smokey Mary," a train that ran along the New Basin Canal,
provided public access from downtown. Many of the lakefront
venues have since closed or been blown away by hurricanes.
There are a few new restaurants, but this prime area is no longer
the popular venue for food, nightlife, and entertainment it once
was. The open spaces along the lake, however, remain busy,
particularly on evenings and weekends.

Canal; Bayou St. John), are late-nineteenth-century versions of
the "pleasure gardens" that populated the city from the early
nineteenth-century. This open-space typology has remained
obscure not only in New Orleans but elsewhere in America;
recent scholarship suggests there were nearly twenty such examples throughout New Orleans that offered varying degrees
of musical entertainment, spectacle (such as balloon ascensions
and demonstrations of early photography), food and drink
(often associated with cultural identity), sport (including com-

petitive and solo games), and political activities, with varying degrees of public accommodation. These privately owned, quasi-public spaces, accessible via a small admission fee, were available to the general public. By the beginning of the twentieth century, with the rise of amusement venues on Lake Pontchartrain and larger public parks elsewhere in the city, pleasure gardens had disappeared, victims of changing tastes, increasing options for entertainment elsewhere in the community, and the commercial pressures of the real-estate marketplace. Today, the park is an open green space, dotted with oak trees, a lagoon, and a central fountain, and surrounded by the marina, boats, and boathouses. The wooden three-stage New Canal Lighthouse of 1890, destroyed by Hurricane Katrina and rebuilt in 2013, can be seen from the north end of N. Roadway Street.

11.2 Lake Vista Development

1936, Hampton Reynolds. Bounded by Robert E. Lee and Marconi blvds., Beauregard Ave., and Lakeshore Dr.

Planned and implemented by the Orleans Levee Board, the 404-acre Lake Vista development was the first of the lakefront's residential neighborhoods to be built on the reclaimed land. The consulting engineer, Hampton Reynolds, a member of the New Orleans city planning board and father-in-law of Louisiana's then-governor, Richard W. Leche, based Lake Vista on such garden city schemes as Radburn, New Jersey (1928). Lake Vista was laid out with streets that terminate in culs-de-sac and curving, landscaped pedestrian lanes, accommodating more than 800 individually designed dwelling units (including a few low-rise apartment buildings) on variably sized lots. Covenants restricting the development to white ownership and to low housing density were written into the articles of incorporation, as elsewhere (Gentilly, for example) in twentieth-century suburban developments.

The first residents arrived in 1939, but most of the houses were built after World War II. At the heart of the development, and within walking distance for all residents, was the Lake Vista Community Shopping Center, on Spanish Fort Boulevard. Built in 1946 by Wogan and Bernard and August Perez Jr. Associate Architects, this smooth-curved building has horizontal lines that are emphasized by a continuous canopy shading the shopfronts. The stores did not prosper; by the time they

opened, shoppers favored larger retail centers, and the spaces are now used by service businesses rather than retail. Behind the shopping center are a school and two churches. St. Pius X School (1953–1954, Burk, Le Breton and Lamantia) initially served as both a school and a church until the completion of St. Pius X Church (**11.3**). August Perez and Associates designed the elliptical Lake Vista United Methodist Church (1961), which has lacelike, aluminum-screened glass walls creating an interior of mottled sunlight, and a folded-plate roof. Several houses are significant examples of modernist design, notably Lawrence and Saunders's Shalett House (1955) at 15 Tern Street; Lawrence, Saunders and Calongne's widely published Mossy House (1956) at 28 Tern; and the Higgins House (1949) by Sporl and Maxwell at 30 Tern, which is constructed of Thermo-Con, a cellular concrete building material developed by Andrew Higgins, the designer and manufacturer of landing craft used in World War II (see **6.29**). Unfortunately, new (and old) residents in Lake Vista, particularly post–Hurricane Katrina, are razing houses dating from the 1950s and 1960s in order to build enormous homes, many in neohistoric styles that are profoundly insensitive to the scale and character of the community.

11.3 St. Pius X Church

1964–1966, James Lamantia Jr. for Burk, Le Breton and Lamantia; 2013 addition, Eskew+Dumez+Ripple. 6666 Spanish Fort Blvd.

Sheltered by an enormous copper roof that sweeps down almost to ground level, St. Piux X is a powerful expression of the

liturgical changes effected by Vatican II. The plan is octagonal in shape, with the altar at the center, reflecting the shift from the traditional axial organization to a nondirectional, unified space. Light fills the interior, from the bands of colored glass separating the roof from the low walls below it to the golden and green stained glass window on the north face of the central tower, which focuses light directly onto the altar. The roof, supported on steel trusses, has a complex folded shape that is suggestive of an origami figure. New Orleans architect James Lamantia Jr. (1923–2011) created a bold design, but one whose size, scale, and concept fit harmoniously within Lake Vista. A small chapel added beside the church in 2013 acknowledges the geometry of the church without attempting to imitate it, though perhaps its white exterior is a little too forceful.

11.4   Milneburg Lighthouse (Port Pontchartrain Lighthouse)
1855. Lakeside of Lakeshore Dr. at the terminus of Elysian Fields Ave.

One of a series of federal lighthouses erected around Lake Pontchartrain from the Rigolets to Madisonville, this 56-foot-high, hourglass-shaped brick tower was stranded inland when the Orleans Levee Board completed the landfill project along the lakeshore in 1929. A concrete levee wall now forms a backdrop to the lighthouse. It was named for Milneburg, the former lakefront resort at this location, which was developed by Scotsman Andrew Milne in 1831. Near the lighthouse are buildings housing the Navy Information Technology Center (1999) in the Research and Technology Park of the University of New Orleans, designed by Perez Ernst Farnet, Architects and Planners.

11.5　Lakefront Airport (Shushan Airport)

1932–1934, Weiss, Dreyfous and Seiferth; 2013 restored, Alton Ochsner Davis. 6001 Stars and Stripes Blvd.

Planned to accommodate seaplanes as well as land-based craft, Lakefront Airport was built on land dredged from Lake Pontchartrain to create a site that projects into the lake. The initial plans for the airport were drawn up by William E. Arthur of Los Angeles, who was replaced in 1932 by Weiss, Dreyfous and Seiferth. Following Arthur's earlier concept, the airfield's buildings were laid out on the triangular-shaped site in a winged arrangement symbolizing flight; the central terminal building was given a similar outline. Both the exterior and interior are lavishly ornamented with relief sculptures that allude to flight. Above the main entrance is a figure of man as a flying machine, flanked by window panels with similar representations; on the side walls are sculptures representing the four winds. Among the sculptors who created these works were Enrique Alferez, William Proctor, and John M. Lachin. This beautiful facade—Weiss, Dreyfous and Seiferth had reached their peak in the integration of sculpture and architecture by the early 1930s—was covered in 1964 by a windowless wall in order to save the expense of needed exterior repairs and to enable the airport to function as an atomic fallout shelter. The wall was removed and the building renovated to its former Art Deco glory in 2013. Inside, the double-height lobby's terrazzo floor; rose-, cream-, and beige-colored marble paneling; streamlined aluminum stair railings and light fixtures; and plaster friezes of mechanical tools and of cloud and sun motifs all convey the magical and modern aura of early flight. At balcony level eight murals by Xavier

Gonzalez, now restored under the direction of Elise Grenier, depict exotic destinations from the air (a compass on the lobby floor points to these destinations, noting the mileage from New Orleans).

Funded originally at a cost of $4 million (the recent renovation far exceeded this amount) and supervised by the Orleans Levee Board, the airport was named, despite considerable public protest, for the board's president Abe Shushan, who had his initials inscribed throughout the terminal, reputedly in more than a thousand places, from doorknobs to roof. Shushan, a friend of Governor Huey P. Long, was indicted for income-tax evasion in 1935. He was subsequently acquitted, but in 1939 the Orleans Levee Board nonetheless renamed the airport and ordered the removal of every trace of Shushan's name. Shushan was jailed for mail fraud the following year. The restored building is now a venue for events and a destination for private and charter air traffic.

On either side of the terminal are two of the original aircraft hangars, each with metal gable ends inscribed with the image of an airplane. Adjacent to the airport's entrance is Enrique Alferez's *Fountain of the Four Winds* (1938), which is composed of four nine-foot-high nude figures of cast stone representing the winds, grouped around a hemisphere and surrounded by a pool. Three of the figures are female; the male figure, representing the north wind, was heavily criticized in its time by citizens who regarded its nudity as harmful to public morals. Although the building has been restored, the fountain has not, though there is speculation it might be moved to a new site and restored.

Gentilly and East to the Parish Line

The elevated strip of land, known as Gentilly Ridge, that runs through this area was occupied by Native Americans before Europeans began to settle here in the eighteenth century. The surrounding swamps and marshes, however, were not drained until the early twentieth century. In 1909, the real estate firm of Baccich and de Montluzin formed the Gentilly Terrace Land Company and laid out Gentilly Terrace (now called Old Gentilly) for white homeowners. Today this racially diverse neighborhood is considered New Orleans's California-style suburb because of its tree-lined streets of stucco-covered, red pantile–roofed bungalows with Arts and Crafts details.

Gentilly Woods, also initially restricted to whites, was developed in 1951 by Hamilton Crawford, who hired architect J. W. Leake to design residences in thirteen different styles. North of it, the Pontchartrain Park neighborhood was laid out in the 1950s for professional and middle-income African Americans. Like Gentilly Woods it borders the Industrial Canal and was built on drained swamp, and thus was inundated by a levee break in the aftermath of Hurricane Katrina. These neighborhoods have largely recovered.

In the 1960s and 1970s, residential subdivisions continued to creep eastward, crossing the Industrial Canal onto former swamplands, hastened with the opening of I-10. This area, known as New Orleans East, suffered heavy flood and wind damage from Katrina and has only partially recovered. Joe W. Brown Memorial Park, at 187 acres the largest park in eastern New Orleans, was developed on vacant land in the mid-1970s (Charles Caplinger, landscape architect); the Audubon Louisiana

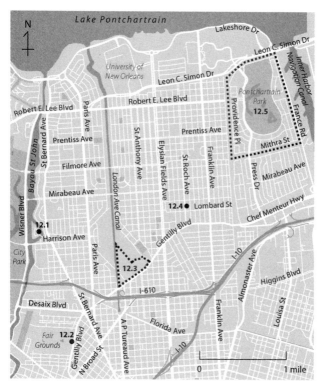

Nature Center followed in 1980. Ninety percent of the park's tree canopy was lost from saltwater intrusion due to Katrina. The park has been rehabilitated with basic recreational amenities (Billes Partners); the Nature Center reopened in 2017.

Alcée Fortier Boulevard forms the center of a Vietnamese community, which has expanded since 1975 when, following American withdrawal from Vietnam, the Orleans Parish Catholic Diocese provided housing in the neighborhood for approximately one thousand people.

Heading east, U.S. 90 follows a ribbon of land between Lake Pontchartrain and Lake Borgne to reach the waterway known as the Rigolets, which links Lake Pontchartrain with the Gulf of Mexico via Lake Borgne and divides Orleans Parish from St. Tammany Parish. Guarding the entrance to the Rigolets stand the ruins of Fort Pike. Constructed between 1820 and 1827, it was one of the first forts built under a national coastal fortification program that began at the end of the War of 1812 and continued to the Civil War in order to withstand attack from land or sea. Pointed, earth-filled brick bastions flank the land side of the structure and a curved wall faces the Rigolets. The fort was decommissioned in 1890; it now lies in ruins due to neglect and coastal erosion, and is open to the public by appointment only.

12.1   Sunkel House (Ashtray House)
1961–1962, Albert C. Ledner. 28 Park Island Dr.

Nestled in the center of Park Island, a small and verdant enclave surrounded by Bayou St. John and developed in the 1950s, is this unusual house. From the porte-cochere at one end, the one-story building stretches along its lot to a glass-walled two-story unit at the other. The flat-roofed, one-story portion is composed of three layers: a painted brick wall, a band of windows, and a tall white-painted cornice. A surprising row of closely spaced amber-colored glass ashtrays decorate the cornice. The house's idiosyncrasies of plan, form, and ornamentation characterize both Ledner's interpretation of the International Style and attention to his clients' personalities. Adrian and Patricia Sunkel wanted something decorative on the exterior of their house and, because they both were both smokers, Ledner proposed the ashtrays, a suggestion the clients loved. Albert Ledner studied briefly under Frank Lloyd Wright, and Wright's influence is apparent in the horizontality of the one-story unit. The house, which was flooded by Hurricane Katrina, has been restored for its current owners.

Ledner also designed the two-story house (1962) at 11 Park Island for Leonie Galatoire, using materials (inside and out) salvaged from demolished local structures. A later addition now installed on a waterfront deck is the aluminum *Tree Domes* by sculptor Kent Bloomer that was part of the 1984 Louisiana World Exposition.

12.2   Fair Grounds Entrance Gates
1866, Gallier and Esterbrook. 1751 Gentilly Blvd.

Laid out in 1852, this racetrack was known as the Union Race Course until the City of New Orleans renamed it the Creole Race Course and built these gates, resembling little cottages. Each gate has a Carpenter Gothic front porch, the upper section covered by panels with trefoil and quatrefoil cutouts; the gable roof has serrated-edged bargeboards. The New Orleans Fair Grounds purchased the track in 1872. Rathbone DeBuys's clubhouse and grandstand of 1919, destroyed by fire in 1993, was replaced by a similar design in 1997 by Eskew Filson Architects.

Horse races are held at the fairgrounds during the winter months, and the annual New Orleans Jazz and Heritage Festival takes place here in late April.

12.3   Dillard University

1934, Moise Goldstein; William Wiedorn, landscape architect; many later additions. 2601 Gentilly Blvd.

Formed from the merger of two African American colleges, Straight College and New Orleans University, Dillard University opened in 1935 on its new sixty-two-acre campus designed by Goldstein. Named in honor of James Hardy Dillard, educator and administrator of funds for African American schools in the South, the university was funded in part by the American Missionary Association, as well as by Edgar and Edith Stern (see **10.12**; Edith Stern's father was philanthropist Julius Rosenwald, president of Sears Roebuck, and with Booker T. Washington, helped build thousands of schools for African Americans in the South). According to the architect's son, Louis Goldstein, his father offered three different designs to Dillard's board of trustees—Gothic Revival, modern, and classical—and the last was selected. The master scheme for Kearny Hall, a building with columns and a pediment dominating an open-ended court, followed the model of Thomas Jefferson's design for the University of Virginia. An avenue of oak trees (replanted after Hurricane Katrina) that extends the length of the court from Gentilly Boulevard to Kearny Hall establishes a major axis and formal entrance to the campus. All the original buildings are painted white, with classical details of the simplest kind.

Flooded following Katrina, the campus buildings were restored and several new structures have been added, all of which interpret the campus's classicism in modern forms, notably in their stylized unornamented entrance colonnades. These include the two-story International Center for Economic Freedom (2006, Davis Brody Bond), the three-story Professional Schools and Sciences Building (2010, Sizeler Thompson Brown Architects), and the Student Union (2010, Campo Architects).

Dillard now owns the parcel facing Gentilly Boulevard that includes a small lagoon, the last remnant of Metairie Bayou, together with the handsome 1920s brick entrance gates and fountain (non-working, with low-relief decoration) that formerly led to the City's Parkway and Parks office and greenhouses. No efforts have yet been made to integrate these striking features into Dillard's landscape.

12.4 Henry W. Bihli House
1912, Morgan Hite. 4615 St. Roch Ave.

Built by the design department of the Gentilly Terrace Land Company, perhaps as a model house, this small Arts and Crafts residence is one of the most attractive of the Gentilly Terrace bungalows. Bihli purchased it in 1912. The deep entrance porch is covered with a wide, low-pitched roof, its gable end crafted from interlocking wood beams, brackets, and slats in the manner of California architects Greene and Greene. Indeed, one of Gentilly Terrace's developers, Colonel R. E. Edgar de Montluzin, traveled to California to study suburbs there before

Gentilly Terrace was begun, and Los Angeles foremen, familiar with building bungalows there, were brought here to oversee construction of the earliest houses. The stucco-covered, red pantile–roofed bungalow at 4486 St. Roch Avenue, with a capacious front porch supported on massive obelisk-shaped brick piers, is a fine example of the California type, as is the house at 4468 Music Street, with its rubble stone piers and gabled dormer. More unusual in this neighborhood is H. Jordan MacKenzie's 1910 design for a two-story house for Rosella Bayhi at 4437 Painters Street, which with its Dutch-styled gable is similar to designs by the early-twentieth-century Secession architects at the Darmstadt Colony. Gentilly Terrace developed slowly at first; then a building boom in the late 1930s generated the yellow-brick houses and Cape Cod cottages in this area.

12.5   Pontchartain Park and Neighborhood

1955–present. Bounded by Leon C. Simon Dr., France Rd., Mithra St. and Providence Pl.

The park of Pontchartrain Park is located in a neighborhood of the same name. (It is now informally known as Pontilly, a port-manteau of Pontchartrain Park and the adjacent Gentilly Woods neighborhood). The Pontchartrain Park neighborhood, the city's first suburban-style subdivision for African Americans, was developed in the 1950s during a period of racial segregation, with notable financial support from Edgar and Edith Stern who had also supported nearby Dillard University (**12.3**). The suburb was marketed to middle-class professional families and featured modern, single-family brick-on-slab ranch-style houses that were distinctly different from the multifamily wooden frame structures in older neighborhoods. Movement into this neighborhood (and the eastern part of the city) corresponded with movement of white families out of older neighborhoods into the Lakeview and Lakewood subdivisions west of here as well as into Metairie in Jefferson Parish, a pattern that continued well into the 1970s.

In the center of the neighborhood is a rectangular public park of just over 180 acres defined on its north–south sides by Press and Congress drives. In the center of the park is a golf course designed in the 1950s by African American golf course designer Joseph M. Bartholomew (1885–1971), a native of New Orleans. Bartholomew had caddied as a teenager on local golf

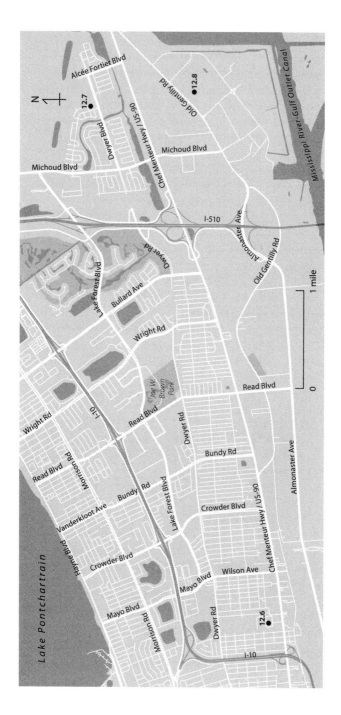

courses, including the Metairie Country Club, and his skill and knowledge about golf soon became apparent. In the early 1920s a wealthy member of the Metairie Country Club persuaded the membership to send him to New York to learn golf course design, and Bartholomew returned to New Orleans in 1922 to redesign the Metairie club's course. Later he designed courses in City Park, which, like the Metairie club, was segregated, and where he could not play. In 1956, he designed the course for Pontchartrain Park and, following his retirement, continued to be active in the park until his death. The refurbished golf course, named after its designer, reopened in 2011.

The Pontchartrain Park neighborhood, like Gentilly Woods which borders it to the south, was built on drained swampland, and its houses, park, and golf course suffered significantly from post–Hurricane Katrina flooding. While some residents abandoned these neighborhoods, many returned, determined to reoccupy houses purchased by their parents or grandparents, for whom owning a house here was a measure of social and economic status and evidence of having achieved the American dream, even during segregated times. At 4533 Mendez Street, Bethany United Methodist Church (1979) designed by African American architect Robert H. "Skip" Perkins (1936–1990), is a modernist beige brick building with a broad tapering spirelike roof over the sanctuary.

12.6   Sisters of the Holy Family Motherhouse and Novitiate
1955, Diboll-Kessels and Associates. 6901 Chef Menteur Hwy.

In 1955, the Sisters of the Holy Family founded by Henriette Delille in 1842 (see **2.10**) moved to these new quarters. Their

Motherhouse occupies a large site preceded by extensive lawns dotted with trees. The building is roughly M-shaped in plan with end wings and a central rear wing reaching back to enclose cloister-like spaces. The facade is a bold modern design with a first story of glass that is slightly recessed. Above, a screen of closely spaced vertical columns covers two stories of colored glass organized in an abstract gridded pattern. A canopy shelters the central entrance and is surmounted by a freestanding low-relief sculpture in aluminum of Christ flanked by Mary and Joseph organized in a curved composition. The facade has all the more impact because the building is set far back from the street and approached by a long central driveway that is processional in effect; up close, however, the impact is diminished by a landscape design insensitive to the building's modernist aesthetic.

12.7 Mary Queen of Vietnam Church
1986, Sauviac+Dang Architectural Design. 14001 Dwyer Blvd.

In 1975, following the fall of Saigon when many South Vietnamese refugees came to the United States, New Orleans was one of the cities where they put down roots. Because many were Catholic, Catholic Charities facilitated their settlement. The immigrants first held services in a mobile home until they built a chapel in 1978. Mary Queen of Vietnam Parish was established in 1983, the first in the nation for a Vietnamese congregation; this church, consecrated in 1986, is a modernist design, square in form, with a shed roof that slopes gently toward the rear, and a one-story portico with a folded-plate roof carried on six slender columns. An education building was added in 1987. The neutral ground in front of the church in the center of Dwyer Boulevard has been landscaped with a parterre garden, and across Dwyer from the church is a community/cooperative vegetable garden.

The growth of the Vietnamese community in New Orleans has given rise to several new religious buildings. Among them is Our Lady of Lavang (6054 Vermillion Boulevard), designed by Louis Kong and consecrated in 1992. While the church building is plain, with two massive dormer clerestory windows illuminating the interior, the associated structures are particularly striking. The church grounds include a grotto and a pagoda sheltering a statue of Our Lady of Lavang.

12.8 NASA Michoud Assembly Facility
1942; 1960s, August Perez and Associates; later additions.
13800 Old Gentilly Rd.

The National Aeronautics and Space Administration's (NASA) Michoud Assembly Facility inhabits an 832-acre site occupied by plantations in the nineteenth century. From the 1960s to 2010 the facility was used for the assembly of the first-stage external booster tanks for the Saturn V rockets. Some of the buildings, however, date back to 1940 when Higgins Industries acquired the site for the production of landing craft for use in World War II (see **6.29**); in 1942, production shifted to aircraft. When the plant closed in 1945 and was transferred to the War Assets Administration, the site included a long reinforced-concrete-framed brick building, which is highlighted at its center with a frontispiece of eight piers, giving it a classical dignity. From 1951 to 1954, the facility was used by the Chrysler Corporation to build tank engines for the U.S. government for the Korean War. In 1961, NASA selected the site for the space program. The facility was enlarged, including a massive H-shaped engineering and office building (August Perez and Associates), and, in 1964, a 203-foot vertical Assembly Building for assembling the booster tanks. The structure was constructed with a brick base and corrugated asbestos walls above. The first booster tank was completed in 1977, loaded on a barge, and shipped to the Stennis Space Center in Mississippi; in 1979 it was delivered to the Kennedy Space Center. Between 1979 and 2010 the facility produced 136 booster tanks. The site is now a multi-tenant manufacturing facility. In front of the brick building facing Old Gentilly Road are two brick chimneys, the remnants of the early-nineteenth-century sugar mill that once stood here on Antoine Michoud's plantation.

Algiers

Algiers, on the west bank of the Mississippi River opposite the Vieux Carré, was annexed by New Orleans in 1870. In the eighteenth century it was the site of the Company of the Indies's first plantation, Louisiana's first slave-trading depot, and New Orleans's gunpowder magazines. In the nineteenth century, dry docks and shipbuilding brought prosperity to the town and after 1853, when the New Orleans, Opelousas and Great Western Railroad (later the Southern Pacific) arrived, it became a center for freight transportation via steamship and rail from the Eastern Seaboard to the West Coast until the 1960s. Pacific and Atlantic streets were named to commemorate that trade. The older section of Algiers, known as Algiers Point, was rebuilt after a fire in 1895, primarily with small cottages and shotgun houses, many elaborately decorated with Eastlake ornament, as along the 200 block of Olivier Street. Construction of the Mississippi River bridge (now with a duplicate span of 1988 and known as the Crescent City Connection) in 1958 made Algiers more accessible to east-bank New Orleanians and triggered new suburban development. Algiers has two small Beaux-Arts classical buildings: a Carnegie-funded public library (725 Pelican Avenue), designed in 1907 by Rathbone DeBuys, and the former Canal Commercial Trust and Savings Bank (505 Patterson Road)

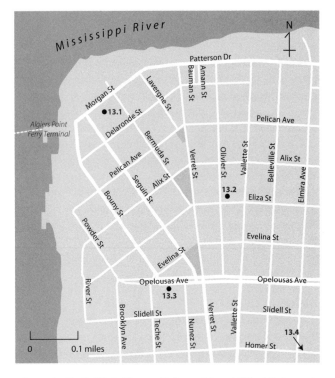

of 1907 by Emile Weil. The small, frame Mount Olivet Episcopal Church (526 Pelican Avenue) dates to 1854. A ferry, operating since 1827, continues to link Algiers Point with Canal Street and provides spectacular views of both banks of the river and of downtown New Orleans.

13.1 Algiers Courthouse

1896, Linus Brown and Alonzo Bell; 1984 renovated, Lyons and Hudson Architects; 2017 restored, Linfield, Hunter and Julius. 225 Morgan St.

This brick, twin-towered courthouse was constructed after the fire of 1895, which destroyed several blocks of downtown Algiers, including the former Duverje plantation house, which had served as the courthouse since 1869. City engineers Brown and Bell designed this awkwardly proportioned but picturesque courthouse in a round-arched Italianate style; the builder was John McNally. The two-story building's facade, rather too wide for its height, features square towers at each end, one three

stories tall and the other four stories with a clock. The facade and towers have paired, round-arched windows set between shallow pilasters and emphasized by prominent hood moldings. Small-scale brick dentil bands adorn the cornice, and a pediment-shaped parapet tablet marks the facade's center. The small central portico is supported on doubled Doric columns.

13.2 Trinity Evangelical Lutheran Church
1875; 1911 renovated. 620 Eliza St.

Built for a German American congregation formed in 1875, this pretty, white frame church has steeply pitched gables inset with small rose windows on its two principal facades. Two square towers have pyramid-shaped steeples supported on brackets; the larger tower anchors the church to its corner site.

Opposite the church at 502 Olivier Street, the three-story former Holy Name of Mary School (1924, Alexander W. Norman), a handsome red brick Collegiate Gothic building, is now the home of the International School of Louisiana. One block away at 446 Vallette Street, the former Rosetree (formerly the Algy) Theater (1930s), an Art Deco movie house, has been converted into an art glass studio and gallery.

13.3 Old Algiers Main Street Fire Station (Fire Engine No. 17)
1925, Andrew S. Montz. 425 Opelousas St.

The main fire station for Algiers was designed to blend in with the residential character of the neighborhood. It is one of several that are English Tudor in style, which city architect E. A Christy introduced to New Orleans in his design of 1909 for the fire station at 436 S. Jefferson Davis Parkway, and used in 1916 for the former fire station at 1421 St. Roch Avenue, both on the east bank of New Orleans. This Algiers station by Montz (c. 1882–1963) is a particularly fine example of the style. The two-story building of red brick trimmed with white stone has a wide Tudor-arched entrance for the fire trucks, a band of square-topped windows on the second story, and a crenellated parapet. Fire stations are extremely important in New Orleans, where most buildings are constructed of wood and closely spaced, making fires a constant hazard.

13.4   Brechtel Memorial Park

Mid-1970s, Charles Caplinger, landscape architect. 4001 Lennox Blvd.

This 110-acre public park was created in the mid-1970s during a period of municipal park expansion and renovations and named for Joseph Berengher Brechtel II, the administrator of the New Orleans Recreation Department in the 1940s and 1950s who established one of the nation's most innovative municipal recreation departments during that time. Although in Orleans Parish, this park is adjacent to Jefferson and Plaquemines parishes and therefore serves the entire West Bank region. Among its features were a golf course (now closed), lagoons, and areas of native plants and natural habitats for migrating birds. Severely damaged by hurricanes Katrina (2005) and Gustav (2008), the park became severely degraded with unrepaired damage, invasive vegetative species, and hydrological problems. A master plan for a restored "Regional Ecological Park" was completed in 2011 by landscape architects Brown and Danos of Baton Rouge, but it has not been fully implemented.

Jefferson Parish

Gretna

Modern-day Gretna was formed from three nineteenth-century communities: Mechanikham, Gretna, and McDonogh-ville. Mechanikham, laid out in 1836 by Nicolas Destrehan from a plan by Benjamin Buisson, consisted of a common (now Huey P. Long Avenue) stretching southeast from the Mississippi River, with two streets on each side. In 1838, the St. Mary's Market Steam Ferry Company developed a four-block-wide community immediately downriver from Mechanikham, named Gretna, although from the mid-nineteenth century on the two villages were often together referred to as Gretna. The town is said to have been named for Gretna Green in Scotland because of its reputation during the 1840s as a mecca for quick marriages and elopements performed by a justice of the peace

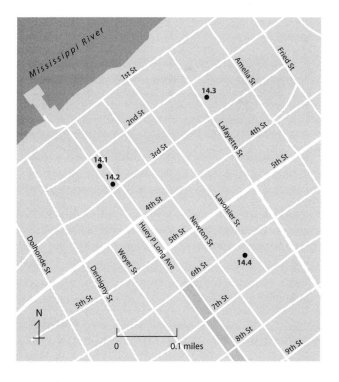

at any hour. In 1913, the adjoining downriver community of McDonoghville, laid out by John McDonogh on his land in 1815, was incorporated into Gretna.

Many of Gretna's early settlers were Germans, and its early industries included shipbuilding and sawmills, both stimulated by the arrival of the New Orleans, Opelousas and Great Western Railroad. In 1884, Gretna became the Jefferson Parish seat. Although commercial establishments now favor U.S. 90 rather than Huey P. Long Avenue, the latter retains several significant early-twentieth-century buildings. In addition to the old courthouse (**13.1**), these include the Beaux-Arts classical First National Bank of Jefferson Parish (c. 1925; 203 Huey P. Long) and, at number 519, a three-story brick elementary school, designed by Stevens and Nelson in 1910, which now serves as the German-American Cultural Center.

14.1   Gretna City Hall (Jefferson Parish Courthouse)
1907, Robert S. Soulé and Francis J. McDonald. 740 2nd St.

Gretna's city hall (formerly the Jefferson Parish Courthouse) occupies a narrow site in the center of Huey P. Long Avenue. The three-story brick building is conventional in its Beaux-Arts classical forms, but squeezed onto a narrow site it is a compact composition with a vertical emphasis. Its central projecting portico has a triple-arched entrance, four Corinthian columns in front of the second and third stories, and a pediment. The building is finished with a projecting cornice lined with modillions and a parapet. At the center of each of the side elevations, the second and third stories together form a single projecting curved bay, which correspond to the concave-curved walls of the courtroom's interior. A columned loggia fronting the second story of the bay further articulates the exterior. The courthouse is painted in a lively color scheme: beige walls, white columns, gray windowsills, and a burnt-orange cornice. In 1929, a plain three-story boxlike annex was added to the rear of the building. In 1964 the building was converted to the city hall when a new courthouse by Claude E. Hooton was constructed, itself since replaced.

The courthouse faces a small public square containing the Jefferson Memorial Arch (1923). Dedicated to Jefferson Parish's citizens who served in all wars, the memorial's single round arch topped by a tall entablature was inspired by Roman triumphal arches. Constructed of red brick with white trim, it has shallow niches on each side of the central opening. Aligned with and located between the former courthouse and the former ferry landing, the arch gives presence to Gretna's historic heart.

14.2 Louisiana Railroad Museum (Texas Pacific Railroad Depot)

c. 1905. 739 3rd St.

Two surviving depots in Gretna's center affirm the importance of the railroad to the town's growth. This brick one-story former passenger and freight railroad depot has a gabled parapet and deep overhangs along three sides carried on battered brick piers and iron brackets. One block away at 4th Street and Huey P. Long Avenue is the former Southern Pacific Railroad Depot (1906), a small wooden structure with a pitched roof and gable in the center of its long side, which was used primarily as a relay station for railroad employees. A caboose is on display beside the building.

14.3 David Crockett Firehouse

1859. 205 Lafayette St.

In 1841, a group of local citizens formed a volunteer fire-fighting company, incorporating as the Gretna Fire Company No. 1 in 1844. The company's name was changed in 1874 to honor David "Davy" Crockett, who was killed at the Alamo. The two-story wooden structure has a wide-arched opening on the ground floor. The front gable is finished to resemble a pediment; at its peak is a large openwork hexagonal bell tower surmounted by

a small cupola. The firehouse shelters a fire engine manufactured in 1876 by the R. Gould Company of Newark, New Jersey.
Weighing 3,000 pounds, it was first propelled by teams of
firemen; later, when it was horse-drawn, a driver's seat was installed at the front. The fire engine's water pump was powered
by a steam engine resting upon four wooden wagon wheels
and could propel a constant stream of water to the height of a
five-story building.

Next door at 201 Lafayette, the Gretna Historical Society
Museum occupies the former Kitty Strehle House of c. 1845.
This single-story, four-room wooden house with a front gallery
supported on wooden posts is typical of the area's early residential stock.

14.4 St. Joseph's Catholic Church
1926–1927, William R. Burk. 600 6th St.

St. Joseph's serves a parish founded in 1857 whose earliest
members were mostly of German origin. Replacing a Gothic
Revival structure, this Spanish Colonial Revival church was built
during the pastorate of Father (later Monsignor) Peter M. H.
Wynhoven, who founded the Hope Haven and Madonna Manor
Homes (**14.6**) for children in Marrero, also Spanish Colonial Re-

vival in style. The church's stuccoed-brick facade and bell tower are almost identical to Bertram Grosvenor Goodhue's design for the California Building at the Panama-California Exposition of 1915–1916 in San Diego. Ornamentation covers the center of the facade in a dense, high-relief composition incorporating scalloped-arched openings, twisted columns, foliate vines, angels, a sculpted head of Christ, and a continuous band of shell-shaped motifs surrounding the round-arched entrance; above the upper window, shallow niches hold a row of statues of saints. The outer sections of the facade are unadorned, intensifying the impact of the ornament. The entire facade is framed by a scalloped parapet which climbs from the outer edges to the taller center in a series of reverse curves and is decorated along the top with ball-shaped urns. A round-arched open arcade extends along each side of the church. The square tower is at the rear of the church rather than beside the facade, as in Goodhue's scheme, and its upper section rises to a pair of setbacks, with a small cupola above. The church's nave has a barrel vault with transverse arches, and a half-dome defines the apse; the interior is modest in its decoration.

Marrero

In 1904, when Louis "Leo" H. Marrero organized the Marrero Land and Improvement Association to develop the town, it was known as Amesville. In 1914, the town was renamed to honor Marrero, who at one time served concurrently as president of

the Jefferson Parish Police Jury and as state senator, and later as sheriff of Jefferson Parish.

14.5   Immaculate Conception Church

1957, Walter J. Rooney Jr. for Curtis and Davis, with Harrison B. Schouest. 4401 7th St.

The most noticeable feature of this rectangular church, built of reinforced concrete, is its sweeping folded-plate gable roof. The pie-shaped panels of structural steel form a rhythmic zig-zag pattern on both the exterior and interior. The roof, which rests on triangular-shaped reinforced-concrete piers that act as buttresses against outward thrust, appears to float over the body of the nave and extends at the front to form a sheltering portico. The textured brick walls are laid in Flemish bond and the bricks have the pink-hued beige color favored by Curtis and Davis in the 1950s. Rooney, the project architect for the firm, stated that he sought to create "an emotional impact . . . by using dim illumination in the low ceiling peripheral areas to lend great emphasis to the vaulted nave. The undulating ceiling hovers lightly over the congregation and focuses all attention on the sanctuary and main altar." Decorative elements inside include a narthex screen of perforated precast concrete panels, designed by New Orleans's sculptor Jack B. Hastings. Stained glass windows by Ruth Goliwas, also of New Orleans, were added later.

14.6   Hope Haven Center (Hope Haven and Madonna Manor Homes)

1925–1940s. 1101 Barataria Blvd.

This complex of homes built for orphans and other children in need is set in spacious grounds on both sides of Barataria Boulevard: Hope Haven on the west and Madonna Manor on the east. The largest ensemble of Spanish Colonial Revival buildings in Louisiana, they are especially fine, offering a splendid panorama of white stuccoed walls, red tile roofs, round-arched arcades, curved parapets, towers, elaborate sculptural decoration, and ornamental ironwork. The earliest structures were Hope Haven, founded in 1925 by Peter M. H. Wynhoven, pastor of St. Joseph's Church in Gretna (**14.4**), as a home for teenage boys of all religions. Madonna Manor was established in 1932 for boys and girls under the age of twelve (although later restricted to boys) and was administered by the Sisters of Notre Dame.

The former administration building (1925) for Hope Haven, in the center of the structures on the west side of the boulevard, was designed by William R. Burk and was the first built. The three-story building has a projecting single-story, round-arched arcade that wraps around the front and sides, a square off-center tower topped by a small, red-tiled dome, and slender spiral columns between the windows. The two-story building (1931) to the far left served as the vocational school for the approximately 125 boys housed at Hope Haven. The tools of their future trades—axes, pliers, planes, and hammers—are indicated in relief sculpture in a frame around the school's central entrance. To the rear of this group of buildings (not visible from the street) is the former Julian Saenger Gymnasium (1930), which, from the front, is shaped like a church, with an arcaded portico and flanking square tower.

On the east side of the boulevard, Madonna Manor (1932, Jack J. H. Kessels for Diboll and Owen) is the largest building in the complex. By 1940, it housed approximately 100 boys and 40 girls (girls were then more commonly adopted). The three-story building has a five-part composition with a curved parapet, and the second-story windows are fronted by iron balconies. A circular stained glass window on the upper facade features a Star of David to recognize the financial contributions of the Jewish community to this Catholic-founded home. The rich mix of forms, materials, colors, and textures, along with the play of light and shade over the facade, are essential to the building's drama. A square tower on the right side of the building has small semicircular balconies around its openwork top and a red-tiled pyramid roof.

The St. John Bosco Chapel (1941, Diboll-Kessels and Associates; 2014 restored) has the most ornate facade in this group of buildings. Rendered in light gray stone, vertically organized across the center of the facade in various shapes and sizes, are columns, niches holding statues of saints, moldings, arches, rams' heads, shields, obelisks, and crosses. Floral scrolls and shells embroider bands around the arched frame of the entrance door. Along each side of the chapel is an open round-arched arcade. To the right of the facade a square bell tower has two setbacks and a miniature red-tiled dome.

The two-story School Building (1932, Jack J. H. Kessels for

Andrew S. Montz) completes the row of buildings. It lacks applied ornamentation but has a squat round tower and a projecting single-story round-arched arcade across the front. The building's ornamental restraint speaks to the serious nature of its scholarly function and, at the same time, offers a further interpretation of the Spanish-inspired theme that unifies the entire complex. The complex, owned by the Archdiocese of New Orleans, is closed, but some buildings are used by organizations for community care programs.

14.7 Education Center, Barataria Preserve, Jean Lafitte National Historical Park and Preserve
1993, Eskew Filson Architects. 6588 Barataria Blvd.

The Barataria unit of the multi-unit Jean Lafitte National Historical Park encompasses 8,600 acres of hardwood forest, cypress swamp, and freshwater marsh that closely represents the eighteenth-century landscape early settlers found here. The Education Center, a linear structure with a steel-truss frame, an exterior of wood paneling and glass, and a metal roof, is raised on concrete piers above soggy soil that is sometimes inundated by spring floods. The steel-truss frame is both a strong formal and a structural element of the design, piercing the wooden skin at the front to give the effect of a ship's prow, appropriate imagery for its watery setting. A raised translucent roof panel runs the length of the building, marking the circulation spine and linking the rangers' offices, study rooms, and screened amphitheater overlooking the swampland. The different textures and colors of the structure's materials echo the tactile qualities of its swampy and wooded site. The park is named for the notorious Jean Lafitte, who used the bayous, shallow bays, and islands of this region for his smuggling operations in the early nineteenth century.

Avondale

Avondale was home to one of the nation's biggest shipbuilding facilities and was once the largest employer in Louisiana. Established in 1938 as Avondale Marine Ways, it later became a unit of Northrop Grumman Corporation, then Huntington Ingalls; it closed in 2014. In its early years, the facility specialized in all-steel construction and primarily built and repaired river barges. During World War II, Avondale manufactured seagoing craft for the war effort. Postwar it expanded its range to include seagoing vessels for the U.S. Coast Guard and the U.S. Navy, tankers for oil companies, and container ships for commercial companies. Encompassing 268 acres along the bank of the Mississippi River, the shipyards presented a formidable sight, with cranes and structural equipment (some still in use) rising high above the levee, reiterating the centrality of the river to the area's culture as the facility and docks seek a new use.

Metairie

This suburb of New Orleans experienced phenomenal growth in the mid-twentieth century, although the area was rural throughout most of its earlier history. Because of the swampy nature of the soil, the remnants of the alluvial Metairie Ridge became the locus of the town's early development. Metairie Road now traverses this ridge, overlying what was once a Native American footpath. The name Metairie is believed to derive from the French word *métairie*, which designated a type of small farm operated on the basis of *métayage*, whereby the farm's products were split evenly between tenant and landowner. An electric streetcar line from downtown New Orleans to the suburb in 1915 encouraged a construction boom in the 1920s and 1930s. This included development of an exclusive residential area promoted as Metryclub Gardens, now known as Old Metairie. While many of the original houses remain, others began to be replaced in the 1990s, with large houses in historically derived styles and more crowded together, diluting the neighborhood's original garden-like character.

In the second half of the twentieth century, expansion far-

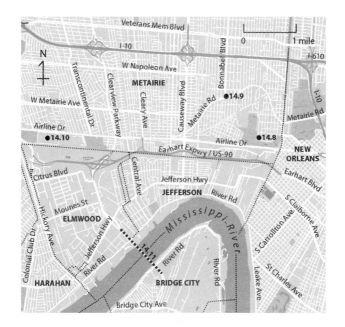

ther west and toward Lake Pontchartrain became possible after the completion of effective drainage systems and the lakefront levee system, the latter in 1948. Nevertheless, at approximately six feet below sea level, the area flooded following Hurricane Katrina in large part because the pumping system backed up; the area generally has recovered. The construction of the Lake Pontchartrain Causeway (1956, Ford, Bacon and Davis), followed by a second span in 1969, contributed to Metairie's growth, spawning an undistinguished row of boxlike high-rise office buildings on Causeway Boulevard near the lake. By the 1980s, Veterans Memorial Boulevard, a multilane divided thoroughfare, offered approximately four miles of strip commercial development with accompanying parking areas, catering to and fostering the appetite for shopping via automobile.

14.8   Feibleman House

1938, Weiss, Dreyfous and Seiferth. 12 Nassau Dr.

Inspired by photographs of houses designed by German architect Walter Gropius, James Feibleman requested a design from Weiss, Dreyfous and Seiferth that expressed the most modern architectural forms. Constructed of brick covered with white-painted stucco, the house is an asymmetrical composition of angled and curved forms. The latter are most evident in the front bay and at the second story, executed with a pronounced horizontal emphasis. Larger window frames have replaced the original modest frames on some of the windows, interrupting the continuity of the building's smooth, streamlined image, and removal of window mullions on the front bay window has diminished the relationship of grid to curve that was fundamental to the design. Nevertheless, this house, handsomely set behind a large front yard, is the most original in Old Metairie.

Demonstrating Weiss, Dreyfous and Seiferth's skill in working across the entire range of fashionable styles is the two-story Colonial Revival house (1929–1930) designed for Solis Seiferth, a partner in the firm, at 608 Iona Street.

14.9 St. Catherine of Siena Roman Catholic Church
1956–1957, James Lamantia Jr. for Burk, Le Breton and Lamantia. 105 Bonnabel Blvd.

Asked to design a large and important church for this congregation to replace a smaller building, Lamantia produced a contemporary interpretation of the traditional basilica form, one he described as the most baroque of all his compositions. The reinforced-concrete frame is pulled to the church's exterior, revealing and clarifying the logic of the structure while creating a dramatic play of vertical and diagonal lines. At the east and west ends, stained glass windows are recessed into vaultlike spaces to provide a contrasting dynamic to the angularity of the external frame and to give a hint of the space within. Placement of the choir stairs on the exterior, at each side of the entrance, adds another sculptural note and allows more interior space by reducing the size of the narthex. Vertical precast concrete louvers alternate with stained glass windows (featuring stylized biblical figures in primary colors) along the clerestory; the lower walls are of beige brick. The interior is impressively lofty. The rectangular concrete piers that separate the tall, wide nave from the narrow aisles echo the external frame, as do the laminated wooden arches that form the ceiling. A freestanding circular baptistery (now occupied by offices) is crowned by a tall openwork bell tower that responds to the skeletonlike frame of the church, to which it is connected by a covered walk. The church's facade faces the street, whereas the baptistery was intended to be seen from Metairie Road.

14.10 Shrine on Airline (Zephyr Field, Jefferson Baseball Park)

1992–1997, HOK, with Perez Ernst Farnet, Architects and Planners. 6000 Airline Dr.

In 1990, a 113-acre parcel of land was purchased from the Illinois Central Gulf Railroad, and during the next two years, then-governor Edwin Edwards brokered a deal to finance the stadium, which included issuing a $52.2 million bond. The Denver Zephyrs, a Triple A–rated minor-league team, was selected in 1992, the first professional baseball team to play in New Orleans since 1977. Construction finally began on the ballpark in 1995, two years behind schedule, in an area now known as LaSalle Park. The medium-sized stadium seats 10,000 people on three levels: two levels of grandstands, along with air-conditioned press and luxury boxes on the third tier. The stands are of typical stepped-concrete construction, supported by an exposed steel structure. The exposed structure allows visual access to the field from the circulation and concessions area and encourages the passage of cooling breezes. A canopy shades the top level. The design is dominated by an industrial aesthetic, evident in the clarity of structure, the materials, and the five circulation towers that ring the exterior. The principal facade overlooking the parking lot is, however, faced with brick—the requisite material of southern regionalism—red below the buff color on the second and third stories, with brown brick pilasters on the first level.

Nearby, at 6400 Airline Drive, is the 1000-seat Jefferson Performing Arts Center (Wisznia and Associates; opened 2015), controversial because of its cost overruns and construction delays. Its open spaces contribute to making LaSalle Park a regional venue for active and passive recreation in Jefferson Parish.

Harahan and Vicinity

In 1894, the Illinois Central Railroad established railroad yards and a roundhouse at what is now the town of Harahan, which was incorporated in 1920 and named for James T. Harahan, a former president of the railroad. In 1915, Harahan was linked to New Orleans by the Orleans-Kenner Traction Company (O-K Line). An early building of interest is the two-story stuccoed-brick Harahan Elementary School (1926; 6723 Jefferson Highway), designed by William R. Burk in the Spanish Colonial Revival style. Its central domed rotunda is covered by a red-tiled conical roof, and the main entrance is decorated with scalloped arches and twisted columns. St. Rita Catholic Church (1964; 7100 Jefferson Highway), designed by James Lamantia Jr. for Burk, Le Breton and Lamantia, is a small but monumental basilican church of blond brick with a steeply pitched roof and a tapered tower made from concave panels of precast concrete at each end.

14.11   Huey P. Long Bridge

1932–1935, 2006–2013, Modjeski and Masters. U.S. 90 across the Mississippi River

Improved transportation systems were one of the hallmarks of Governor Huey P. Long's political platform and this combined rail and road bridge was a highlight of his term of office. The bridge, the first to cross the Mississippi River in Louisiana, replaced a train ferry and gave New Orleans a continuous rail line and highway to the west. Celebrations on the bridge's opening day in December 1935 included a pageant and an airplane flyover while a Southern Pacific train crossed the Mississippi 135 feet above the river's surface. Huey Long was absent from

Cont #4   #133
Mississippi River Bridge
Superstructure Main Bridge

the event because he had been assassinated three months
previously.

Including its approach structure, the bridge is 4.4 miles in
length, with the center span across the river measuring 790 feet
in length. The steel cantilevered bridge is composed of a series
of truss spans carried on six Gothic-arched concrete supports,
the deepest resting 170 feet below sea level. When built, the
highway component of the structure comprised two nine-foot-
wide lanes in each direction, but the bridge was widened in the
early twenty-first century to create three eleven-foot-wide
lanes each way. Spectacular views of the river can easily dis-
tract a driver when traveling across the bridge and, before the
lane-widening, made the journey a thrilling but nerve-wracking
experience. Although the bridge's supports are now reinforced
to strengthen and carry its additional width, the shape and
sequence of the pointed-arched footings striding across the
river originally brought to mind the nave of a Gothic cathedral.
The long, seemingly endless geometry of cross-braced metal
trestles that carry the inclined approaches to the bridge is
now accompanied by concrete supports. Huey Long's favored
architectural firm of Weiss, Dreyfous and Seiferth designed a
one-story brick administration building at the base of the bridge
on River Road, which was demolished to make way for the new
construction.

Kenner

Kenner (first known as Kennerville) extends across the former plantation lands of Minor Kenner and William B. Kenner (brothers of Duncan F. Kenner of Ashland Plantation upriver in Ascension Parish; see **Day Trip 2**). Much of the original town, laid out by surveyor W. T. Thompson in 1855, was absorbed into a new Mississippi River levee in the twentieth century, and thus few of its early buildings have survived. Kenner remained a community of truck farms until New Orleans's International Airport opened in 1945. Initially named for pioneer aviator John B. Moisant, who died in a plane crash in New Orleans in 1910, the airport was renamed Louis Armstrong International Airport in 2000 to honor the New Orleans–born musician. Ongoing expansions include new terminals and parking garages. Airline Highway (now Airline Drive), the original route to the airport from New Orleans, blossomed with motels and restaurants, sadly deteriorated or demolished after I-10 superseded the older highway. One of Kenner's earliest buildings is the two-story Felix and Block General Mercantile Store (1907; 303 Williams Boulevard); its brick facade is ornamented with pilasters, a cornice with dentils, and a sawtooth brick panel in the center of a small pediment.

St. Bernard Parish

Arabi

15.1   Domino Sugar Corporation (American Sugar Refinery)
1905–1912; later additions. 7417 N. Peters St.

The American Sugar Refinery, which owned refineries in Brooklyn, Jersey City, Boston, and Philadelphia, began construction on this plant beside the Mississippi River in 1905 and started processing sugarcane here in 1909. Constructed to plans prepared by the company, the refinery, which was described as one of the largest in the world at the time, included a wharf on the Mississippi River and vast warehouses. Of the many concrete-frame and brick-faced structures in this plant, the fourteen-story filter house is the tallest. Here the liquid sugar solution flows by gravity from storage tanks on the upper floor through filter tanks filled with bone char, which removes impurities and whitens the sugar. Other structures include the twelve-story pan house and nine-story granulator, where the sugar is dried, granulated, and pulverized. A pair of 225-foot-high cylindrical brick smokestacks flanks the powerhouse, glorifying it as a twin-towered cathedral of industry. The powerhouse, which originally supplied all the plant's electrical needs, has a facade articulated by an enormous inverted V-shaped vent. Bricks for the buildings were manufactured in brickyards north of Lake Pontchartrain. The contractor for the building was James Stewart & Co. of St. Louis, Missouri. Over the years additional processing buildings have been added to the site.

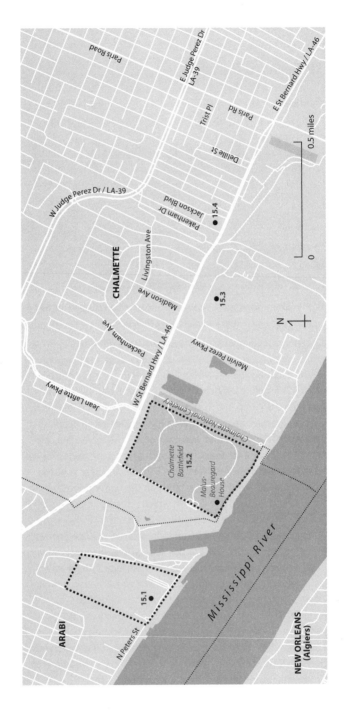

ARABI

15.1

N Peters St

NEW ORLEANS
(Algiers)

Mississippi River

Chalmette Battlefield
15.2

Malus-
Beauregard
House

Chalmette National Cemetery

Jean Lafitte Pkwy

W St Bernard Hwy / LA-46

Packenham Ave

Melvin Perez Pkwy

CHALMETTE

W Judge Perez Dr / LA-39

Madison Ave

Livingston Ave

Packenham Dr

Jackson Blvd

15.3

15.4

Delille St

Paris Rd

Trist Pl

E Judge Perez Dr
LA-39

E St Bernard Hwy / LA-46

Paris Road

0   0.5 miles

Within the refinery's grounds is Cavaroc House (c. 1840), built by the Paul Darcantel family on its brickyard, though the house is now known by the name of businessman Pierre Charles Cavaroc, who owned it from 1860 to 1880. The two-story, stucco-covered brick structure is surrounded by a two-story gallery on square Doric piers and has a hipped roof with dormers on all four sides. The American Sugar Company acquired the house when it purchased the land for its refinery.

Just upriver (to the left) of Domino is the two-story former Ford Assembly Plant (1922–1923, Albert Kahn), where the company's automobiles were assembled, tested, and distributed for the southern market. The reinforced-concrete building has red brick spandrels and a narrow dentiled cornice. The plant closed in 1930, then operated sporadically under different ownerships as a testing or distribution center until 1977 when it became a warehouse. Flooded in Hurricane Katrina, the building awaits a new use.

Chalmette

In the neutral ground of Louisiana 46 (near Paris Road) are several brick piers, the sole remains of Versailles, the sixteen-room plantation house built in 1805 by Pierre Denis de la Ronde, destroyed by fire in 1876. Extending from the ruins toward the river is the allee of oaks planted c. 1821 by de la Ronde. The trees are known as both the de la Ronde Oaks and the Pakenham Oaks, named for British Major General Sir Edward Pakenham, who was incorrectly said to have died beneath one of the trees after his defeat by Andrew Jackson at the Battle of New Orleans (he died on the Chalmette battlefield). De la Ronde dreamed of creating two cities in this area that would overshadow and absorb New Orleans. The city focused around his plantation would be named Versailles, and the other, beside Lake Borgne, was to be called Paris. The modern highway Paris Road (LA 47) gets its name from the Chemin de Paris, the road planned by de la Ronde to link the two cities. Today near the river end of Paris Road is Our Lady of Prompt Succor Church (2320 Paris Road), designed by James Lamantia Jr. for Burk, Le Breton and Lamantia in 1957. The church's gabled facade of colored glass is articulated with mullions, and a multifaceted roof encloses a column-free, amphitheater-like space; a recent barrel-vaulted addition is beside the church.

15.2 Chalmette Battlefield and Cemetery (Jean Lafitte National Historical Park)

1815 battlefield; 1832, 1856 Malus-Beauregard House;
1855–1908 monument, Newton Richards; 1864 cemetery.
8606 W. St. Bernard Hwy.

Chalmette Battlefield and Cemetery are named for Ignace de Lino de Chalmet, whose late-eighteenth-century plantation land they now occupy. The Battle of New Orleans, which took place here on January 8, 1815, sixteen days after the signing of the Treaty of Ghent on December 24, 1814, was the last engagement of the War of 1812. Under the command of Major General Andrew Jackson, American forces defeated British troops led by Major General Sir Edward Pakenham in a battle that took place on a strip of land approximately one-half mile wide and that lasted less than two hours. British casualties exceeded 2,000, and Pakenham was among those killed; the Americans reported only 71 mortalities. The British retreat to Lake Borgne on January 18, 1815, marked the end of the Louisiana campaign and preserved America's claim to the territory acquired from France in the Louisiana Purchase. A section of the American earthworks has been restored, and battery positions are identified by artillery displays. Visitors can take a 1.5-mile tour by automobile or on foot that links important sites on the battlefield. A visitor center provides additional information.

Marking the site of Jackson's position during the battle on January 8, 1815, is a 102-foot-high obelisk designed by Newton Richards. Originally planned to be 200 feet high and modeled after the Washington Monument in the nation's capital, the obelisk is of Tuckahoe and Georgia marble on a marble-faced brick foundation. Its cornerstone was laid in January 1840 a few days after Andrew Jackson visited the field on the twenty-fifth anniversary of the battle. Construction began in 1855 but was halted at the outbreak of the Civil War, when the obelisk was only 55 feet high. It was completed as a shortened version of the original design in 1908 by the U.S. War Department one year after the federal government acquired the monument from the State of Louisiana. The obelisk sits on a stepped podium and has neo-Egyptian entrance porticoes on all four sides; three of them are blind, and one opens to the shaft's interior, where an iron spiral staircase surrounds a brick central support.

Also on the battlefield site is the Malus-Beauregard House. This two-story house of stucco-covered brick, never part of a plantation, was built for Madeleine Pannetier Malus between 1832 and 1834; she died in 1835. The house was purchased from her family in 1856 by Caroline Fabre Cantrelle, who replaced the wooden columns of the galleries with full-height Doric columns of stuccoed brick at front and rear. The house has a hipped roof with six dormers, with three rooms on each floor, and its principal entrance was from the river side. The Greek Revival moldings were probably added in the 1850s. The house later

served as a country residence for a succession of owners, one of whom was Judge René Beauregard, son of Confederate General P. G. T. Beauregard, who purchased it in 1880. The National Park Service acquired the house in 1949 and it was restored in the late 1950s by architect Samuel Wilson Jr. Changes were made to the interior to accommodate exhibits on the Battle of New Orleans.

Occupying a long, narrow site next to Chalmette Battlefield is the cemetery established in 1864 for Union soldiers who died in Louisiana during the Civil War. It also contains the graves of veterans of the Spanish-American War, World Wars I and II, the Vietnam War, and four Americans who fought in the War of 1812. Many of the 15,000 graves are unidentified, and all are marked by small plain headstones that vary in design according to the era they were placed here. The cemetery is surrounded by a brick wall, completed in 1873.

15.3 Smokestack of the Kaiser Aluminum and Chemical Corporation

1951–1953. 9000 W. St. Bernard Hwy.

This 500-foot-high air-control tower looming over Chalmette, visible from miles away, was built for the Kaiser Aluminum Corporation plant, which in its heyday employed up to 2,700 people. The tower, 80 feet in diameter at its base and said to be one of the tallest in the world, was shut down in the late 1960s for environmental reasons. Kaiser opened this aluminum-producing plant a mere ten months after construction began at the 280-acre site. It was the nation's largest aluminum reduction plant. Bauxite from Gramercy (St. James Parish; see **Day Trip 2**) and Baton Rouge plants were processed into aluminum here. Engineer Frank A. Backman, chief of construction for the Kaiser company, who had previously worked on the Hoover Dam, supervised construction of the plant's approximately eighty buildings. Kaiser shuttered the plant in 1983. Most of the buildings are now demolished and the site is used as an industrial park and for container storage.

15.4 St. Bernard Parish Courthouse

1939, Weiss, Dreyfous and Seiferth; 2013 restored, Architects Beazley Moliere. W. St. Bernard Hwy. at Jackson Blvd.

This PWA-funded courthouse, constructed when the parish seat was transferred from St. Bernard to Chalmette, is an austere Moderne structure, with a central section four stories in height and wider than the slightly recessed three-story wings. Faced with smooth limestone and sparely ornamented, the reinforced-concrete structure projects an image of weight and serious purpose—characteristics of Weiss, Dreyfous and Seiferth's designs. Narrow foliate-patterned carved bands placed to define architectural parts enhance the building's linear qualities. Occupying the full width of the interior central section is a two-story lobby with curved staircases at each end leading to a balcony, a geometrically patterned terrazzo floor, and walls sheathed in gray-veined marble. The principal courtroom has wood paneling and narrow vertical windows with metal mullions on the exterior that are decorated with stylized female representations of Justice, alternating with magnolia flowers. The courthouse was flooded by seven feet of water from Hurricane Katrina but was restored and reopened in 2013.

St. Bernard

15.5 St. Bernard's Old Courthouse (Historic Beauregard Courthouse)

1914–1915, Toledano and Wogan; 2012 restored, Architects Beazley Moliere. 1201 Bayou Rd.

This three-story building served as the parish courthouse until completion in 1939 of the present courthouse in Chalmette (**15.4**). The building was converted for use as a school until flooded from Hurricane Katrina, after which it was restored for various parish uses, including a library and a sheriff's office, and rental space for events. It is a handsome Beaux-Arts classical design with paired Corinthian columns outlining a loggia in front of the second and third stories. An entablature and balustrade complete the building.

15.6 Los Isleños Museum and Village

1980 established. 1357 Bayou Rd.

The museum and several historic buildings occupy a twenty-two-acre site dedicated to the interpretation and preservation of the Spanish influence in Louisiana, particularly as it relates to the two thousand or so Canary Islanders who settled in St. Bernard Parish between 1779 and 1783. All the structures exemplify the parish's early building stock. The museum is in a one-and-a-

half-story front-galleried wooden house, which was altered in the late nineteenth or early twentieth century by the addition of two dormers, a curved side gallery, and gingerbread trim for both its new and original galleries. Among the other buildings (rebuilt or restored after flooding from Hurricane Katrina) are a trapper's cabin and the one-and-a-half-story former Ducros House (c. 1800), which has a front gallery with six columns and French doors.

Day Trips from New Orleans

These three driving trips from New Orleans along the Mississippi River each take a day. Tour 1 goes downriver toward the river's delta. Tours 2 and 3 travel upriver, the first along the river's east bank and the second along the west bank. All three tours highlight significant places in the region's history and culture, with key stops set **boldface.**

Day Trip 1: The Mississippi River Delta

To travel the Mississippi River's west bank to the Gulf of Mexico is to encounter a landscape under constant change and threat. The river, essential to the nation's commerce as a route for oceangoing vessels, has been manipulated over the years to improve navigation and to protect New Orleans from floods. But these projects have prevented the Mississippi from carrying silt to rebuild wetlands and the low, unstable barrier islands that help protect the coastline from hurricanes and tidal surges. Canals and pipelines dug to support the offshore oil and gas industry have furthered erosion, encouraging salt water from the Gulf of Mexico to invade the fragile freshwater marshes. More than 2,000 square miles of delta land have been lost in the last eighty years (current loss is about a football field per day), and buildings and entire communities have disappeared, a pressing problem more recently and forcefully underscored by the impact of hurricanes Katrina and Rita in 2005. To combat land loss, the State of Louisiana established the Coastal Restoration Authority that year to mitigate erosion and to master-plan protection and restoration projects.

The earliest structures along the river's delta were earth and shell mounds and middens constructed 1,500 years ago by Native Americans; practically nothing remains of these features. The Balize, a small fort built in 1734 on an islet at the mouth of the Mississippi River, is now submerged, and Manila Village, a Filipino fishing settlement that became a hub of the shrimp-drying industry in the 1890s, was destroyed by Hurricane Betsy in 1965. Little survives from the sugar plantations along this route, and citrus-fruit cultivation is a mere shadow of what was once a vigorous industry. After engineer James B. Eads

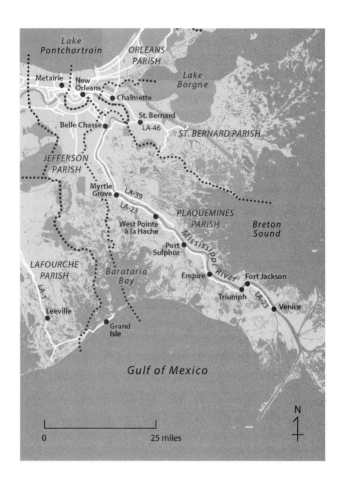

constructed jetties at the South Pass of the Mississippi River in 1879, the region's importance as a route and a port for ocean-going ships was assured. The U.S. Army Corps of Engineers now controls the navigation channels.

Land along the Mississippi River was subdivided on the French long-lot pattern, with the narrow side of the lot bordering the waterway to give property owners access to the principal means of transportation. Communities and towns tend to be linear in plan, following the ridge of higher land next to the river. Consequently, lines of vernacular structures, rather than any individual monument or building, give the delta its character, as do the ships, visible from the highway, threading their way to the Gulf of Mexico. The route from New Orleans to Venice at the end of the road is 75 miles.

The route downriver along LA 23 begins at **Belle Chasse,** home to a Naval Air Station Joint Reserve Base. Just before **West Pointe à la Hache** is **Woodland Plantation House** (now an inn) at 21997 LA 23, built c. 1855. The one-and-a-half-story raised house of the former sugar plantation was constructed of cypress for retired river pilot William Bradish Johnson. The house faces the river, so its rear view is visible from the highway. Nevertheless, front and rear facades are alike, each with a full-width gallery and a row of five dormer windows in the pitched roof.

Nine miles south of West Pointe à la Hache is what remains of the town of **Port Sulphur,** founded by the Freeport Sulphur Company in 1933 to house employees for the company's mine ten miles west at Grande Ecaille and to serve as a processing and shipping point. Approximately two hundred houses were built in the new town, along with churches, a hospital, and a school. After the mine closed in 1978, the town continued to process sulphur from the company's other Gulf Coast mines, but is now much diminished after being inundated by more than twenty feet of water from Hurricane Katrina.

Farther south, **Fort Jackson** was begun in 1822 on a bend of the river and was occupied in 1832. Named to honor Andrew Jackson, the fort, along with the scant, inaccessible remains of Fort St. Philip on the east bank of the river, was designed to safeguard the river approaches to New Orleans from the Gulf

Fort Jackson, with bastion on right

of Mexico. Like Fort Pike in eastern New Orleans (see **page 244**), it was one of first forts built under a national coastal fortification program that extended from the end of the War of 1812 to the Civil War and was designed to withstand attack from land or sea. The forts were singularly ineffectual in this effort; after a five-day bombardment early in the Civil War, forts Jackson and St. Philip failed to stop the Union fleet, under the command of Admiral David Farragut, from proceeding upriver to New Orleans, which surrendered on April 28, 1862. Fort Jackson was built on the site of Fort Bourbon, a Spanish redoubt of c. 1792 that was destroyed by a hurricane in 1795. Pentagonal, with a large bastion at each corner, it has twenty-foot-thick brick walls and rises twenty-five feet above a surrounding moat. At the time of the Civil War, a large citadel occupied the center of the parade area; this was destroyed during the 1862 attack, along with the wooden quarters outside the fort. Repairs were made to the fort after the war, and it received additional guns during the Spanish-American War in 1898. In World War I, several units based at Jackson Barracks in New Orleans received training at Fort Jackson. In 1926, the fort was declared surplus property and sold into private ownership. Donated to Plaquemines Parish in 1960, it was restored and opened to the public in 1962. Although the fort's interior is now closed following damage from Hurricane Katrina, a walk around its perimeter reveals the impressive size and importance of this ambitious structure.

Venice, the last habitable community on the Mississippi River before land dissolves into water, is a popular point of departure for sport fishing. It cannot be said to resemble its more famous eponym, but it does have a distinctive character of its own. Like its Italian counterpart, it is laced with and surrounded by water channels. As a base for helicopters transporting workers and supplies to offshore oil rigs and for various marine-related structures, Venice has that untidy but purposeful and fascinating industrial appearance that characterizes other Louisiana Gulf communities.

Day Trips 2 and 3: Upriver from New Orleans

Mark Twain described his journey by steamboat along the Lower Mississippi River in *Life on the Mississippi* (1883): "From Baton Rouge to New Orleans, the great sugar plantations border both sides of the river all the way, and stretch their league-wide levels back to the dim forest-walls of bearded cypress in the rear. Plenty of dwellings all the way, on both banks—standing so close together, for long distances, that the broad river lying between the two rows, becomes a sort of spacious street." Today the vista along the 132 miles of river between the two cities is as memorable as it was in the nineteenth century. Vast grain silos, fields of circular oil-storage tanks, and shiny petrochemical plants have displaced many of the plantations, but their products, transported by water for export throughout the world, make the Mississippi River as much a corridor now as it was then.

Native Americans first inhabited this area, and although nothing survives of their culture on this stretch of the river, there are two mounds on the Louisiana State University campus in Baton Rouge, remnants of the ancient nomadic mound-building native cultures that also built Poverty Point (a World Heritage site) in northeast Louisiana. From the 1720s, European settlers, mostly Germans and Acadians, established small farms along the river. Anglo-Americans arrived in significant numbers after the Louisiana Purchase of 1803, some bringing their enslaved workers with them. Soon, wealthy planters consolidated small farms into vast landholdings, transformed the hinterland of cypress swamp into fertile fields, and built elegant houses.

Early crops were indigo and perique tobacco (in St. James Parish), but by the beginning of the nineteenth century sugarcane reigned supreme, and by its end increasingly large sugar mills were built as the manufacturing process was consolidated. In some cases, new towns developed around the mills, such as Gramercy for Colonial Sugars. Lumber, mostly cypress, was also a major industry until the late nineteenth century, but by the 1930s it had declined as sources were depleted. The railroad accelerated industrial growth, as did maintenance of a deep-water channel that allowed oceangoing vessels to travel upriver as far as Baton Rouge.

In the twentieth century, grain elevators were built on the river's bank, where grain harvested in the Midwest was received and loaded onto ships. Thereafter, petroleum, chemical, and fertilizer companies saw the potential of this transportation route. Between 1945 and 1961 alone, one hundred and fifty industrial plants were established along the river between

Baton Rouge and Port Sulphur below New Orleans. These twentieth-century changes inevitably led to the destruction of important historic buildings, which galvanized local citizens to preserve and maintain what remained. These, together with the newer structures, tell the story of the river's evolution and offer a diverse and fascinating journey. The following tours along its east and west banks offer some of the highlights.

Day Trip 2: The East Bank

The first notable structure after leaving the New Orleans metro area is the **Bunge Grain Elevator** at 12442 LA 48 (known as River Road) in **Destrehan** (St. Charles Parish), a landmark along the Lower Mississippi. Grain from America's Midwest is stored in the concrete silos and then moved to the waiting ships via covered conveyer belts that span the highway and levee. Bunge chose this site for its grain elevator, as did Archer Daniels Midland (1963) at 12710 LA 48, because of the availability of barge, rail, and truck transportation and the Mississippi's deep-water channel that accommodates oceangoing ships. Driving along the highway underneath the conveyer shafts is akin to passing through a series of triumphal arches.

At 13034 LA 48 is **Destrehan Plantation House.** In 1787 indigo planter Robert Antoine Robin de Logny hired free man of color Charles Paquet, a carpenter and mason, to build the house, which has a pegged cypress frame with *bousillage* infill, a double-pitched roof, and a gallery on slender wooden supports.

Destrehan Plantation House

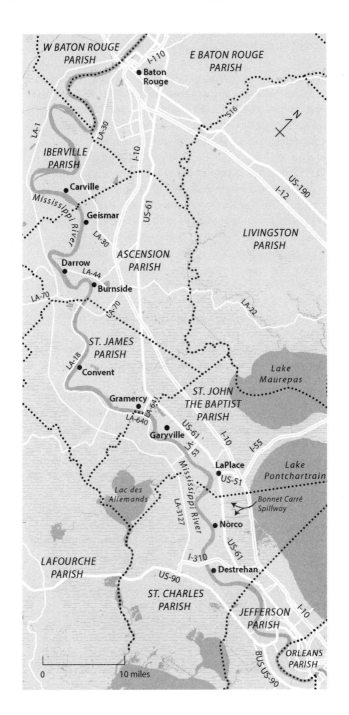

At de Logny's death in 1792, an estate inventory recorded the house, a kitchen, a storehouse, two hospitals, a *pigeonnier*, a coach house, nineteen slave cabins, and nine pairs of vats for indigo processing. De Logny's daughter Marie-Claude Céleste and her husband, Jean Noël Destrehan, acquired the house, added two-story wings, and turned to sugar cultivation. Under the ownership from 1838 of the Destrehans' daughter Louise and her husband, Pierre Rost, they refashioned the house in Greek Revival style by encasing the gallery supports in plastered brick to form double-height columns, among other changes. The house's exterior yellow stuccoed walls (scored to resemble stone), dark green shutters, and red-painted gallery rails replicate the mid-nineteenth-century color scheme.

From 1865 to 1866, Destrehan served as a headquarters for the Louisiana Freedmen's Bureau; it was then returned to the Rosts. Following a number of later owners, including a petroleum company, the River Road Historical Society acquired the then-deteriorated house in 1971. It was restored under the direction of architect Eugene D. Cizek. In 1997, a mule barn, 162 × 35 feet, constructed in the 1830s of pegged timber, was moved here from Glendale Plantation and reconstructed. Destrehan is open to the public.

One-half mile from Destrehan is the **Hale Boggs Bridge** (1975–1983) designed by engineers Modjeski and Masters, with Frankland and Lienhard. The sleek form of this bridge derives from its cable-stayed design. With a center span of 1,222 feet, it soars over the river, conveying both lightness and strength through the two dark brown Cor-Ten steel pylons, battered like Egyptian gateways.

The town of **Norco** was founded in 1916 by the New Orleans Refining Company (Norco) on a former sugar plantation. The refinery began operation in 1920. After Shell Petroleum Corporation (now Motive Enterprises) acquired the refinery in 1929, it built housing for workers, along with the amenities common to company towns, some of which survive. The complex stretches approximately two miles back from the river,

Just beyond Norco is the **Bonnet Carré Spillway** constructed between 1929 and 1936 by the U.S. Army Corps of Engineers, which protect New Orleans from downriver Mississippi River floods by providing a passage for excess floodwaters to discharge into Lake Pontchartrain and thence

Bonnet Carré Spillway

to the Gulf of Mexico. The Spillway is one of the flood-control structures along the Lower Mississippi authorized by the Flood Control Act of 1928 in response to the floods of 1927 that devastated the Mississippi River Valley, described by John M. Barry in *Rising Tide: The Great Mississippi Flood of 1927 and How It Changed America* (1997). This site was selected because previous crevasses indicated it was a weak point in the river's levee system. The dam's 350 bays, each 20 feet wide, set between reinforced-concrete piers and closed by vertical timbers, can be opened singly or in combination. The vast width of this Spillway illustrates the force and power of the Mississippi River, and dramatizes the fact that the river is at a higher elevation than the Spillway. The Spillway, 5.7 miles in length and a major feat of twentieth-century engineering, has become a recreation area (when not inundated), popular for biking and camping. As of 2017, the Spillway has been opened eleven times. From here the Spillway must be skirted along LA 61, rejoining LA 44 on the other side.

San Francisco Plantation (c. 1853–1860) on LA 44 in **Garyville** shows the juxtaposition of old and new in its situation among the adjacent oil tanks. The house's first floor is constructed of brick, and the second floor of brick between posts. A wide double flight of stairs leads to the principal living spaces on the second floor. The interior is organized according to the Creole plan of rooms en suite (without halls). Creole tradition was also followed in the use of the ground floor for dining and service rooms and the upper for the principal living spaces. The house's picturesque exterior includes a gallery with Corinthian columns, a balustrade screening the louvered windows that ventilate the attic, and a widow's walk. Creole families often favored colorfully painted houses, as here. Cisterns with reconstructed onion-domed copper covers stand on each side of the house; water was pumped from them to a tank in the attic, and was fed to sinks through a system of lead pipes. No buildings survive from the plantation's wealthy years before the Civil War. Late-nineteenth-century photographs show an elaborate garden in front of the house; this fell victim to a twentieth-century relocation of the levee, which also rerouted River Road uncomfortably close to the building's front. The house is open for tours.

A few yards farther at 2858 LA 44 is **Emilie Plantation House** (1882), an attractive raised house of brick-between-posts construction, and a plan that is two rooms wide with rear cabinets and loggia. A square cupola flanked by identical chimneys crowns the steep pyramidal roof.

Garyville was a lumber town established in 1903 when the Lyon Lumber Company of Illinois purchased the former Glencoe sugar plantation and acres of cypress swamp for the Lyon Cypress Lumber Company. Southron Duval (1862–1916) laid out Garyville and designed the buildings. As was typical of its time, housing was racially segregated. The white areas on the west were further subdivided for executives, managers, and workers, with houses ranging in size according to the rank of the employee. The Lyon Lumber Company ceased production here in 1931 and departed for the forests of Oregon. Of the 230 original buildings, some 60 residences (now in private ownership) and the Lyon Company headquarters, now the **Garyville Timbermill Museum,** survive. The museum, a two-story frame building, is one of the few extant lumber company headquarters from Louisiana's timber boom of the early twentieth century. The large sign across the front of the building imitates in size a sign that originally identified the building as the Lyon Cypress Lumber Company.

A few miles before the town of Gramercy in St. James Parish, the vast red-dusted processing and storage structures of the **Noranda Alumina and Bauxite** plant appear. Here the ore is processed into red alumina, the key ingredient in aluminum. The plant was built in 1958 for Kaiser Aluminum Corporation and the alumina was transported to Kaiser's aluminum plant (see **15.3**) in Chalmette until it closed; it is now sold to other companies.

Gramercy, the company town for the Gramercy Sugar Company (now **Colonial Sugar Company**), was founded in 1895 by New York investors and built mostly between 1895 and 1920. Among the many historic buildings is McKim, Mead and White's powerhouse, a three-story Beaux-Arts classical brick structure with a rusticated base, Doric pilasters separating the large windows, and gable ends outlined to resemble a pediment. The powerhouse is not accessible but is partially visible from the company's gated entrance on E. Main Street.

At 5858 LA 44, just before the town of **Convent,** is the **Manresa House of Retreats,** a Jesuit retreat house for laymen, which occupies the former College of Jefferson, founded in 1831 by a group of Louisianians of French ancestry for the education of their children. A fire destroyed most of the buildings in 1842, and though it was rebuilt, the college never recovered and was sold in 1848. The main building, fronted by twenty-two giant columns, was probably completed in 1843. The architect is unknown. After various owners, the Jesuits acquired the property in 1931. The Gothic Revival chapel (c. 1860), was perhaps designed by James Gallier Jr. The town of Convent was named after the now-demolished Convent of the Sacred Heart, established here in 1825.

The next few miles showcase the surviving grand plantation houses on the east side of the river. All are Greek Revival, but their differences reveal the aesthetic possibilities of the style.

Houmas House (40136 LA 942) near **Burnside** in Ascension Parish occupies land acquired in 1774 from the Houma Indians. A house built c. 1809 is now the two-story structure attached to the rear of the Greek Revival house constructed for John and Caroline Preston in 1840. Shaded by a monumental Tuscan-columned gallery, the stucco-covered brick house has a wide central hall and is three rooms deep, with hexagonal brick *garçonnières* flanking the building. In 1857 the Prestons sold the house, 12,000 acres, and 550 slaves to John Burnside, an Irish immigrant and New Orleans merchant, who by 1862 was the nation's foremost sugar producer. None of the plantation's original outbuildings survive. In 2003 the house was purchased and "restored," with questionable authenticity, and cottages along with other outbuildings were constructed for use as an inn and destination event venue. The gardens now include exotic features designed more as dramatic settings for events than as an accurate representation of an antebellum plantation's garden.

Around the bend of the river at 39050 LA 942 is **Bocage.** This sophisticated and unusual interpretation of Greek Revival, built c. 1837, is attributed to James Dakin. The front gallery has double-height plastered brick Tuscan piers that rise to a tall wooden entablature hiding the hipped roof. Two thinner piers mark the center of the facade. Because the house is not wide, it gives the impression that its upper story, much taller than the lower, is pushing the building into the ground, but this curious imbalance of proportions achieves a most satisfying aesthetic.

The twenty-four monumental stuccoed-brick Tuscan columns that surround **Hermitage Plantation House** at 38308 LA 942 give it an impressive exterior, belying its actual size and relatively modest interior. The house was built in 1819 shortly after the marriage of Louise du Bourg of Baltimore to Michel Doradou Bringier, and the columns probably were added c. 1840. The first floor is constructed of brick, and the second of brick between posts. The house has a symmetrical plan and a central hall, but as is typical of Louisiana's early houses, the windows and doors on the first floor do not align with those on the second, nor with the spacing of the columns, but instead respond to interior spaces. All the plantation's original outbuildings were demolished over the years.

The last of Ascension Parish's east-bank plantation houses is **Ashland–Belle Helene,** at the junction of LA 75 and LA 3521 near **Geismar.** Perhaps more than any other plantation house, Ashland–Belle Helene epitomizes the popular image of the grand Greek Revival southern mansion. It was built in 1839–1841 for planter and politician Duncan Farrar Kenner and Anne Bringier, daughter of Michel Doradou Bringier of Hermitage Plantation. The architect is unknown. The house essentially is a square brick box surrounded by twenty-eight thirty-foot-high piers supporting a two-story gallery and a simple but massive wooden entablature. Yet the effect is magnificent in size, proportions, and clarity of the design. Although none of the plantation's dependency buildings survives, excavations

Ashland–Belle Helene

have established that the enslaved workers lived in wooden cabins laid out in two parallel rows between the big house and the sugarhouse. Foundations of Kenner's brick sugarhouse, an overseer's house, and a blacksmith shop have been unearthed. The 1850 census lists 169 enslaved workers at Ashland. By 1860, Kenner owned a total of 473 slaves on three plantations, making him the eighth-largest slaveholder in the state. In 1992, the owners sold the house to Shell Chemical Company, which

Indian Camp

owned a petrochemical plant on land behind the property; it is not open to the public.

Around another bend in the river, at 5445 LA 141, is the **National Hansen's Disease Museum** in **Carville** (Iberville Parish). In 1894, the nation's first state-operated leprosarium, the Louisiana Leper Home (popularly known as Carville), opened here at an isolated and abandoned former sugar plantation, **Indian Camp.** The first seven patients were housed in the former slave cabins. In 1896, four nuns of the Sisters of Charity of St. Vincent de Paul arrived to provide nursing care, living at first in the dilapidated plantation house. In 1921, the U.S. Public Health Service took over the facility, designated it the national leprosarium, and built a new hospital and numerous support buildings, completed in 1934 with PWA funding. Carville was also a research center and made medical history in 1941 with the introduction of a sulfone drug (Promin) that successfully treated Hansen's disease. The government closed the facility in 1999, and the museum opened in 2000; portions of the landscaping done by the patients have been redone. Some of the buildings are now occupied by the Louisiana National Guard. The former plantation house, built 1858–1859 to a design by Howard and Diettel, has a lively facade, with fluted Corinthian columns on the gallery's second level, an entablature busily dotted with dentils, a projecting cornice, and a tall parapet.

Day Trip 3: The West Bank

Leaving New Orleans, the west bank of the Mississippi River can be reached via I-10, turning onto I-310 across the cypress swamps and the cable-stayed **Hale Boggs Bridge.** Approximately three miles north of the bridge on LA 18 in **Hahnville** is **Homeplace Plantation House.** Built c. 1800, this raised house is typical of southern Louisiana's early plantation houses. Its Creole plan is four rooms wide and two rooms deep, arranged en suite, and all rooms open onto the sixteen-foot-deep gallery that surrounds the house. Ground-floor walls and columns are of brick, and the upper story's timber frame is filled with *bousillage*. Slender wooden columns on the upper gallery rise to a high, hipped roof that has three front dormers. The front stairs were added in 1900.

One of the largest and most intact plantation complexes in the South is **Evergreen,** located at 4677 LA 18 in **Edgard.** The present house is a remodeling and expansion of a two-story Creole house built in 1790. After Pierre Clidament Becnel acquired the property in 1830, he hired builder and carpenter John Carver to update the house in the Greek Revival style, completed in 1832. Tuscan columns two stories in height support a ten-foot-deep gallery that stretches across the front of the house and wraps the corners. A pedimented portico at the center implies the house has a central hall, but Becnel retained the Creole plan of three rooms across the front, with a loggia

Evergreen

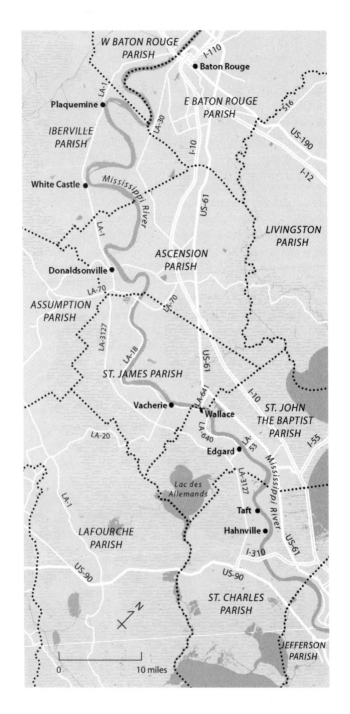

flanked by cabinets behind. Square brick *pigeonniers* flank the house, beyond which is a matching pair of *garçonnières*, a kitchen, a guest house, and a brick privy, all Greek Revival and painted white, thus creating an idealized framing for Becnel's elegant house. A double row of twenty-two wooden slave dwellings, built between 1830 and 1860, is the largest surviving group in Louisiana (and was famously documented by local surrealist photographer Clarence John Laughlin in the 1940s). The sugar mill (now demolished) stood at the end of the row. When oil heiress Matilda Gray purchased Evergreen in 1944, it was dilapidated. Architect Richard Koch began the restoration for Gray, and Douglass V. Freret continued it into the early 1950s. The rear parterre garden was laid out in 1944, probably designed by Koch and likely not authentic. Evergreen offers a remarkable picture of the social hierarchies and dynamics of slaves and masters in the years preceding the Civil War. Its layout and design also illuminate the image that plantation owners sought to express their achievements, wealth, and aesthetic pretensions. Evergreen is open to the public.

Heading toward the town of **Wallace** (St. John the Baptist Parish) is **Whitney Plantation,** formed from several tracts beginning in the 1760s by the Haydel family. In 1803, Jean-Jacques Haydel enlarged a c. 1790s house on the plantation, which was remodeled and decorated on the interior with murals between 1836 and 1839. Numerous nineteenth-century dependency buildings survive at Whitney, among them a barn, a pair of square brick *pigeonniers* (the one on the right is reconstructed) and a one-story plantation store of c. 1890. The census of 1860 recorded ninety-seven enslaved workers housed in twenty cabins. In 1867, Bradish Johnson of New Orleans purchased the plantation and named it Whitney. Following a succession of owners, the plantation's structures fell into disrepair. The current owner has restored the buildings. Numerous artifacts and small buildings related to the antebellum slave experience have been added, with mixed effect.

Upriver from Whitney at 2247 LA 18 in **Vacherie** (St. James Parish) is **Laura Plantation.** French-born Guillaume DuParc built the house in 1805. Raised on brick piers and constructed of brick between posts, the house, five rooms wide and two rooms deep with front and rear galleries, is painted in the varied bright colors preferred by Creole families. Laura's history is rare in that for nearly a century the plantation was managed by women, first by Guillaume's widow, Nanette, then by her daughter, Elizabeth. Laura and neighboring plantations are the setting of the Br'er Rabbit and Br'er Fox stories based on tales brought from Africa by slaves and handed down to their descendants.

Just before Oak Alley at 3535 LA 18 is **St. Joseph Plantation,** built in the 1830s. The galleried house is raised on brick piers and has a vast hipped roof with three dormers. Architect H. H. Richardson (see **6.26, 6.30**) was born here in 1838. It is open for tours.

The eight-hundred-foot-long allee of twenty-eight massive live oak trees leading from the river to **Oak Alley** constitutes one of the most familiar and evocative images of Louisiana's grand plantation houses. Built 1837–1839 by Jacques Roman, Oak Alley (3645 LA 18) is square in plan, constructed of brick, stuccoed and colored pale peach, and surrounded by a gallery supported on twenty-eight colossal Tuscan columns. Inside, the rooms are large but not ostentatious. No original buildings survive documenting the slaves who worked this nine-thousand-acre plantation, but records indicate that there were twenty-four dwellings, each forty feet square and divided into four rooms. Recently, and based on a single surviving photograph, six have been reconstructed to show where they once stood. The structures are used as exhibit spaces to interpret plantation life. Oak Alley is open to the public.

Just beyond Oak Alley are remains of **Le Petit Versailles** (burned in the 1920s) and its elaborate garden, denoted now by a historical marker on LA 18 and visible only as a clump of vegetation in an agricultural field. This plantation was built by one of Louisiana's wealthiest men, Valcour Aime, brother-in-law of Jacques Roman, who built Oak Alley. Aime had an elaborate *jardin anglaise*, with a pagoda, ornamental bridges, exotic plants and animals, and other features. The small parcel with the garden's remains was purchased by Baton Rouge landscape architect/garden historian Suzanne Turner to preserve these ruins of an important nineteenth-century garden.

The route upriver to **Donaldsonville** in Ascension Parish passes several oil and petrochemical plants, as well as farmland. Engineer Barthélemy Lafon laid out Donaldsonville in 1806. The town prospered as a riverboat stop, and it retains much of

Ascension Parish Courthouse

its nineteenth-century character. James Freret designed the **Ascension Parish Courthouse** (1889; 300 Houmas Street), a red brick two-story Romanesque Revival building with a square tower, that faces the square Lafon included in his plan. Other notable buildings include the former **B. Lemann and Bro. Store** (1878; 318 Mississippi Street), attributed to James Freret. Its departments for dry goods, notions, hardware, and groceries are unified on the exterior by a continuous Italianate facade with cast-iron pilasters between the display windows and a one-story gallery supported on cast-iron columns. The diminutive Carpenter Gothic **First United Methodist Church** (1844; 401 Railroad Avenue) contrasts with the **Ascension of Our Lord Catholic Church** completed in 1896 at 716 Mississippi Street, a massive brick church with an immense square tower and a spire. The **Ascension of Our Lord Catholic Church Cemetery** (Opelousas Street at St. Vincent Street) contains two impressive Classical Revival raised tombs. The Bringier family tomb (c. 1845), attributed to J. N. B. de Pouilly, is four vaults high and four wide, and the Landry tomb (c. 1845), attributed to James H. Dakin, rises in two stages, each treated as small temples.

Upriver from Donaldsonville at 31025 LA 1 at **White Castle** in Iberville Parish is **Nottoway,** the largest surviving plantation house in Louisiana. Completed in 1859 and designed by Howard and Diettel for John Hampden Randolph, it is richly ornamented, outside and in. The house's central hall is twelve feet wide and forty feet long, but the principal interior space is the ballroom, which is all white (including the floor), with a freestanding Corinthian arch. The house had indoor plumbing and gas lighting. The census of 1860 records that Randolph owned 155 enslaved workers, who lived in 42 cabins. Nottoway is now a destination venue. (The best view of the house's front is at 31112 LA 405).

The town of **Plaquemine,** situated at the confluence of the Mississippi River and Bayou Plaquemine, thrived as a steamboat stop and trading center. The **Plaquemine Lock** (1895–1909), now part of a State Historic Site, allowed ships to pass from the river through the bayou to Louisiana's interior;

Nottoway

Plaquemine Lock and Gary J. Hebert Memorial Lockhouse

the lock closed in 1961. The lock's pumphouse (now the **Gary J. Hebert Memorial Lockhouse**) has an exterior facing of white glazed brick, a material chosen for its ability to reflect light, as there were no lighthouses along the river. The building's stepped gables are said to reflect the Dutch heritage of designer Colonel George Goethals of the Army Corps of Engineers. The pumphouse now serves as a museum.

Across the road is the **Iberville Parish Museum,** built in 1849 as the parish courthouse. Nearby, **St. John the Evangelist Catholic Church** (1926–1927), designed by architects Emile Weil and Albert Bendernagel, was modeled on Italian Romanesque churches. It has a freestanding square campanile and a magnificent interior featuring a round-arched arcade with Ionic columns and open-truss ceiling.

Bibliography

This bibliography collects, briefly and thematically, titles essential to a more detailed understanding of New Orleans and its environment, subjects that the authors of this guide maintain are inextricably linked. Analysis and documentation of the region's architectural heritage began years ago. Yet examination of connections between built form and environment has just started, notably with studies in the last decade inspired by the impact of Hurricane Katrina. Works on the community's architecture and its cultural landscape continue to emerge as new investigative approaches, information, and perspectives provide different lenses through which we might view built form and the environment. Astute readers will detect observations in some of the following works, particularly older ones, that are challenged or refuted by newer works, an inevitable situation that occurs in all areas of scholarship. While this may reflect the nature of earlier methodologies and assertions, it also speaks to the value of such early works as inspiration to later scholarship that, through different and more sophisticated approaches, adds new perspectives on the past to the continuing conversation.

An essential resource for information on New Orleans's buildings is the ongoing series *New Orleans Architecture*, begun in 1971, which devotes each of its volumes to a single neighborhood. Written by many authors (and listed collectively below under Friends of the Cabildo), these carefully researched, illustrated books provide a street-by-street guide to the city's buildings. Other valuable resources include the plan-book drawings in the City's Notarial Archives, which feature more than 5,000 watercolor depictions of its buildings, dating mostly from the nineteenth century.

The Williams Research Center of The Historic New Orleans Collection (www.hnoc.org) possesses a vast archive of historical documents about and photographs of the city. The Collection's *The Historic New Orleans Quarterly* publishes information and short essays on materials in its collection. City records, archives, and special collections are held in the New Orleans Public Library (www.nolalibrary.org; see also http://nutrias.org/spec/speclist.htm), along with a wide variety of other materials relating to the city's history. The Louisiana Supreme Court Archives, together with other material related to the history and culture of Louisiana and New Orleans, is found at the Earl K. Long Library, University of New Orleans (http://libguides.uno.edu/c.php?g=149946&p=986528). Another resource is the Southeastern Architectural Archive at Tulane University (https://seaa.tulane.edu/), which contains plans, documents, and photographs of the works of Louisiana architects (and a few landscape architects) who practiced in New Orleans and the region. Other such papers and collections of architects and landscape architects are found at Louisiana State University (Baton Rouge) at Special Collections in Hill Memorial Library (www.lib.lsu.edu /special/) and at the Robert Reich School of Landscape Architecture (though unprocessed at present). The Louisiana State Museum (http://louisianastatemuseum.org/) has an extensive collection of photographic images and objects related to the history of New Orleans and Louisiana. Researchers seeking photographic images will benefit from the State Library of Louisiana Historic Photograph Collection (http://cdm16313.contentdm.oclc.org/cdm/landingpage /collection/LHP), an online resource linking photographic resources of multiple Louisiana public and private universities, archives, and libraries, searchable by general themes, locations, names, collection, and numerous other topics. The Division of Historic Preservation at the Louisiana Department of Culture, Recreation and Tourism in Baton Rouge holds the documentation on buildings nominated to the National Register of Historic Places, and that information can be accessed at www.crt.la.gov. For direct access to State Museum holdings, see: http://www.crt.state.la.us/louisiana -state-museum/collections/visual-art/works-on-paper/.

The many publications of Samuel Wilson Jr. (1911–1993) are essential to understanding New Orleans's early architecture for many reasons, not the least of which is that they are among the first to record built form in Louisiana from both archival scholarship and in situ documentation. Those most relevant to this volume are listed below. Information on many aspects of New Orleans's history and culture can be found in the *Louisiana Purchase Bicentennial Series in Louisiana History.* Listed collectively below under general editor Glenn Conrad, this multiple-volume series consists of essays drawn from different journals. *Preservation in Print*, published every month by the Preservation Resource Center (https://prcno.org/), gives information on recent National Register listings, short histories of Louisiana's historic buildings, and preservation issues. And the Louisiana Endowment for the Humanities' digital encyclopedia KnowLouisiana (www.knowlouisiana.org) and magazine *Cultural*

Vistas similarly provide a wealth of information on the city's history, art, and architecture.

Historic Descriptions and Guidebooks, and General History

Brasseaux, Carl A., ed. *A Comparative View of French Louisiana, 1699 and 1762: The Journals of Pierre le Moyne d'Iberville and Jean-Jacques-Blaise d'Abbadie.* Lafayette: Center for Louisiana Studies, University of Southwestern Louisiana, 1979.

Caillot, Marc-Antoine. *A Company Man: The Remarkable French-Atlantic Voyage of a Clerk for the Company of the Indies: A Memoir.* Edited by Erin M. Greenwald, translated by Teri F. Chalmers. New Orleans La.: The Historic New Orleans Collection, 2013.

Conrad, Glenn, gen. ed. *Louisiana Purchase Bicentennial Series in Louisiana History.* Multiple volumes and editors. Lafayette: Center for Louisiana Studies, University of Southwestern Louisiana, 1995–2006.

Didimus, H. [Edward Henry Durrell]. *New Orleans as I Found It.* New York: Harper and Brothers, 1845.

Federal Writers' Project of the WPA for the City of New Orleans. *New Orleans City Guide.* Boston: Houghton Mifflin Company, 1938. Rev. ed., New York: Pantheon Books, 1983.

Hall, Gwendolyn Midlo. *Africans in Colonial Louisiana: The Development of Afro-Creole Culture in the Eighteenth Century.* Baton Rouge: Louisiana State University Press, 1992.

Jewell, Edwin L., ed. *Crescent City Illustrated: The Commercial, Social, Political and General History of New Orleans.* New Orleans: [s.n.], 1873.

Latrobe, Benjamin H. *Impressions Respecting New Orleans: Diary and Sketches, 1818–1820.* Edited by Samuel Wilson Jr. New York: Columbia University Press, 1951.

——. *The Journals of Benjamin Henry Latrobe, 1799–1820: From Philadelphia to New Orleans.* Edited by Edward C. Carter II, John C. Van Horne, and Lee W. Formwalt. New Haven: Yale University Press, 1980.

Latrobe, John H. B. *Southern Travels: Journal of John H. B. Latrobe, 1834.* Edited by Samuel Wilson Jr. New Orleans: The Historic New Orleans Collection, 1986.

Lemmon, Alfred E., John T. Magill, and Jason R. Wiese, eds. *Charting Louisiana: Five Hundred Years of Maps.* New Orleans: The Historic New Orleans Collection, 2003.

Louisiana Endowment for the Humanities. *New Orleans and the*

World: 1718–2018 Tricentennial Anthology. New Orleans: Louisiana Endowment for the Humanities, 2017.

Norman, Benjamin Moore. *Norman's New Orleans and Environs*. New Orleans: B. M. Norman, 1845. Reprint, Baton Rouge: Louisiana State University Press, 1976.

Olmsted, Frederick Law. *The Cotton Kingdom: A Traveller's Observations on Cotton and Slavery in the American Slave States*. Edited with an introduction by Arthur M. Schlesinger. New York: Modern Library, 1969.

———. *A Journey in the Seaboard Slave States, with Remarks on Their Economy*. New York: Dix and Edwards, 1856.

Powell, Lawrence N. *The Accidental City: Improvising New Orleans*. Cambridge, Mass.: Harvard University Press, 2012.

Wharton, Thomas Kelah. *Queen of the South: New Orleans, 1853–1862: The Journal of Thomas K. Wharton*. Edited by Samuel Wilson Jr., Patricia Brady, and Lynn Adams. New Orleans and New York: The Historic New Orleans Collection and The New York Public Library, 1999.

New Orleans Architecture, Urban Planning, and Landscape Architecture

Architecture in Times of Need: Make It Right Rebuilding New Orleans' Lower Ninth Ward. Edited by Kristin Feireiss, with contributions by Brad Pitt. Munich and New York: Prestel, 2009.

Campanella, Richard. *Delta Urbanism: New Orleans*. Chicago and Washington, D.C.: APA Planners Press, 2010.

———. *Time and Place in New Orleans: Past Geographies in the Present Day*. Gretna, La.: Pelican Publishing Company, 2002.

Casey, Powell A. *Encyclopedia of Forts, Posts, Named Camps, and Other Military Installations in Louisiana, 1700–1981*. Baton Rouge, La.: Claitor's Publishing Division, 1983.

Christian, Marcus. *Negro Ironworkers of Louisiana, 1718–1900*. Gretna, La.: Pelican Publishing Company, 2002.

Christovich, Mary Louise Mossy, and Roulhac Bunkley Toledano. *Garden Legacy*. New Orleans: The Historic New Orleans Collection, 2016.

Colten, Craig E., ed. *Transforming New Orleans and Its Environs: Centuries of Change*. Pittsburgh: University of Pittsburgh Press, 2000.

———. *An Unnatural Metropolis: Wresting New Orleans from Nature*. Baton Rouge: Louisiana State University Press, 2005.

Conrad, Max Z. *Landscape Architecture and New Orleans: Room for Only One?: A Memoir.* Baton Rouge: Robert Reich School of Landscape Architecture, Louisiana State University, 2011.

Cultural Landscape Foundation. *What's Out There New Orleans.* Washington, D.C.: TCLF Publications, 2017. Available online at https://tclf.org/sites/default/files/New-Orelans_WOTW -booklets_2016_lowspreads.pdf.

Curtis, Nathaniel Cortlandt. *New Orleans: Its Old Houses, Shops and Public Buildings.* Philadelphia: J. B. Lippincott Company, 1933.

Dedek, Peter B. *The Cemeteries of New Orleans: A Cultural History.* Baton Rouge: Louisiana State University Press, 2017.

Douglas, Lake. "Cultural Determinants in Landscape Architectural Typologies: Plants and Gardens in New Orleans from the Colonial Era to the Civil War." *Journal of Garden History* 16, no. 2 (Summer 1996): 87–110.

——. "Pleasure Gardens in Nineteenth-Century New Orleans: 'Useful for All Classes of Society.'" In *The Pleasure Garden, from Vauxhall to Coney Island,* ed. Jonathan Conlin, 150–76. Philadelphia: University of Pennsylvania Press, 2013.

——. *Public Spaces, Private Gardens: A History of Designed Landscapes in New Orleans.* Baton Rouge: Louisiana State University Press, 2011.

Douglas, Lake, and Jeannette Hardy. *Gardens of New Orleans: Exquisite Excess.* San Francisco: Chronicle Books, 2001.

Edwards, Jay. *Louisiana's Remarkable French Vernacular Architecture, 1700–1900.* Monograph No. 1, Fred B. Kniffen Cultural Resources Laboratory. Baton Rouge: Department of Geography and Anthropology, Louisiana State University, 1988.

——. "The Origins of Creole Architecture." *Winterthur Portfolio* 29, no. 2/3 (Summer–Autumn 1994): 155–89.

Evans, Freddi Williams. *Congo Square: African Roots in New Orleans.* Lafayette: University of Louisiana at Lafayette Press, 2011.

Ferguson, John C. "The Architecture of Education: The Public School Buildings of New Orleans." In *Crescent City Schools, Public Education in New Orleans, 1841–1991* by Donald E. DeVore and Joseph Logsdon, 308–39. Lafayette: Center for Louisiana Studies, University of Southwestern Louisiana, 1991.

Filipich, Judy Ann, and Lee Taylor. *Lakefront New Orleans, Planning and Development, 1926–1971.* New Orleans: Urban Studies Institute, Louisiana State University, New Orleans, 1971.

Forman, L. Ronald, Joseph Logsdon, and John Wilds. *Audubon Park: An Urban Eden.* Baton Rouge, La.: Friends of the Zoo, 1985.

Friends of the Cabildo. *New Orleans Architecture.* Text by Samuel Wilson Jr. et al., compiled and edited by Mary Louise Christovich et al. 8 vols. Gretna, La.: Pelican Publishing Company, 1971–97.

Gandolfo, Henri A. *Metairie Cemetery: An Historical Memoir: Tales of Its Statesmen, Soldiers, and Great Families.* New Orleans: Stewart Enterprises, 1981.

Guilbeau, James. *The St. Charles Streetcar or the History of the New Orleans and Carrollton Rail Road.* New Orleans: Louisiana Landmarks Society, 1992.

Heard, Malcolm. *French Quarter Manual: An Architectural Guide to New Orleans' Vieux Carré.* Jackson: University Press of Mississippi, 1997.

Huber, Leonard V. *Jackson Square through the Years.* New Orleans: Friends of the Cabildo, 1982.

———. *Landmarks of New Orleans.* Rev. ed. New Orleans: Louisiana Landmarks Society, 1991.

Huber, Leonard V., and Samuel Wilson Jr. *Baroness Pontalba's Buildings: Their Site and the Remarkable Woman Who Built Them.* New Orleans: Louisiana Landmarks Society, 1964.

———. *The Basilica on Jackson Square: The History of St. Louis Cathedral and Its Predecessors, 1727–1965.* New Orleans: St. Louis Cathedral, 1972.

Irvin, Hilary. "The Impact of German Immigration on New Orleans Architecture." *Louisiana History* 27, no. 4 (Fall 1986): 375–406.

Janssen, James S. *Building New Orleans: The Engineer's Role.* New Orleans: Waldemar S. Nelson and Company, 1987.

Johnson, Jerah. *Congo Square in New Orleans.* New Orleans: Louisiana Landmarks Society. 1995.

Kelman, Ari. *A River and Its City: The Nature of Landscape in New Orleans.* Berkeley: University of California Press, 2003.

Kemp, John R. *New Orleans: An Illustrated History.* Woodland Hills, Calif.: Windsor Publications, 1981.

Kingsley, Karen. *Buildings of Louisiana.* New York: Oxford University Press, 2003.

———. "Designing for Women: The Architecture of Newcomb College." In *Newcomb College: 1886–2006,* ed. Susan Tucker and Beth Willinger, 97–113. Baton Rouge: Louisiana State University Press, 2012.

Klingman, John P. *New in New Orleans Architecture.* Gretna, La.: Pelican Publishing Company, 2012.

Leighninger, Robert D., Jr. *Building Louisiana: The Legacy of the Public Works Administration.* Jackson: University Press of Mississippi, 2007.

Lemann, Bernard, Malcolm Heard Jr., and John P. Klingman, eds. *Talk About Architecture: A Century of Architectural Education at Tulane.* New Orleans: Tulane University School of Architecture, 1993.

Lewis, Peirce F. New Orleans: *The Making of an Urban Landscape.* 2nd ed. Santa Fe, N.Mex., and Staunton, Va.: Center for American Places, 2003. Reissued with a foreword by Karen Kingsley, Charlottesville: University of Virginia Press, 2017.

Longstreth, Richard. "New Orleans New and Old: St. Francis Cabrini Church, Liturgical Reform, and Historical Association." In Longstreth, *Looking Beyond the Icons: Midcentury Architecture, Landscape, and Urbanism,* 69–90. Charlottesville: University of Virginia Press, 2015.

Mahé, John A., II, and Rosanne McCaffrey, eds. *Encyclopedia of New Orleans Artists, 1718–1918.* New Orleans: The Historic New Orleans Collection, 1987.

Masson, Ann M., and Lydia H. Schmalz. *Cast Iron and the Crescent City.* New Orleans: Louisiana Landmarks Society, 1995.

McDowell, Peggy. "New Orleans Cemeteries: Architectural Styles and Influences." *Southern Quarterly* 20, no. 2 (Winter 1982): 9–27.

Nolan, Charles E. *Splendors of Faith: New Orleans Catholic Churches, 1727–1930.* Baton Rouge: Louisiana State University Press, 2010.

Olshansky, Robert B., and Laurie A. Johnson. *Clear as Mud: Planning for the Rebuilding of New Orleans.* Chicago and Washington D.C.: American Planning Association, 2010.

Parkerson, Codman. *New Orleans, America's Most Fortified City.* New Orleans: The Quest, 1990.

Powell, Lawrence N., and Clarence L. Mohr, eds. "Through the Eye of Katrina: The Past as Prologue?" Special issue, *Journal of American History* 94, no. 3 (December 2007).

Reeves, Sally K. "The Plan Book Drawings of the New Orleans Notarial Archives: Legal Background and Artistic Development." *Proceedings of the American Antiquarian Society* 105, no. 1 (1995): 105–25.

Reeves, Sally K. Evans, and William D. Reeves. *Historic City Park, New Orleans.* New Orleans: Friends of City Park, 1982.

Rivet, Hilton L. *The History of the Immaculate Conception Church in*

New Orleans. New Orleans: Immaculate Conception Church, 1978.

Starr, S. Frederick. *Une Belle Maison: The Lombard Plantation House in New Orleans's Bywater.* Jackson: University Press of Mississippi, 2013.

——. *Southern Comfort: The Garden District of New Orleans.* Rev. and updated ed. New York: Princeton University Press, 1998.

——. "St. Charles Avenue, New Orleans, Louisiana." In *The Grand American Avenue, 1850–1920,* ed. Jan Cigliano and Sarah Bradford Landau, 153–75. San Francisco: Pomegranate Artbooks, 1994.

Toledano, Roulhac B. *A Pattern Book of New Orleans Architecture.* Gretna, La.: Pelican Publishing Company, 2010.

Upton, Dell. "The Master Street of the World: The Levee." In *Streets: Critical Perspectives on Public Space,* ed. Zeynep Çelik, Diane Favro, and Richard Ingersoll, 277–88. Berkeley: University of California Press, 1994.

Van Zante, Gary A. *New Orleans 1867: Photographs by Theodore Lilienthal.* London: Merrell, 2008.

Vlach, John Michael. "The Shotgun House: An African Architectural Legacy." In *Common Places: Readings in American Vernacular Architecture,* ed. Dell Upton and John Michael Vlach, 58–78. Athens: University of Georgia Press, 1986.

Wilson, Samuel, Jr. *The Architecture of Colonial Louisiana: Collected Essays of Samuel Wilson, Jr., F.A.I.A.* Compiled and edited by Jean M. Farnsworth and Ann M. Masson. Lafayette: Center for Louisiana Studies, University of Southwestern Louisiana, 1987.

——. *The Beauregard-Keyes House.* New Orleans: The Keyes Foundation, 1993.

——. *The Church of St. Alphonsus.* New Orleans: Friends of St. Alphonsus, 1996.

——. *A Guide to the Architecture of New Orleans, 1699–1959.* New York: Reinhold Publishing Corporation, 1959.

——. "The Howard Memorial Library and Memorial Hall." *Louisiana History* 28, no. 3 (Summer 1987): 229–44.

——. *The Pitot House on Bayou St. John.* New Orleans: Louisiana Landmarks Society, 1992.

——. *The Presbytère on Jackson Square.* New Orleans: Friends of the Cabildo, 1981.

——. *St. Patrick's Church, 1883–1992: A National Historic Landmark, Its History and Its Pastors.* New Orleans: The Church, 1992.

———. *The Vieux Carré, New Orleans: Its Plan, Its Growth, Its Architecture.* New Orleans: Vieux Carré Historic District Commission, 1968.

Wilson, Samuel, Jr., and Leonard V. Huber. *The Cabildo on Jackson Square.* New Orleans: Friends of the Cabildo, 1970.

Architects and Builders

"The Architect and His Community: Curtis and Davis, New Orleans." *Progressive Architecture* 41, no. 4 (April 1960): 141–55.

Banks, William Nathaniel. "The Galliers, New Orleans Architects." *Antiques* 151 (April 1997): 600–611.

Brady, Patricia. "Florville Foy, F.M.C.: Master Marble Cutter and Tomb Builder." *Southern Quarterly* 31, no. 2 (Winter 1993): 8–20.

Brantley, Robert S., with Victor McGee. *Henry Howard: Louisiana's Architect.* New Orleans and New York: The Historic New Orleans Collection and Princeton Architectural Press, 2015.

Davis, Arthur Q. *It Happened by Design: The Life and Work of Arthur Q. Davis.* Jackson: University Press of Mississippi, in association with the Ogden Museum of Southern Art, University of New Orleans, 2009.

Dufour, Charles L. "Henry Howard: Forgotten Architect." *Journal of the Society of Architectural Historians* 11, no. 4 (December 1952): 21–24.

"The Equal Arts of James Lamantia." *Architectural Forum* 109 (November 1958): 134–39.

Gallier, James. *Autobiography of James Gallier, Architect.* Introduction by Samuel Wilson Jr. New York: Da Capo Press, 1973.

Masson, Ann M. "Mortuary Architecture of Jacques Nicolas Bussière de Pouilly." Master's thesis, Tulane University, 1992.

Raised to the Trade: Creole Building Arts of New Orleans. Edited by Jonn Ethan Hankins and Steven Maklansky. New Orleans: New Orleans Museum of Art, 2002.

Scully, Arthur, Jr. *James Dakin, Architect: His Career in New York and the South.* Baton Rouge: Louisiana State University Press, 1973.

Weil, Emile, H. A. Benson, and Albert Bendernagel. *Illustrations of Selected Work of Emile Weil, Architect, New Orleans, La., 1900–1928.* New York: Architectural Catalog Co., 1928.

New Orleans Vicinity and Plantation Architecture

Banks, William Nathaniel. "The River Road Plantations of Louisiana." *Antiques* 111 (June 1977): 1170–83.

Bonner, James C. "Plantation Architecture of the Lower South on the Eve of the Civil War." *Journal of Southern History* 11, no. 3 (August 1945): 370–88.

Fricker, Jonathan. "The Origins of the Creole Raised Plantation House." *Louisiana History* 25, no. 2 (Spring 1984): 137–53.

Krotzer, Henry W., Jr. "The Restoration of San Francisco (St. Frusquin), Reserve, Louisiana" *Antiques* 111 (June 1977): 1194–1203.

Lewis, Richard Anthony. *Robert W. Tebbs: Photographer to Architects: Louisiana Plantations in 1926*. Baton Rouge: Louisiana State University Press, 2011.

Menn, Joseph Karl. *The Large Slaveholders of Louisiana, 1860*. New Orleans: Pelican Publishing Company, 1964.

Sternberg, Mary Ann. *Along the River Road: Past and Present on Louisiana's Historic Byway*. 3rd. ed. Baton Rouge: Louisiana State University Press, 2013.

Swanson, Betsy. *Historic Jefferson Parish: From Shore to Shore*. Gretna, La.: Pelican Publishing Company, 1975.

Vlach, John Michael. *Back of the Big House: The Architecture of Plantation Slavery*. Chapel Hill: University of North Carolina Press, 1993.

———. "Plantation Landscapes of the Antebellum South." In *Before Freedom Came: African-American Life in the Antebellum South*, ed. Edward D. C. Campbell Jr. and Kym S. Rice, 21–49. Charlottesville: University Press of Virginia, 1991.

Wilson, Samuel, Jr. "Architecture of the Early Sugar Plantations." In *Green Fields: Two Hundred Years of Louisiana Sugar*, 51–82. Lafayette: Center for Louisiana Studies, University of Southwestern Louisiana, 1980.

———. "The Building Contract for Evergreen Plantation, 1832." *Louisiana History* 21, no. 4 (Winter 1990): 399–404.

Illustration Credits

CMH-LC   Carol M. Highsmith Archive, Prints and Photographs
          Division, Library of Congress
DPC   Detroit Publishing Company Photograph Collection,
          Prints and Photographs Division, Library of Congress
HABS   Historic American Buildings Survey, Prints and Photo-
          graphs Division, Library of Congress
HAER   Historic American Engineering Survey, Prints and Pho-
          tographs Division, Library of Congress
KK   Karen Kingsley
LD   Lake Douglas
PP-LC   Panoramic Photographs Collection, Prints and Photo-
          graphs Division, Library of Congress

Maps by Nat Case, INCase, LLC. Some map base data © Open-
StreetMap contributors, openstreetmap.org.

Front Matter

Page iv, Guy W. Carwile

Orleans Parish

Page 6, The Historic New Orleans Collection, 1987.65 i-iii; 1.1, 1.2
CMH-LC; 1.3 Robert S. Salzar; 1.5 LD; 1.7, 1.8 KK; 1.9 Robert S. Salzar; 1.10, 1.12, 1.13, 1.14 KK; 1.17 Joan Kay; 1.19 HABS; 1.21 Joan Kay;
1.23 CMH-LC; 1.26, 1.28, 1.29, 1.30 KK; 2.1, 2.4 HABS; 2.5 Joan Kay;
2.6, 2.7, 2.8, 2.10, 2.11 LD; 2.12 KK; 3.1, 3.3 LD; 3.6, 3.7 KK; 3.8, 3.10
LD; 3.11 KK; 3.12 LD; 3.15 KK; 3.16 CMH-LC; 3.18 PP-LC; 4.1 KK; 4.3,
4.5, 4.7, 4.9, 4.10, 4.11 LD; 4.13 KK; 4.14 DPC; 4.15 Joan Kay; 4.16 KK;
5.2 Jennifer V. O. Baughn; 5.3 LD; 5.4 CMH-LC; 5.5, 5.6, 5.7, 5.8 LD;
5.11, 5.12 KK; 5.13 LD; 5.14 KK; 5.16 D Hughes; 5.17 KK; 6.1 KK; 6.2 LD;
6.4 KK; 6.6, 6.7 LD; 6.8, 6.9, 6.10 KK; 6.11 KK; 6.14 KK; 6.15 Guy W.
Carwile; 6.17 KK; 6.18 Dell Upton; 6.20 KK; 6.21 Mark Mones; 6.22
CMH-LC; 6.24 HABS; 6.25, 6.26 KK; 6.27, 6.28; 6.29, 6.30 LD; 6.31
KK; 6.32, 7.1 LD; 7.2 KK; 7.4 LD; 7.5, 7.6, 7.8, 7.9, 7.10, 7.12, 7.13 KK;
7.17 HABS; 7.19 LD; 7.20 HABS; 7.21 LD; 7.22 KK; 7.23 LD; 7.24
HABS; 7.25 LD; 7.27, 7.28, 7.29 KK; 8.1 LD; 8.2 KK; 8.3, 8.5 LD; 8.7,
8.8 KK; 8.9 LD; 8.10, 8.14 KK; 8.15, 8.17 Southeastern Architectural
Archive, Special Collections Division, Tulane University Libraries,

Frank Lotz Miller, photographer; 8.18, 8.19, 9.1 KK; 9.2 Guy W. Carwile; 9.3 KK; 9.4 CMH-LC; 9.6, 9.9 LD; 9.10 KK; 9.11, 9.12, 9.14 LD; 10.1 Jennifer V. O. Baughn; 10.2 LD; 10.3, 10.4, 10.6, 10.7 KK; 10.8 LD; 10.9 KK; 10.10 LD; 10.11 Dell Upton; 10.12 Jennifer V. O. Baughn; 11.2 KK; 11.3, 11.5 D Hughes; 12.1 LD; 12.2 Joan Kay; 12.3, 12.4 LD; 12.6, 12.7, 12.8 KK; 13.1 photograph by Dieter Karner (with thanks to the Algiers Historical Society, www.algiershistoricalsociety.org)

Jefferson Parish

14.1, 14.3, 14.4, 14.6, 14.9 KK; 14.11 PP-LC

St. Bernard Parish

15.1 PP-LC; 15.2 HABS, Richard Koch, photographer, and DPC-LC; 15.6 KK

Day Trips from New Orleans

Page 283, photograph by John Stanton, FortWiki.com; page 286, Jennifer V. O. Baughn; page 289, U.S. Army Corps of Engineers; page 293, Guy W. Carwile; pages 294, 295, 299, 300, 301, KK

Index

Note: Properties named for individuals or families with a given surname are indexed in the form *surname (first name).* Page numbers in **boldface** refer to illustrations.

BUILDINGS OF THE UNITED STATES is a series of books on American architecture compiled and written on a state-by-state basis, with separate guides for specific cities. The primary objective of the series is to identify and celebrate the rich cultural, economic, and geographical diversity of the United States as it is reflected in the architecture of each state. The series has been commissioned by the Society of Architectural Historians, an organization dedicated to the study, interpretation, and preservation of the built environment throughout the world. To date, twenty-three volumes have been published, covering Alaska, Arkansas, Colorado, Delaware, the District of Columbia, Hawaii, Iowa, Louisiana, Massachusetts (Metropolitan Boston), Michigan, Nevada, North Dakota, Pennsylvania (including Pittsburgh), Rhode Island, Texas (Central, South, and Gulf Coast), Vermont, Virginia, West Virginia, and Wisconsin.

SAH/BUS City Guide

Buildings of New Orleans, Karen Kingsley and Lake Douglas (2018)

> Karen Kingsley, Professor Emerita of Architecture at Tulane University and Editor-in-Chief of the Buildings of the United States series, is the author of *Buildings of Louisiana* and coauthor (with Guy W. Carwile) of *The Modernist Architecture of Samuel G. and William B. Wiener: Shreveport, Louisiana, 1920-1960*. Lake Douglas, FASLA, Associate Dean for Research and Development in Louisiana State University's College of Art and Design and Professor of Landscape Architecture in the Robert Reich School of Landscape Architecture, is the author of a number of books, including *Public Spaces, Private Gardens: A History of Designed Landscapes in New Orleans*.

Buildings of Savannah, Robin B. Williams, with David Gobel, Patrick Haughey, Daves Rossell, and Karl Schuler (2015)